TRINITY POETS

TRINITY POETS

an anthology of poems by
members of Trinity College, Cambridge
from the sixteenth to the twenty-first century

edited by
ADRIAN POOLE and ANGELA LEIGHTON

with
JOE MOSHENSKA, CHRIS SCOTT,
ANNE TONER, and ROSS WILSON

CARCANET

First published in Great Britain in 2017 by
Carcanet Press Ltd
Alliance House, 30 Cross Street
Manchester M2 7AQ
www.carcanet.co.uk

A CIP catalogue record for this book is available from
the British Library:
ISBN 9781784103569 (paperback)
9781784105235 (hardback).

Typeset by XL Publishing Services, Exmouth.
Printed and bound in England by SRP Ltd.

The publisher acknowledges financial assistance
from Arts Council England.

Supported by
**ARTS COUNCIL
ENGLAND**

ACKNOWLEDGMENTS

We gratefully acknowledge the bequest by Anne Barton, Fellow of Trinity College, Cambridge from 1985 to 2013, that sparked the idea for this volume and helped to support its production; the approval of the Master and Fellows of Trinity College, Cambridge; the enthusiasm of our publisher, Michael Schmidt, and the work of our editor at Carcanet Press, Luke Allan. This volume is the product of collaboration between eight members of the College. Angela Leighton, Joe Moshenska, Adrian Poole, Anne Toner and Ross Wilson are Fellows in English, and Chris Scott is a post-graduate student. Particular recognition is due to Chris for his work in preparing the volume for publication. We are also grateful to two further members of the College, Lauren Brown and Cal Revely-Calder, for their valuable assistance; to Anthony Baker, Santanu Das, Janar Davletov, Orlando Gibbs, Boyd Hilton, Luke Ingram, James Kirwan, August Kleinzahler, Javed Majeed, Harriet Marland, Keith Moffatt, Jacqueline Norton, Sandy Paul, Marion Shaw, Nigel Smith and Clive Wilmer for their advice and support; and to Nicolas Bell, Trinity's Librarian, for facilitating searches and providing help with the reproduction of manuscripts and other illustrations.

TO THE MEMORY OF
ANNE BARTON
(1933–2013)

CONTENTS

EDITORIAL NOTE

All the poets included in this volume have been (or continue to be) members of Trinity College, Cambridge, the great majority of them as undergraduates, some as graduate students, as Fellows, or Visiting Fellow Commoners.

Sources for the texts may be found on pp. 377–84. Texts of the earlier poems in this volume have been modernised with respect to spelling and punctuation. Annotation has been kept to a minimum.

We are grateful for permission to re-print the following:

WILLIAM ALABASTER 'Upon the Crucifix (1)', 'Upon St Paul to the Corinthians', 'Upon the Crucifix (2)', 'Ego Sum Vitis', 'Lord, I have left all and myself behind', 'The Difference 'twixt Compunction and Cold Devotion'. *The Sonnets of William Alabaster*, ed. Helen Gardner and G. M. Story (Oxford University Press, 1959). Reproduced by permission of Oxford University Press.

MUHAMMAD (ALLAMA) IQBAL 'Beauty's Essence', 'Two Planets', 'Six Rubáiyát', 'Reproach', 'Civilisation's Clutches', 'God and Man', 'Solitude'. V. G. Kiernan (trans.), *Poems from Iqbal* (John Murray, 1955). We are grateful to Hodder & Stoughton, an imprint of Hachette, for raising no objection to our reproduction of this material. 'The Night and the Poet'. Mustansir Mir (trans.), *Tulip in the Desert* (Hurst, 2000). Reproduced by permission of C. Hurst & Co.

A. A. MILNE Extract from *When We Were Very Young* by A. A. Milne. Text copyright © The Trustees of the Pooh Properties 1924. Published by Egmont UK Ltd and used with permission. Extract from *Now We Are Six* by A. A. Milne. Text copyright © The Trustees of the Pooh Properties 1927. Published by Egmont UK Ltd and used with permission. Extract from *Winnie the Pooh* by A. A. Milne. Text copyright © The Trustees of the Pooh Properties 1926. Published by Egmont UK Ltd and used with permission. Extract from *The House at Pooh Corner* by

A. A. Milne. Text copyright © The Trustees of the Pooh Properties 1928. Published by Egmont UK Ltd and used with permission.

E. H. SHEPARD Illustrations to 'The Old Sailor' and 'Poem' reproduced by permission of Curtis Brown.

EDWARD SHANKS 'The Rock Pool', 'Armistice Day, 1921'. *Collected Poems* (William Collins & Sons, 1926). We are grateful to HarperCollins Publishers LLC for raising no objection to our reproduction of this material.

VLADIMIR NABOKOV 'On Translating "Eugene Onegin"', 'A Literary Dinner', 'Ode to a Model'. *Poems and Problems* (McGraw-Hill, 1969). 'The University Poem', 'Spring'. *Collected Poems* (Penguin, 2012). Reproduced by permission of Penguin Random House UK. *Eugene Onegin: A Novel in Verse* (The Antioch Press, 1964), *Lolita* (G. P. Putnam's Sons, 1955). Reproduced by permission of the Dmitri Nabokov Estate, c/o The Wylie Agency.

JOHN LEHMANN 'This Excellent Machine', 'A Death in Hospital', 'After Fever', 'Greek Landscape with Figures'. *Collected Poems* (Eyre & Spottiswoode, 1963). Reproduced by permission of David Higham Associates.

THOM GUNN 'The Secret Sharer', 'Tamer and Hawk', 'The Outdoor Concert', 'His Rooms in College', 'The Hug', 'The Man with Night Sweats', 'Lament', 'The Gas-Poker'. *Collected Poems* (Faber, 1994). Reproduced by permission of Faber and Faber Ltd. 'The Missed Beat'. *The Missed Beat* (The Gruffyground Press, 1976). Reproduced by permission of The Gruffyground Press, August Kleinzahler and Clive Wilmer.

KIT WRIGHT 'The Roller in the Woods', 'Stabat Mater', 'Cold Harbor'. *Ode to Didcot Power Station* (Bloodaxe Books, 2014). Reproduced by permission of Bloodaxe Books Ltd. www.bloodaxebooks.com. 'George Herbert's Other Self in Africa'. *Short Afternoons* (Hutchinson, 1989). Reproduced by permission of the author.

PETER ROBINSON 'Autobiography', 'A Woman a Poem a Picture'. *Overdrawn Account* (The Many Press, 1980). 'Cleaning'. *This Other Life* (Carcanet, 1988). 'Convalescent Days'. *Lost and Found* (Carcanet,

1997). 'Unheimlich Leben'. *The Look of Goodbye* (Shearsman Books, 2008). 'Like a Railway Station'. *Buried Music* (Shearsman Books, 2015). All reproduced by permission of the author.

ANGELA LEIGHTON 'Crack-Willow', 'Library'. *The Messages* (Shoestring Press, 2012). Reproduced by permission of Shoestring Press; 'Sluice', 'Crocus', 'Sicilian Road', '"Aftermath: Parasite"', 'Even-Song'. *Spills* (Carcanet, 2016). Reproduced by permission of Carcanet Press Ltd.

JAMES HARPUR 'Cranborne Woods (17 May, 1994)'. *Oracle Bones* (Anvil, 2001). Reproduced by permission of Carcanet Press Ltd. 'The White Silhouette'. Reproduced by permission of the author.

BEN OKRI 'An Undeserved Sweetness'. *An African Elegy* (Jonathan Cape, 1992). 'Migrations', 'Heraclitus' Golden River'. *Wild* (Random House, 2012). 'Angled willows of the river'. Reproduced by permission of the author c/o Ed Victor Ltd.

SOPHIE HANNAH 'Long For This World', 'The Cancellation', 'Unbalanced', and 'The Storming'. *Marrying the Ugly Millionaire* (Carcanet, 2015). Reproduced by permission of Carcanet Press Ltd.

SEAN BORODALE 'Apple Jelly (On-going)', 'Washing-Up'. *Human Work: A Poet's Cookbook* (Jonathan Cape, 2015). '23rd July: Noise & Waste', '7th August: Property', '2nd May'. *Bee Journal* (Jonathan Cape, 2012). 'Soil at Cockle's Field'. All reproduced by permission of the author c/o Rogers, Coleridge & White Ltd.

JACOB POLLEY 'A Jar of Honey'. *The Brink* (Picador, 2003). Reproduced by permission of Pan Macmillan Publishers. 'The Owls', 'You' from *Little Gods* by Jacob Polley. Published by Picador, 2006. Copyright © Jacob Polley. 'Langley Lane' from *The Havocs* by Jacob Polley. Published by Picador, 2012. Copyright © Jacob Polley. 'Peewit' from *Jackself* by Jacob Polley. Published by Picador, 2016. Copyright © Jacob Polley. All reproduced by permission of the author c/o Rogers, Coleridge & White Ltd, 20 Powis Mews, London W11 1JN.

EMMA JONES 'Farming', 'Conversation'. *The Striped World* (Faber & Faber, 2009). Reproduced by permission of Faber & Faber Ltd. Extracts from 'The Hawk Man'. Reproduced by permission of the author.

ILLUSTRATIONS

Cover image adapts a notebook sketch by Alfred Tennyson (Trinity College MS 0.15.36, fol. 54v and 0.15.36, fol. 55r).

All the illustrations described above are reproduced by kind permission of the Master and Fellows of Trinity College, Cambridge.

We are grateful to Anthony Baker, publisher of The Gruffyground Press, and to Clive Wilmer and August Kleinzahler, Gunn's literary executors, for permission to reproduce it here.

INTRODUCTION

Trinity College, Cambridge is well known for having nurtured many famous scientists and mathematicians, including Isaac Newton, James Clerk Maxwell and Srinivasa Ramanujan. It is less often noted that many great poets have also passed through its doors: George Herbert, Andrew Marvell, John Dryden, George Gordon Lord Byron, Alfred Tennyson, A. E. Housman, and Thom Gunn. Other major figures with whom the College has been associated include the many writers who have delivered the Clark Lectures, starting in 1884 with Sir Leslie Stephen: Walter de la Mare, T. S. Eliot, E. M. Forster, Harley Granville-Barker, C. Day Lewis, Robert Graves, Louis MacNeice, L. P. Hartley, Stephen Spender, V. S. Pritchett, Donald Davie, Tom Stoppard, Geoffrey Hill, Toni Morrison, Alison Lurie, Adrienne Rich, Seamus Heaney, Paul Muldoon, and Alice Oswald.

This anthology represents the great range of poetry produced by members of the College over the last four centuries and more, from the later sixteenth to the early twenty-first. At one extreme we find the restless, volatile spirit of a Byron – dissident, heterodox, recalcitrant, deviant: 'What should I have known or written had I been a quiet, mercantile politician or a lord in waiting? A man must travel, and turmoil, or there is no existence.'[1] Some have shared Byron's appetite for travel and turmoil, most spectacularly perhaps Aleister Crowley. Others, such as Herbert and Housman, have forged an apparently more conventional existence within which their poetry flourished. All bear the imprint of their times, the pressure of historical events and of dominant literary forms, but readers will be struck by the variety of ways in which they have responded to them.

A handful of the authors represented here also achieved success for reasons other than their poetry. The statesman, philosopher and essayist Francis Bacon, for example, the translation of whose ideas into action resulted in the founding of the Royal Society in 1660; Charles Montagu, Earl of Halifax, founder of the Bank of England, a major political figure in the years following the revolution of 1688; Thomas Babington Macaulay, essayist, historian and politician; and James Clerk Maxwell, often called the father of modern physics, whose theory of electromagnetism paved the way for many crucial developments in twentieth-century science. Then there is William Makepeace Thackeray, far better known for his novels, *Vanity Fair* and *The History of Henry Esmond*, than for his poetry. The same is true of the Russian émigré writer Vladimir Nabokov, author of *Lolita* and *Pale Fire*, as well as the autobiography *Speak, Memory*, which contains wonderful vignettes of life at Trinity shortly after the First World War. Even Muhammad Iqbal, whose poetry won him eminence in the Indian Muslim community, is at least as well-known as a philosopher, and as the intellectual or spiritual father of Pakistan.

Throughout history most poets have had something else to do, whether their poetry was central or marginal to their lives. The biographer of Sir John Suckling makes the point that although his subject was known as a poet and playwright, his writing was not central to his short life (he died in 1641, aged thirty-two): 'He was first and last a wit and a courtier to Charles 1, being occupied mainly as a gentleman officer, socio-political observer, gamester, amorist, and marital fortune seeker […].'[2] Allowing for changes in manners between the 1630s and 1830s, a similar thing could be said about the rising young Tory politician Winston Mackworth Praed, his life also cut short at the age of thirty-seven.

These individuals, for whom poetry did not absorb their central energies, remind us that most poets *have* to do something else as well, whether they wish to or not. Very few have enjoyed the independent means that allowed figures such as Byron and Crowley to follow their own whims and appetites. The sources of their support have varied from the aristocratic and royal patronage of the sixteenth and seventeenth centuries to the employment opportunities in journalism and teaching in the later periods. For a few such as Herbert there has been the refuge, itself uncertain and unpredictable, of the Church.

At a mundane level, money (or rather the lack of it) has featured prominently in the lives of many, more clearly in earlier periods than now. Amongst those celebrated for their prodigality we can count George Gascoigne, Thomas Randolph (whose loss of a finger in a tavern brawl prompted the poem reprinted here), Suckling, and Robert Lloyd (who died in a debtors' prison). More broadly speaking, of the many life-threatening forms of insecurity, political upheaval has certainly afflicted (and inspired) some authors, especially in the sixteenth and seventeenth centuries, from Gascoigne to Dryden. Again in the twentieth century, war and revolution have left deep marks on the lives and works of Maurice Baring, Edward Shanks, Nabokov, John Lehmann, and A. A. Milne, author of the best-selling *Peace with Honour* (1934) and *War with Honour* (1940), as well as *Winnie-the-Pooh* and *The House at Pooh Corner.*

But of course there are writers for whom poetry *has* been close to the heart of their life's endeavour: Herbert, Marvell, Dryden, Byron, Tennyson and Gunn, to go no further. Some have enjoyed greater fame in their own time, or at their passing, than they do now. In 1667 Abraham Cowley received a tremendous send-off, 'the most lavish funeral which had ever been given to a mere man of letters in England'.[3] Two hundred years or so later Tennyson's public funeral in Westminster Abbey drew thousands. But time has not been as kind to Cowley's reputation as Tennyson's – nor to that of Suckling, who enjoyed his highest esteem in the years after the Restoration. Dryden too, the dominant figure of these critical decades from 1660 to 1700, no longer commands the high respect or wide interest that he once did.

For virtually all the poets featured in this anthology, Trinity has provided a temporary haven, a place of respite and relative calm in a troubled world, at a formative point in their youth. Edmund Gosse is an exception. Despite his lack of formal qualifications, his success as a man of letters led to his lecturing in English literature at Trinity from 1885 to 1889.[4] Others who have come to Trinity later in life include A. E. Housman, appointed to the Chair of Latin and arriving as a Fellow in 1911. He had already gained a name as a poet through *A Shropshire Lad*, but he went on to publish a second, immensely popular volume, *Last Poems* (1922), while at Trinity. For him the haven proved permanent. James Clerk Maxwell studied at Edinburgh University before migrating to Cambridge; after posts in Aberdeen and King's College London, he returned to the Chair of Experimental Physics, 1871–9. Angela Leighton was elected to a Senior Research Fellowship in poetry in 2006 after many years at the University of Hull. Several of the more recent names in this collection came to Trinity as Fellow Commoners in Creative Arts, a post inaugurated in 1967: Kit Wright (1977–9), Ben Okri (1991–3), Sophie Hannah (1997–9), Jacob Polley (2005–7), and Sean Borodale (2013–15).[5]

However, most of the poets in this volume entered Trinity at an earlier age and stage, as undergraduates. A certain number stayed on to become (however briefly) Fellows, including William Alabaster, Giles Fletcher, Herbert, Randolph, Cowley, Charles Montagu (elected a Fellow in 1683 by royal command, 'notwithstanding any statute or custom to the contrary'), Laurence Eusden, Mackworth Praed, and Clerk Maxwell. Until the Statutes were changed in 1882, most Fellows of Trinity – as of other Colleges – were required to take Holy Orders within seven years of becoming MAs, thus preserving the strong character of the College as a religious foundation. For the majority, then, Trinity provided hospitality, and the guest travelled on in life. A contemporary of John Dryden's reflected that, fine scholar as his friend had been, 'his head was too roving and active, or what else you'll call it, to confine himself to a College Life; & so he left it & went to London into gayer company, & set up for a Poet.'[6] A fair number of authors here, including Suckling, Leonard Welsted, Byron, Tennyson, Thackeray, and Baring, never completed their degrees, the obligation to do so being less stringently enforced before the twentieth century.

The haven of calm has not always been undisturbed, to be sure. It should come as no surprise that not all of these poets have felt at ease in Trinity, or relished the world of learning, or indeed expressed as much gratitude to the College as John Hacket (1592–1670), contemporary of George Herbert's in the early seventeenth century and later Bishop of Coventry and Lichfield. Hacket is supposed to have thanked God

> that he was not bred among rude and barbarian people, but among civil and learned Athenians; that he was not disposed to some monkish society, or ignorant cloister; but to the Greece of Greece itself, the most learned and royal society of Trinity College, which in that and all other ages since the foundation equalled any other college in Europe for plenty of incomparable divines, philosophers and orators.[7]

Some two hundred years later Byron took a dimmer view of the place, to put it mildly, complaining that 'college improves in everything but Learning, nobody here seems to look into an author ancient or modern if they can avoid it'. At first he was, so he later declared, 'miserable and untoward to a degree [...] about as unsocial as a wolf taken from the troop'. On his arrival in 1805, however, he declared to his half-sister Augusta that 'I like a College Life extremely', not least because he had escaped 'the Trammels or rather *Fetters* of my domestic Tyrant Mrs Byron'. He was 'most pleasantly situated in *Super*excellent Rooms, flanked on one side by my Tutor, on the other by an old Fellow, both of whom are rather checks upon my *vivacity*.' He retaliated against such checks by installing his famous bear (whom he said should '*sit* for a *Fellowship*'), and holding 'eternal parties' including a large assortment of '*Jockies*, Gamblers, *Boxers, Authors, parsons*, and poets'.[8] The poem 'Granta, a Medley' speaks of the 'daring revels' with which he whiled away his time, nicely rhyming 'student' with 'impudent' and scorning the College choir as 'a set of croaking sinners'.

Twenty years or so later Tennyson thought no better of Cambridge:

'The country is so disgustingly level, the revelry of the place so monot-
onous, the studies of the University so uninteresting, so much matter
of fact – none but dryheaded calculating angular little gentlemen can
take much delight in [algebraic formulae].'[9] His 'Lines on Cambridge
of 1830' express a similarly severe judgment, though he regretted them
later. Yet he too was glad to escape from a large family that included a
violent father and several troubled brothers. Through Trinity he was
able to make new friendships, with Edward FitzGerald for example,
author of the extraordinarily popular *Rubáiyát of Omar Khayyám*, and
above all with Arthur Hallam, a passion that would endure long after
the latter's early death in Vienna, and fuel Tennyson's great poem of
mourning, *In Memoriam: A.H.H.*

There was a time when the route to Trinity was much narrower
than it is now. Through the late sixteenth and seventeenth centuries
most of the poets featured here were schooled at Westminster and
won scholarships to Trinity (Bacon and Marvell are signal exceptions,
the former being educated at home, the latter at the Grammar School
in Hull): Alabaster, Fletcher, Herbert, Randolph, Cowley, Dryden,
Montagu; Welsted and Lloyd continued the tradition in the eighteenth
century, and A. A. Milne in the early years of the twentieth. Needless
to say, the sources from which Trinity now draws its students are wider
and more varied than at any previous point in its history.

The image of a haven is one that the College naturally attracts. Yet
the very idea of refuge and respite is itself a reaction to the peril and
excitement of exposure, as Marvell stages it in his fine version of a well-
known chorus from Seneca's *Thyestes* (not included here):

> Climb at Court for me that will
> Tottering favour's pinnacle;
> All I seek is to lie still.
> Settled in some secret nest
> In calm leisure let me rest;
> And far off the public stage
> Pass away my silent age.

This plea for the quiet life may seem the antithesis of Byron's call for
travel and turmoil, but throughout the poetry gathered here the two
appeals are in constant dialogue with each other. One is for exposure
and risk, the other is for peace and quiet: the active and contemplative
lives, if you like. The deep origins of the College before Henry VIII (the
pre-existing institutions of King's Hall and Michaelhouse) may have
been in the monastic tradition of meditation and withdrawal from the

world, but with the foundation of Trinity as we know it in 1546, the world has always pressed in on it – and pressed its occupants out again.

Elected a scholar in 1609, at the age of sixteen, George Herbert became a major Fellow of Trinity in 1615. But over the next few years his future was radically uncertain as he sought and gained the significant office of University Orator, a post fraught with political potential. As one of his biographers puts it, 'Sacred ambitions were in growing tension with secular ones [...] there was a contradiction between writing flowery eulogies and the honest truth, between courtliness and Christian simplicity. It would get worse.'[10] Out of such contradictions Herbert would forge his finest poetry. Trinity provided the setting for some crucial turning-points and decisions in his life, but the trajectory that took him from birth in the Welsh town of Montgomery, near the border with England, to death in the Wiltshire parish of Bemerton was never easily predictable.

So it is to be expected that the poetry of the sixteenth and seventeenth centuries bears witness, however obliquely, to the political and religious conflicts of the age. Travel and turmoil are exactly what characterise the life of one of the earliest poets featured here, William Alabaster (1568–1640), who began and ended his career in apparent conformity to type: that is, a brilliant student, destined for more or less high office in the Church of England, eventually settling in the quiet living of Little Shelford, near Cambridge. But to tell his story like this is to leave out the turbulent fifteen or so years in the middle, between 1597 and 1613, when Alabaster was perilously converted to Roman Catholicism, escaped to Rome, was captured at La Rochelle and imprisoned in the Tower, turned double agent and eventually secured royal absolution. A contemporary account summarised the final figure he struck as 'A papist formerly now a zealous Protestant against them'. The knowledge of such turbulence may help readers appreciate the religious sonnets printed here, known only in manuscript before the twentieth century.

Other figures buffeted by the pressures of allegiance in this tumultuous century include Abraham Cowley, who by the beginning of 1646 had left England to follow Queen Henrietta Maria into France, and was then employed in passing secret correspondence between the exiled queen and Charles 1. Arrested as a royalist agent in 1655, he was fortunate to survive. If one wishes to consider the predicament of the poet in the traumatic decade of the Commonwealth, one could do worse than visualise this real scene at Cromwell's funeral procession in 1658: three men walking together, John Dryden, John Milton and Andrew Marvell (see the headnote to 'Dryden', p. 91).[11] What would Milton or Marvell have said to Dryden, had they known he would later convert to Roman Catholicism? In their very different ways both Marvell's verse and Dryden's testify to the difficulty of negotiating these perilous times, during the Interregnum, the Restoration of the Stuarts, and – for Dryden – through the Glorious Revolution of 1688.

If the period between the major figures of Dryden and Byron represents a relatively dry period for Trinity poets – both Eusden and Welsted were the objects of Alexander Pope's brilliant scorn – the century from Byron to Housman contains some of this volume's highlights. Not only the great figures of Byron, Tennyson and Housman, but a host of lesser but accomplished authors, including one of Tennyson's two older brothers, Charles (Tennyson) Turner, and his friend Edward FitzGerald, and other significant literary figures such as Macaulay and Gosse, plus the remarkable James Clerk Maxwell.

With the poets born from the mid-1870s onwards, the world begins to seem larger, more diverse, more radically unpredictable. In a sense Gosse's poem on '1870–71', the date of the Franco-Prussian War and the birth of the third French Republic, announces this turn in a larger cultural climate. It is one in which the consequences of Britain's imperial ambitions begin to emerge more clearly. While Thackeray was born in India and Macaulay was significantly employed there, India now began to send students to Trinity. Most notably, Muhammad Iqbal, admitted to read philosophy and study law in 1905, who went on to write widely about Islam and supported the movement for a Muslim State in the Indian subcontinent. The Russian Revolution of 1917 brought another major figure to Trinity: that of Vladimir Nabokov. Meanwhile the Great War and its aftermath spurred lesser but still significant men of letters to new kinds of engagement and disenchantment with domestic politics and the world beyond (Maurice Baring, Edward Shanks, John Lehmann). Thom Gunn stands at a pivotal point in the history of this volume in that he is the last author no longer living. He came up to Trinity shortly after the Second World War, having done his national service; he died in 2004, in California, where he spent most of his life after Cambridge. Only Nabokov, among other writers here, chose similarly to settle in the USA. Both of them were escaping from political and cultural difficulties to a safe, or safer, haven: in one case the taboos surrounding homosexuality in Britain, in the other the nightmare legacy of Russian history and contemporary European politics (Nabokov's father was murdered in Berlin in 1922).

After Gunn all the poets featured here have known a Trinity to which the admission of women for the first time in 1977 has made an historic difference. Quite how sharp and welcome a difference can be gauged from the reminiscence of one woman who was not able to enter.

In *A Room of One's Own* (1929) Virginia Woolf remembers Charles
Lamb coming to Trinity's Wren Library to look at the manuscript of
Milton's 'Lycidas', and wondering how she 'could follow Lamb's foot-
steps across the quadrangle to that famous library where the treasure is
kept'.[12] She does so only to be barred from entering by 'a deprecating,
silvery, kindly gentleman', who regrets, as he waves her back, that she
can only be admitted if accompanied by a Fellow or furnished with a
letter of introduction. This is not her first rebuff; prior to this she has
been shooed off a College lawn 'which has been rolled for 300 years in
succession'.[13] Angela Leighton recalls this incident in her own memories
of first entering Trinity. It is good to think of Woolf's successors finding
fewer obstacles in the way and creating new paths of their own.

An anthology literally means a collection of flowers, and it would
be foolish to make extravagant claims for the coherence of the gathering
culled from this particular meadow. It is the amplitude of the field which
may justify the enterprise. If meadow and field sound too rural, we may
think instead of a garden, an image that Marvell puts to some teasing,
appealing, even outrageous use in two of his finest poems, 'The Garden'
and 'The Mower against Gardens'. It is worth noting that several poems
in this anthology make explicit reference to aspects of Trinity's physical
environment, including Tennyson's famous stanzas in *In Memoriam*
(LXXVII) about returning down the lime tree avenue to find Arthur
Hallam's room; Crowley's 'In Neville's Court',[14] which recalls a happy
evening in its cloisters; Gunn's 'The Secret Sharer', written in and about
his rooms in Whewell's Court; Leighton's 'Crocus', in memory of one
of Trinity's first women Fellows, the dedicatee of this volume; Okri's
'Angled willows of the river'; and Jones's 'The Hawk Man', based on
the hawk brought in to scare off the pigeons from sitting on the clock
in Great Court. The courts and gardens provide an appropriate model
both for the hospitality on which this introduction has laid some stress,
but also for the cultivated space represented by the poems included
here, and indeed for the volume as a whole.

There is room within this large garden-court (let us call it) for
the most solemn meditations on mortality and immortality, such as
Tennyson's *In Memoriam*, even for visions of the end of the world, such
as Byron's terrifying 'Darkness'. Or this, from a great woman writer of
a generation earlier than Virginia Woolf's. Unlike Woolf, George Eliot
had a Fellow to accompany her.[15] In 1881 F. W. H. Myers remembered
walking with her in the Fellows' Garden, 'on an evening of rainy May':

> she, stirred somewhat beyond her wont, and taking as her text
> the three words which have been used so often as the inspiring

trumpet-calls of men – the words *God, Immortality, Duty* – pronounced, with terrible earnestness, how inconceivable was the *first*, how unbelievable the *second*, and yet how peremptory and absolute the *third*. Never perhaps, have sterner accents affirmed the sovereignty of impersonal and unrecompensing Law.[16]

Yet it would be wrong to underplay the sunnier side, or rather, the large space where sun and shade intermingle, where we listen to 'accents' in which it is difficult to distinguish gravity from levity. The tradition of so-called 'light verse' is a serious one, from Gascoigne's 'Sonnet Written in Praise of the Brown Beauty' and Suckling's scandalously nonchalant 'Out upon it! I have loved / Three whole days together', to Kit Wright's 'That Was the Summer' and Sophie Hannah's 'Unbalanced'. Along the way readers will meet various forms of these 'light-hearted' accents, sociable, amicable, colloquial, including Welsted's 'The Invitation', Lloyd's 'A Familiar Epistle, to J. B. Esq', Praed's 'Yes or No', Thackeray's 'Commanders of the Faithful'. The wit is sometimes barbed – one hesitates to call Dryden's 'Mac Flecknoe', of which we provide here just a taste, light-hearted – but it is often more genial than vicious. Think for example of the brilliant coinage by John Byrom of 'Tweedle-dum' and 'Tweedle-dee', more often associated with Lewis Carroll's *Through the Looking Glass*.

Two of the most popular of such voices are Edward FitzGerald's, whose *Rubáiyát* continues to enthral readers at large, and A. A. Milne's, whose Winnie-the-Pooh has become a modern legend. In both cases biography can suggest the darkness from which the make-believe of writing proved a refuge for its author. In a letter of 1833, when he was still in his mid-twenties, FitzGerald tentatively boasts of 'a victory over my evil spirits'. He expresses gratitude for the solace to be found in conversation with friends, including the letter itself, and admiration for a metaphor of Francis Bacon's, when he suggests that with a friend 'a man *tosseth* his thoughts':

> I feel that, being alone, one's thoughts and feelings, from want of communication, become heaped up and clotted together, as it were: and so lie like undigested food heavy upon the mind: but with a friend one *tosseth* them about, so that the air gets between them, and keeps them fresh and sweet.[17]

Writing that lightens, in more than one sense, that lifts readers and aerates their world, is what FitzGerald sought; Milne too, who loathed war's horrors and would write against them, yet enlisted and served at the front. We are told that 'In July 1916 he was in France, on the Somme, in a "nightmare of mental and moral degradation", about which he wrote very little.' As for the poems that made up the first of his four famous children's books, they were mostly written, perhaps as a goodbye to all that, on a wet holiday in Wales in 1923.[18]

Laughter takes many forms and accents, from the demonically derisive to the magnanimously sociable. This brings us back to Byron, who for all the melancholy to which he gave ample expression (*Manfred*, for example), may also be considered the presiding spirit of resistance to it. 'I hope it is no crime / To laugh at *all* things', he mischievously asks in *Don Juan*, not staying for an answer. He stands accused, he tells us, of 'A tendency to under-rate and scoff / At human power and virtue'. He goes on to show, or at least claim, that his exposure of 'the Nothingness of life' aligns him with the most prestigious literary, biblical, philosophical and theological authorities, including – in no particular order other than that required by rhyme and rhythm – Dante, Solomon, Cervantes, Swift, Luther, Plato (to rhyme with 'potato'). Why, even Isaac Newton – the great ornament and icon of Trinity itself –

> Newton (that Proverb of the Mind) alas! –
>   Declared, with all his grand discoveries recent,
> That he himself felt only 'like a youth
> Picking up shells by the great Ocean – Truth.'

A nice conjunction on which to end, between two such Trinity giants as Byron and Newton. To adopt Byron's metaphor, we hope that the shells of poetry in this volume will similarly resonate in rich and various ways to the ear of the reader.

GEORGE GASCOIGNE
c. 1535–77

Little is known about the early life of George Gascoigne; there are no official records of his time at school or at Cambridge. On the basis of his later assertion that Stephen Nevynson was his 'master', he is thought to have attended either Christ's, where Nevynson was a tutor, or Trinity, where the same man was later Master of the college. We know only that Gascoigne appeared at Gray's Inn aged twenty or so, and from there he attempted to launch a legal career, though for the most part he only got himself into heavy debt. Gray's Inn was well known as a school for wits, a place for bright young men to hone their verbal skills and experiment with varying styles and daring turns of phrase. Very little of Gascoigne's work was published before 1572, except some unobtrusive commendatory verses, but he retrospectively described how at Gray's Inn his peers would ask him to write Latin poems to themes of their choice. Two of his plays were also apparently performed there: *Supposes*, an adaptation of Ariosto's *I suppositi*, and the co-authored *Jocasta*, adapted from an Italian version of Euripides' *Phoenician Women*.

In 1561 he married a rich widow who turned out to be married to someone else, which led to some legal battles and actual fist fights between the two husbands. Gascoigne's fortunes did not improve. In 1570, he ended up in jail for debt, later attempting to better his fortunes by joining a disastrous military expedition to the Netherlands, in which he found himself suspected of treachery by both sides. Back in England, he continued to seek patronage from wealthy sources. The poem 'Gascoigne's Woodmanship' is an example of how skilfully he could combine praise for a patron with fine depictions of pastoral scenery. Ivor Winters described it, perhaps a little over-fulsomely, as 'a poem unsurpassed in the century except by a few of the Sonnets of Shakespeare'. Gascoigne's first book-length attempt to secure support was the collection *A Hundred Sundry Flowers* (1573), a fictionalised anthology of poems by gentlemen, intended to charm and tease the court circles it obliquely satirised. This proved another miscalculation. Two years later he prefaced the second edition – re-titled *Posies of Gascoigne* – with an apology for his 'unbridled youth': the role of penitent *enfant terrible* was one he would often have to adopt.

Certainly he was the first poet to deify Elizabeth 1, dedicating sketches, translations and short poems to her, two decades before Spenser's *Faerie Queene*. However, a masque composed for her in 1575 turned out to be another *faux pas*: it was so explicit about her relations with the Earl of Leicester, from whom Gascoigne was hoping for patronage, that it could not be performed. Somehow, despite all his efforts, he seemed fated to miss the financial backing or literary renown for which he hoped. But his last five years saw a steady stream of poetic activity, and after his death in 1577 he would quite soon come to be considered the most significant poet of the early Elizabethan period. Gascoigne's reputation today seems less certain, but he deserves a wider readership, as someone who felt, in the words of Colin Burrow, 'the forces which made English Renaissance literature happen'.

The Green Knight's Farewell to Fancy

Fancy (quoth he) farewell, whose badge I long did bear,
And in my hat full harebrainedly, thy flowers did I wear:
Too late I find (at last), thy fruits are nothing worth,
Thy blossoms fall and fade full fast, though bravery bring them forth.
By thee I hoped always, in deep delights to dwell,
But since I find thy fickleness, *Fancy* (quoth he) *farewell*.

Thou mad'st me live in love, which wisdom bids me hate,
Thou bleard'st mine eyes and mad'st me think, that faith was mine by fate:
By thee those bitter sweets, did please my taste alway,
By thee I thought that love was light, and pain was but a play:
I thought that Beauty's blaze, was meet to bear the bell,
And since I find myself deceived, *Fancy* (quoth he) *farewell*.

The gloss of gorgeous courts, by thee did please mine eye,
A stately sight methought it was, to see the brave go by:
To see there feathers flaunt, to mark their strange device,
To lie along in Ladies' laps, to lisp and make it nice:
To fawn and flatter both, I liked sometimes well,
But since I see how vain it is, *Fancy* (quoth he) *farewell*.

When court had cast me off, I toiled at the plough,
My fancy stood in strange conceits, to thrive I wot not how:
By mills, by making malt, by sheep and eke by swine,
By duck and drake, by pig and goose, by calves and keeping kine:[19]
By feeding bullocks fat, when price at markets fell,
But since my swains eat up my gains, *Fancy* (quoth he) *farewell*.

In hunting of the deer, my fancy took delight,
All forests knew my folly still, the moonshine was my light:
In frosts I felt no cold, a sunburnt hue was best,
I sweat and was in temper still, my watching seemed rest:
What dangers deep I passed, it folly were to tell,
And since I sigh to think thereon, *Fancy* (quoth he) *farewell*.

A fancy fed me once, to write in verse and rhyme,
To wray[20] my grief, to crave reward, to cover still my crime:
To frame a long discourse, on stirring of a straw,
To rumble rhyme in raffe and ruffe,[21] yet all not worth an haw:
To hear it said there goeth, the *Man that writes so well*,
But since I see, what Poets be, *Fancy* (quoth he) *farewell*.

At Music's sacred sound, my fancies eft begun,
In concords, discords, notes and clefs, in tunes of unison:
In *Hierarchies* and strains, in rests, in rule and space,
In monochords and moving moods, in *Burdens* underbass:
In descants and in chants, I strained many a yell,
But since Musicians be so mad, *Fancy* (quoth he) *farewell*.

To plant strange country fruits, to sow such seeds likewise,
To dig and delve for new found roots, where old might well suffice:
To prune the water boughs, to pick the mossy trees,
(Oh how it pleased my fancy once) to kneel upon my knees,
To griff[22] a pippin stock, when sap begins to swell:
But since the gains scarce quite[23] the cost, *Fancy* (quoth he) *farewell*.

Fancy (quoth he) *farewell*, which made me follow drums,
Where powdered bullets serves for sauce, to every dish that comes:
Where treason lurks in trust, where Hope all hearts beguiles,
Where mischief lieth still in wait, when fortune friendly smiles:
Where one day's prison proves, that all such heavens are hell,
And such I feel the fruits thereof, *Fancy* (quoth he) *farewell*.

If reason rule my thoughts, and God vouchsafe me grace
Then comfort of Philosophy, shall make me change my race:
And fond I shall it find, that Fancy sets to show,
For weakly stands that building still, which lacketh grace by low:
But since I must accept, my fortunes as they fall,
I say God send me better speed, and *Fancy now farewell*.

A Sonnet Written in Praise of the Brown Beauty

compiled for the love of Mistress E. P. as followeth

The thriftless thread which pampered beauty spins,
In thraldom binds the foolish gazing eyes:
As cruel spiders with their crafty gins,
In worthless webs do snare the simple flies.
The garments gay, the glittering golden gite,[24]
The teasing talk which flows from Pallas's spools:
The painted pale, the (too much) red made white,
Are smiling baits to fish for loving fools.
But lo, when eld in toothless mouth appears,
And hoary hairs instead of beauty's blaze:
Then had I wist, doth teach repenting years,
The tickle track of crafty Cupid's maze.
'Twixt faire and foul therefore, 'twixt great and small,
A lovely nutbrown face is best of all.

Si fortunatus infoelix.[25]

Gascoigne's Woodmanship

My worthy Lord, I pray you wonder not
To see your woodman shoot so oft awry,
Nor that he stands amazed like a sot
And lets the harmless deer unhurt go by.
Or if he strike a doe which is but carrion,
Laugh not good Lord, but favour such a fault;
Take will in worth, he would fain hit the barren;
But though his heart be good, his hap is naught.
And therefore now I crave your Lordship's leave
To tell you plain what is the cause of this.
First if it please your honour to perceive
What makes your woodman shoot so oft amiss,
Believe me, Lord, the case is nothing strange.
He shoots awry almost at every mark;
His eyes have been so used for to range,
That now God knows they be both dim and dark.
For proof he bears the note of folly now,

Who shot sometimes to hit philosophy,
And ask you why? forsooth I make avow
Because his wanton wits went all awry.
Next that, he shot to be a man in law,
And spent some time with learned Littleton,[26]
Yet in the end, he proved but a daw,
For law was dark and he had quickly done.
Then could he wish Fitzherbert[27] such a brain
As Tully[28] had, to write the law by art,
So that with pleasure, or with little pain,
He might perhaps have caught a truant's part.
But all too late, he most misliked the thing,
Which most might help to guide his arrow straight;
He winked wrong, and so let slip the string,
Which cast him wide, for all his quaint conceit.
From thence he shot to catch a courtly grace,
And thought even there to wield the world at will,
But out, alas, he much mistook the place,
And shot awry at every rover still.
The blazing baits which draw the gazing eye
Unfeathered there his first affection;
No wonder then although he shot awry,
Wanting the feathers of discretion.
Yet more than them, the marks of dignity
He much mistook, and shot the wronger way,
Thinking the purse of prodigality
Had been best mean to purchase such a prey.
He thought the flattering face which fleereth[29] still,
Had been full fraught with all fidelity,
And that such words as courtiers use at will,
Could not have varied from the verity.
But when his bonnet buttoned with gold,
His comely cape beguarded all with gay,
His bombast hose, with linings manifold,
His knit silk stocks and all his quaint array,
Had picked his purse of all the Peter pence[30]
Which might have paid for his promotion,
Then, all too late, he found that light expense
Had quite quenched out the court's devotion.
So that since then the taste of misery
Hath been always full bitter in his bit,
And why? forsooth because he shot awry,

Mistaking still the marks which others hit.
But now behold what mark the man doth find:
He shoots to be a soldier in his age;
Mistrusting all the virtues of the mind,
He trusts the power of his personage.
As though long limbs led by a lusty heart,
Might yet suffice to make him rich again,
But Flushing frays[31] have taught him such a part
That now he thinks the wars yield no such gain.
And sure I fear, unless your lordship deign
To train him yet into some better trade,
It will be long before he hit the vein
Whereby he may a richer man be made.
He cannot climb as other catchers can,
To lead a charge before himself be led.
He cannot spoil the simple sakeless man,
Which is content to feed him with his bread.
He cannot pinch the painful soldier's pay,
And shear him out his share in ragged sheets.
He cannot stoop to take a greedy prey
Upon his fellows grovelling in the streets.
He cannot pull the spoil from such as pill,
And seem full angry at such foul offence,
Although the gain content his greedy will,
Under the cloak of contrary pretence:
And nowadays, the man that shoots not so,
May shoot amiss, even as your woodman doth:
But then you marvel why I let them go,
And never shoot, but say farewell forsooth:
Alas my Lord, while I do muse hereon,
And call to mind my youthful years misspent,
They give me such a bone to gnaw upon,
That all my senses are in silence pent.
My mind is rapt in contemplation,
Wherein my dazzled eyes only behold
The black hour of my constellation
Which framed me so luckless on the mould.
Yet therewithal I cannot but confess,
That vain presumption makes my heart to swell,
For thus I think, not all the world, I guess,
Shoots bet than I, nay some shoots not so well.
In Aristotle somewhat did I learn

To guide my manners all by comeliness,
And Tully taught me somewhat to discern
Between sweet speech and barbarous rudeness.
Old Parkins, Rastell, and Dan Bracton's books,[32]
Did lend me somewhat of the lawless law;
The crafty courtiers with their guileful looks,
Must needs put some experience in my maw:
Yet cannot these with many maistries mo[33]
Make me shoot straight at any gainful prick,
Where some that never handled such a bow
Can hit the white or touch it near the quick,
Who can nor speak nor write in pleasant wise,
Nor lead their life by Aristotle's rule,
Nor argue well on questions that arise,
Nor plead a case more than my Lord Mayor's mule,
Yet can they hit the marks that I do miss,
And win the mean which may the man maintain.
Now when my mind doth mumble upon this,
No wonder then although I pine for pain:
And whiles mine eyes behold this mirror thus,
The herd goeth by, and farewell gentle does:
So that your lordship quickly may discuss
What blinds mine eyes so oft, as I suppose.
But since my Muse can to my Lord rehearse
What makes me miss, and why I do not shoot,
Let me imagine in this worthless verse,
If right before me, at my standing's foot
There stood a doe, and I should strike her dead,
And then she prove a carrion carcass too,
What figure might I find within my head,
To scuse the rage which ruled me so to do?
Some might interpret with plain paraphrase,
That lack of skill or fortune led the chance,
But I must otherwise expound the case;
I say Jehovah did this doe advance,
And made her bold to stand before me so,
Till I had thrust mine arrow to her heart,
That by the sudden of her overthrow
I might endeavour to amend my part
And turn mine eyes that they no more behold
Such guileful marks as seem more than they be:
And though they glister outwardly like gold,

Are inwardly but brass, as men may see:
And when I see the milk hang in her teat,
Methinks it saith, old babe now learn to suck,
Who in thy youth could'st never learn the feat
To hide the whites which live with all good luck.
Thus have I told my Lord, God grant in season,
A tedious tale in rhyme, but little reason.

Haud ictus sapio.[34]

FRANCIS BACON
1561–1626

Francis Bacon's name is seldom associated with poetry: he is more typically remembered, in the words of a later Trinity thinker, Bertrand Russell, as 'the founder of modern inductive method and the pioneer in the attempt at logical systematization of scientific procedure'. The fact that he wrote poetry of some distinction is a reminder that the strict modern division between literature and science came about only gradually. His best-remembered intellectual achievements represent only one aspect of a fully rounded mind, and of a life dogged by scandal. Bacon was born in London, into both intellectual and financial wealth. His mother, Anne, spoke seven languages, while his father was Sir Nicholas Bacon, Keeper of the Great Seal and, as such, one of the most powerful men in the country. All of the Bacon boys went to Trinity, and Francis, aged twelve, followed suit, accompanying his brother up to Cambridge in 1573. They lived in the household of the Master, Dr John Whitgift, a future Archbishop of Canterbury and to all intents and purposes their personal tutor. At this point a Cambridge education continued to follow the long-established mediaeval curriculum – canon law, scholastic philosophy, and so on – but the influence of humanism was already becoming strong. Records of the books Bacon purchased show him reading new works on rhetoric, classical literature, and some emerging philosophical studies. Still, his first moves after graduation were conventional for a young man in his gilded position. Following three years of travel in France under the wing of the English ambassador, he entered Gray's Inn, rising rapidly throughout the 1580s to become a qualified barrister and legal scholar. Simultaneously, he entered Parliament via a rotten borough, and made himself more and more prominent in public life.

It was in the early 1590s that Bacon turned to philosophical writing, as he decided 'not to follow the practice of the law [...] because it drinketh too much time, which I have dedicated to better purposes'. His writing hitherto had consisted of treatises on English law, mostly advocating its reform, and some informal letters of advice, but when his first published book appeared in 1597, it turned out to be called *Essays*, and contained chatty, unbuttoned prose-pieces on topics from marriage to travel, usury to gardens. (Bacon may possibly have met Montaigne; Anthony Bacon, his brother and contemporary at Trinity, certainly did.) The majority of Bacon's philosophical works, meanwhile, would appear in formal Latin; the exception was his first such, *The Advancement of Learning* (1605). In it Bacon discusses what he elsewhere would call 'the great instauration': his desire to sweep away the deadened schools of scholastic and natural-philosophical thought, and replace them with a direct empirical attention to what could be scrutinised and measured.

Over time, Bacon's work – most of which remained unpublished until his death – became more varied and creative. In 1609 he published *De sapientia veterum*, a collection of thirty-one ancient myths with his accompanying interpretations of what they meant, and later he would compose a utopian tract, the *New Atlantis* (1624). His poems have received less attention than his prose, with the notable exception of the enduring theory that gives him credit for Shakespeare's plays. In the *Advancement* he called poetry 'an imitation of history at pleasure' – a pleasure conspicuously absent from the history of his own life, which was spent relentlessly working at reforms of various philosophical and legal kinds. In 1618 his tireless labours led to his appointment as Lord Chancellor, but he fell from this lofty role after two years, punished with a hefty fine and a brief stint in the Tower of London for taking bribes. He openly admitted that he had done so, as did almost everyone in a position of power at the time, but insisted that he had never allowed them to influence his decisions. His reputation never entirely recovered, and over the centuries it has fluctuated: he has been both praised for his intellectual achievements and condemned for venery and treachery. There has also been considerable speculation as to his sexual appetites. John Aubrey, collating gossip about Bacon several decades after his death, summed up these mixed opinions when he bluntly asserted: 'He was a homosexual. His Ganymedes and favourites took bribes; but his lordship always gave judgement according to justice and honesty.'

Aubrey also wrote that Bacon 'was a good poet, but concealed', and suggested that his 'excellent verses' were known only after his death. Bacon's extant poems demonstrate much of the same erudition and learning as his other writings, for example, in the formal precision and linguistic dexterity of his *Translation of Certain Psalms into English Verse* (1625). These seven translations show the same analytical powers as those driving the *Essays*, the legal treatises, and the work on natural philosophy. They are his final work, for he died in London in early 1626. He was reported to have perished from a chill, caught while packing a dead chicken with snow to investigate the nature of refrigeration – characteristically pursuing the values of empirical knowledge until the very end.

Translation of Psalm 126

When God returned us graciously
   Unto our native land,
We seemed as in a dream to be,
   And in a maze to stand.

The heathen likewise they could say,
   'The God, that these men serve,
Hath done great things for them this day,
   Their nation to preserve'.

'Tis true, God hath poured out his grace
   On us abundantly,
For which we yield him psalms, and praise,
   And thanks with jubilee.

O Lord, turn our captivity,
   As winds that blow at south,
Do pour the tides with violence
   Back to the river's mouth.

Who sows in tears shall reap in joy,
   The Lord doth so ordain;
So that his seed be pure and good,
   His harvest shall be gain.

Translation of Psalm 137

When as we sat all sad and desolate,
  By Babylon upon the river's side,
Eased from the tasks which in our captive state
  We were enforced daily to abide,
        Our harps we had brought with us to the field,
        Some solace to our heavy souls to yield.

But soon we found we failed of our account,
  For when our minds some freedom did obtain,
Straightways the memory of Sion Mount
  Did cause afresh our wounds to bleed again;
        So that with present griefs, and future fears,
        Our eyes burst forth into a stream of tears.

As for our harps, since sorrow struck them dumb,
  We hanged them on the willow-trees were near;
Yet did our cruel masters to us come,
  Asking of us some Hebrew songs to hear;
        Taunting us rather in our misery,
        Than much delighting in our melody.

Alas (said we), who can once force or frame
  His grieved and oppressed heart to sing
The praises of Jehovah's glorious name,
  In banishment, under a foreign king?
        In Sion is his seat and dwelling-place,
        Thence doth he show the brightness of his face.

Jerusalem, where God his throne hath set,
  Shall any hour absent thee from my mind?
Then let my right hand quite her skill forget,
  Then let my voice and words no passage find;
        Nay, if I do not thee prefer in all,
        That in the compass of my thoughts can fall.

Remember thou, O Lord, the cruel cry
  Of Edom's children, which did ring and sound,
Inciting the Chaldean's cruelty,
  'Down with it, down with it, even unto the ground'.
        In that good day repay it unto them,
        When thou shalt visit thy Jerusalem.

And thou, O Babylon, shalt have thy turn
  By just revenge, and happy shall he be,
That thy proud walls and towers shall waste and burn,
  And as thou didst by us, so do by thee.
        Yea, happy he, that takes thy children's bones,
        And dasheth them against the pavement stones.

[The world's a bubble, and the life of man]

Ποίην τις βιότοιο τάμοι τρίβον; εἰν ἀγορῇ μέν
  Νείκεα καὶ χαλεπαὶ πρήζιες· ἐν δὲ δόμοις
Φροντίδες· ἐν δ᾽ ἀγροῖς καμάτων ἅλις· ἐν δὲ θαλάσσῃ
  Τάρβος· ἐπὶ ξείνης δ᾽ ἤν μὲν ἔχῃς τι, δέος·
Ἤν δ᾽ ἀπορῇς, ἀνιηρόν. ἔχεις γάμον; οὐκ ἀμέριμνος
  Ἔσσεαι· οὐ γαμέεις; ζῇς ἔτ᾽ ἐρημότερος.
Τέκνα πόνοι. πήρωσις ἄπαις βίος· αἱ νεότητες
  Ἄφρονες· αἱ πολιαὶ δ᾽ ἔμπαλιν ἀδρανέες.
Ἤν ἄρα τοῖνδε δυοῖν ἑνὸς αἵρεσις, ἢ τὸ γενέσθαι
  Μηδέποτ᾽, ἢ τὸ θανεῖν αὐτίκα τικτόμενον.[35]

The world's a bubble, and the life of man
        less than a span:
In his conception wretched, from the womb
        so to the tomb;
Cursed from the cradle, and brought up to years
        with cares and fears.
Who then to frail mortality shall trust,
But limns the water, or but writes in dust.

Yet, since with sorrow here we live oppressed,
        what life is best?
Courts are but only superficial schools
        to dandle fools:
The rural parts are turned into a den

         of savage men:
And where's a city from all vice so free,
But may be termed the worst of all the three?

Domestic cares afflict the husband's bed,
         or pains, his head;
Those that live single take it for a curse,
         or do things worse;
Some would have children: those that have them moan,
         or wish them gone.
What is it, then, to have or have no wife,
But single thraldom, or a double strife?

Our own affections still at home to please
         is a disease:
To cross the sea to any foreign soil,
         perils and toil.
Wars with their noise affright us; when they cease,
         we are worse in peace.
What then remains, but that we still should cry
Not to be born, or being born, to die?

[The man of life upright, whose guiltless heart is free]

The man of life upright, whose guiltless heart is free
From all dishonest deeds and thoughts of vanity:
The man whose silent days in harmless joys are spent,
Whom hopes cannot delude, nor fortune discontent;
That man needs neither towers nor armour for defence,
Nor secret vaults to fly from thunder's violence:
He only can behold with unaffrighted eyes
The horrors of the deep and terrors of the skies;
Thus scorning all the care that fate or fortune brings,
He makes the heaven his book, his wisdom heavenly things;
Good thoughts his only friends, his life a well-spent age,
The earth his sober inn, – a quiet pilgrimage.

WILLIAM ALABASTER
1568–1640

While his is hardly a household name today, William Alabaster's life and work exemplifies the dramatic transformations of identity and belief that energised much of the finest religious poetry of his time. His adaptation of the sonnet form for devotional purposes may have helped inspire the more famous use of the form by John Donne; like Donne, his was a religious fervour both fuelled and destabilised by the experience of conversion. Born into a merchant's family, Alabaster was able to study at Westminster School thanks to the intercession of John Still, who had married Alabaster's cousin Anne in around 1574. Still was Master of Trinity, and thereby on the board that selected Queen's Scholars at Westminster. His young relative was ushered into Trinity in 1583, where a few years later he was invited to become a Fellow of the College. It was following this election that he seems to have begun writing, staging in Trinity a Latin tragedy, *Roxana*, and beginning an epic poem in praise of Elizabeth I, the *Elisaeis*. He showed this poem – never to be finished – to Edmund Spenser in 1591, when the latter was in Cambridge to visit Still at Trinity. Spenser, to whom the subject-matter could hardly have been more appealing, would praise Alabaster's poem in *Colin Clouts Come Home Again* (1595), writing 'Who lives that can match that heroic song?'. Alabaster would later return the favour, by writing a well-known Latin epitaph on Spenser's immortal fame.

After spending the early 1590s largely in Cambridge, Alabaster made his first substantial foray into public life when in June 1596 he travelled to Cadiz with the Earl of Essex, serving as a chaplain; there he had his first substantial contact with Roman Catholicism and practising Roman Catholics. Soon after returning he was sent to convince Father Thomas Wright, a Catholic priest under house arrest, to convert; but after encountering the charismatic Wright, the opposite seems to have occurred. Alabaster returned to Cambridge, began to write religious sonnets, and fatefully told close friends about being drawn to Catholicism. Within months the putative converter of Wright was himself under house arrest. Bishop Bancroft, the fearsome scourge of Puritans and Papists alike, tried to reconcile him to the English Church, as did Still and even the learned Bishop Lancelot Andrewes, but none was successful. Alabaster was imprisoned in the Clink in Southwark; trapped between the unpalatable alternatives of martyrdom or public recantation. Instead he took the *via media* of breaking out of prison. The subsequent arrest-warrant described him as 'a tall young man about the age thirty, sallow coloured, long visaged, lean faced, black haired, [who] speaketh somewhat thick'. With the help of his co-religionists he evaded capture, escaping to Rome in 1598 and Spain the year after, before being caught by English agents and extradited back to London. Upon James I's succession in 1603 he was pardoned, but with his Catholicism never satisfactorily renounced, he was re-arrested in 1604 and sent away to Rome in 1609. Unfortunately, his cabbalistic text *Apparatus in revelationem Jesu Christi* (1607) would catch up with him there, and earn the attention of the Inquisition, who imprisoned him themselves in 1610. Demonstrating once more a gift for jailbreaks, Alabaster escaped and fled back to England via Amsterdam. Once on home shores he made an (overdue) end to life on the run. He regained royal favour by writing a Latin epithalamium for James upon the 1613 marriage of Robert Carr – a court favourite – and the following year was sent, at last, back to Cambridge as a Doctor of Divinity, absolved of all past transgressions and, outwardly at least, renewed in the Protestant faith.

The years that followed were his most productive, and he wrote a series of Latin devotional works in the 1620s and 30s. As a poet, Alabaster's stock was high among his peers, who admired the wit, learning and skill he showed in his Latin versification. His vernacular religious sonnets, highly personal and direct in their expression, circulated in manuscript form, and were little-known until the twentieth century. For the rest of his life, Alabaster managed to stay out of trouble. Samuel Hartlib, who called his more cabbalistic works 'Antick and Phantastical', nevertheless praised him in 1640 as 'A papist formerly [but] now a zealous Protestant against them'. Alabaster would die that year while in London, having lived peacefully in Cambridgeshire since his 1614 return.

Upon the Crucifix (1)

Before thy Cross, O Christ, I do present
My soul and body into love distilled,
As dewy clouds with equal moisture filled
Receive the tincture of the rainbow bent;
And print those wounds which did thy feet torment,
On my affections which to thee I yield,
And leave those marks wherewith thy hands were held,
Upon my works thy works to represent,
And let those thorns that crowned thy head with pain,
Wound all my thoughts to think on thy disdain,
And let my mouth savour of thy distaste,
And love flow from my breast since thine did stream,
And learn my body with thy grief to waste,
And in thy Cross mine honour to esteem.

Upon St Paul to the Corinthians

Behold a conduit that from heaven doth run,
And at Christ's side a double stream doth vent,
Water with blood and blood with water went,
Water of solace and blood of passion.
All faithful souls must drink this potion,
Where pain to passion is ingredient,
Comfort not made to cause the pain relent,
But pain to relish contentation;
For our distaste cannot Christ apprehend,
Unless that sufferings first our sense amend.
Since then I long thy joys to entertain,
And that thy joys with passion must combine,
Lord, let me feel the tartness of thy pain,
Or drink mine own heart's blood to relish thine.

Upon the Crucifix (2)

Behold a cluster to itself a vine,
Behold a vine extended in one cluster,
Whose grapes do swell with grace and heavenly lustre,
Climbing upon a Cross with lovely twine,
Sent down to earth from Canaan divine,
To stir us up unto a warlike muster,
To take that garden where this cluster grew,
Whose nectar sweet the angels doth bedew.
See how the purple blood doth from it drain,
With thorns, and whips, and nails, and spear diffused!
Drink, drink apace, my soul, that sovereign rain
By which heaven is into my spirit infused,
O drink to thirst, and thirst to drink that treasure,
Where the only danger is to keep a measure.

Ego Sum Vitis [36]

Now that the midday heat doth scorch my shame
With lightning of fond lust, I will retire
Under this vine whose arms with wandering spire
Do climb upon the cross, and on the same
Devise a cool repose from lawless flame,
Whose leaves are intertwist with love entire,
That envy's eye cannot transfuse her fire,
But is rebated on the shady frame;
And youthful vigour from the leaved tier,
Doth stream upon my soul a new desire.
List, list, the ditties of sublimed fame,
Which in the closet of those leaves the choir
Of heavenly birds do warble to his name.
O where was I that was not where I am?

Upon the Crucifix (3)

Now I have found thee, I will evermore
Embrace this standard where thou sitst above.
Feed greedy eyes and from hence never rove,
Suck hungry soul of this eternal store,
Issue my heart from thy two-leaved door,
And let my lips from kissing not remove.
O that I were transformed into love,
And as a plant might spring upon this flower;
Like wandering ivy or sweet honeysuckle,
How would I with my twine about it buckle,
And kiss his feet with my ambitious boughs,
And climb along upon his sacred breast,
And make a garland for his wounded brows.
Lord, so I am if here my thoughts might rest.

'Lord, I have left all and myself behind'

Lord, I have left all and myself behind,
My state, my hopes, my strength, and present ease,
My unprovoked studies' sweet disease,
And touch of nature and engrafted kind,
Whose cleaving twist doth distant tempers bind,
And gentle sense of kindness that doth praise
The earnest judgements, others' wills to please:
All and myself I leave thy love to find.
O strike my heart with lightning from above,
That from one wound both fire and blood may spring,
Fire to transelement[37] my soul to love,
And blood as oil to keep the fire burning,
That fire may draw forth blood, blood extend fire,
Desire possession, possession desire.

Incarnationis Profundum Mysterium[38]

The unbounded sea of the Incarnation!
Whither, my thoughts, O whither do ye tend,
To touch the limits of untermed end?
For though I quarter to each region,
Yet find I nought to rest my thoughts upon;
For if to bounty or to power I bend,
Or wisdom or to justice I extend,
I cannot sound the depth of any one:
Power, by which God is finite man become,
Bounty, that did baseness so dear esteem,
Wisdom, that hath unspun man's fatal doom,
And justice, that by man would man redeem.
Then choose thy death, my thought, or else leave thinking,
Where diving never hath an end of sinking.

The Difference 'twixt Compunction and Cold Devotion in Beholding the Passion of Our Saviour

When without tears I look on Christ, I see
Only a story of some passion,
Which any common eye may wonder on;
But if I look through tears Christ smiles on me.
Yea, there I see myself, and from that tree
He bendeth down to my devotion,
And from his side the blood doth spin, whereon
My heart, my mouth, mine eyes still sucking be;
Like as in optic works, one thing appears
In open gaze, in closer otherwise.
Then since tears see the best, I ask in tears,
Lord, either thaw mine eyes to tears, or freeze
My tears to eyes, or let my heart tears bleed,
Or bring where eyes, nor tears, nor blood shall need.

GILES FLETCHER
1585/6–1623

Giles Fletcher was born into an educated and literary family: his father, also named Giles (a cause for confusion) was a poet and diplomat; his brother was the poet Phineas Fletcher; and his cousin the dramatist John Fletcher who collaborated with Shakespeare. The younger Giles was sent to Westminster, where his ability caught the attention of the Master of Trinity, Thomas Nevile, and with Nevile's encouragement he went up to Trinity aged fifteen or sixteen. He was elected a Scholar, obtained his BA, and duly received a Fellowship. Fletcher entered the priesthood in 1613 – all Fellows at that time took holy orders – but his path took him away from Cambridge when, probably through the influence of Francis Bacon, a family friend, he was given the rectory of Helmingham in Suffolk. This seems not to have been to Fletcher's liking, and he returned to Cambridge on winning the post of University Reader in Greek grammar. Before long, however, he left again, probably sent on Bacon's recommendation to a second living in the village of Alderton.

Fletcher wrote poetry from a young age. His elegy 'A Canto upon the Death of Eliza', for the death of Elizabeth I and the accession of James I, was said to have been written when he was no older than eight. Even if this is an exaggeration, it suggests a wide recognition of the precocity that he displayed long before his university years. This poem might have marked the beginning of a long career, but his next poetic work, upon which his reputation rests, appears to have been his last: *Christ's Victory and Triumph, in Heaven, in Earth, over and after Death* was published in 1610 and dedicated to Nevile. It is an epic in four cantos, written correspondingly in four different forms: those of the mediaeval debate, Spenserian allegory, meditation on Christ's passion, and beatific vision. Fletcher himself owed much to his reading of Spenser, and *Christ's Victory and Triumph* was in turn read by Milton. His body of work, however, was exceptionally small, and he added only *The Reward of the Faithful* (1623) – a prose treatise on religious life – to his verse output before his untimely death. His relationship with his parishioners in Alderton had never been good, and his parochial duties seem to have had an impact on his health – Thomas Fuller hints at an unspecified 'melancholy' that made him ill – and he died of unidentified causes in his thirties.

A Canto upon the Death of Eliza

The early hours were ready to unlock
The door of morn, to let abroad the day,
When sad Ocyroe[39] sitting on a rock,
Hemmed in with tears, not glassing as they say
She wont, her damask beauties (when to play
She bent her looser fancy) in the stream,
That sudding[40] on the rock, would closely seem
To imitate her whiteness with his frothy cream.

But hanging from the stone her careful head,
That showed (for grief had made it so to show)
A stone itself, thus only differed,
That those without, these streams within did flow,
Both ever ran, yet never less did grow,
And tearing from her head her amber hairs,
Whose like or none, or only Phoebus wears,
She strowed there on the flood to wait upon her tears.

About her many Nymphs sat weeping by,
That when she sang were wont to dance and leap.
And all the grass that round about did lie,
Hung full of tears, as if that meant to weep,
Whilst, th'undersliding streams did softly creep,
And clung about the rock with winding wreath,
To hear a Canto of Eliza's death:
Which thus poor nymph she sung, whilst sorrow lent her breath.

'Tell me ye blushing corals that bunch out,
To clothe with beauteous red your ragged sire,
So let the sea-green moss curl round about
With soft embrace (as creeping vines do wire
Their loved elms) your sides in rosy tyre,
So let the ruddy vermeil of your cheek
Make stained carnations fresher liveries seek,
So let your branched arms grow crooked, smooth, and sleek.

'So from your growth late be you rent away,
And hung with silver bells and whistles shrill,
Unto those children be you given to play
Where blest Eliza reigned: so never ill

Betide your canes nor them with breaking spill,
Tell me if some uncivil hand should tear
Your branches hence, and place them otherwhere;
Could you still grow, and such fresh crimson ensigns bear?

'Tell me sad Philomel that yonder sit'st
Piping thy songs unto the dancing twig,
And to the waters fall thy music fit'st,
So let the friendly prickle never dig
Thy watchful breast with wound or small or big,
Whereon thou lean'st, so let the hissing snake
Sliding with shrinking silence never take
Th'unwary foot, whilst thou perhaps hang'st half awake.

'So let the loathed lapwing when her nest
Is stolen away, not as she uses, fly,
Cozening the searcher of his promised feast,
But widowed of all hope still Itys⁴¹ cry,
And nought but Itys, Itys, till she die.
Say sweetest chorister of the airy quire
Doth not thy Tereu, Tereu then expire,
When winter robs thy house of all her green attire?

'Tell me ye velvet headed violets
That fringe the crooked bank with gaudy blue,
So let with comely grace your pretty frets
Be spread, so let a thousand Zephyrs sue
To kiss your willing heads, that seem t'eschew
Their wanton touch with maiden modesty,
So let the silver dew but lightly lie
Like little watery worlds within your azure sky,

'So when your blazing leaves are broadly spread
Let wandering nymphs gather you in their laps,
And send you where Eliza lieth dead,
To strow the sheet that her pale body wraps,
Ay me in this I envy your good haps:
Who would not die, there to be buried?
Say if the sun deny his beams to shed
Upon your living stalks, grow you not withered?

'Tell me thou wanton brook, that slip'st away
T'avoid the straggling banks still flowing cling,
So let thy waters cleanly tribute pay
Unmixed with mud unto the sea your king,
So never let your streams leave murmuring
Until they steal by many a secret furt[42]
To kiss those walls that built Eliza's court,
Dry you not when your mother springs are choked with dirt?

'Yes you all say, and I say with you all,
Naught without cause of joy can joyous bide,
Then me unhappy nymph whom the dire fall
Of my joys spring.' But there 'aye me' she cried,
And spake no more, for sorrow speech denied.
And down into her watery lodge did go;
The very waters when she sunk did show
With many wrinkled ohs they sympathised her woe.

The sun in mourning clouds enveloped
Flew fast into the western world to tell
News of her death. Heaven itself sorrowed
With tears that to the earth's dank bosom fell;
But when the next Aurora gan to deal
Handfuls of roses fore the team of day
A shepherd drove his flock by chance that way
And made the nymph to dance that mourned yesterday.

GEORGE HERBERT
1593–1633

George Herbert was born to a noble family in Montgomery, Wales. His father died when he was only three, and the family moved to Oxford. John Donne, godfather to the young boy, played a part in raising him until the Herberts moved again, down to London. Young George went as a day-boy to Westminster, where Lancelot Andrewes was the Dean, a man with a reputation for strict discipline and a fanatical devotion to literary exercises. Andrewes' eloquent and obsessive dissection of Christian language would find its poetic counterpart in Herbert's later poems, and the two would prove pivotal to later narratives in an unbroken Anglican tradition. Thus trained, George went up to Trinity aged sixteen, and went on not only to receive a BA, an MA and a Fellowship, but in due time to become an assistant lecturer at Trinity, University Praelector in rhetoric, deputy to the University Orator, and eventually University Orator. Concurrently, he became MP for Montgomery, and was high in James I's esteem until the King's death in 1625, after which Herbert drifted away from politics and towards religion. He was ordained in 1629.

It was in Cambridge that Herbert began to write poetry. The earliest of the devotional works for which he is now well-known is 'The Church-Porch', which can be dated back to 1614, shortly after his BA was awarded. His first publication of any kind, however, was a pair of Latin elegies on the death of Prince Henry, published two years previously in a university anthology. His verses were strongly individual, devotional, and explored the difficult link between a solitary worshipper and a God whose demands were unignorable but agonisingly hard to bear. Much of this was due to the increasing pain of Herbert's own life. He suffered from tuberculosis, the symptoms of which grew worse and worse – 'He was a very fine complexion and consumptive', John Aubrey wrote – and after only three years of the priesthood, he died aged thirty-nine. He was remembered by his parishioners as a man close to sainthood, who continued to bring them the sacraments even as his own strength failed. Herbert himself bewailed the frustrations of illness to his mother, writing 'I always feared sickness more than death, because sickness hath made me unable to perform those Offices for which I came into the world, and must yet be kept in it.'

None of Herbert's English poems were published during his lifetime. The work for which he is now remembered, *The Temple: Sacred Poems and Private Ejaculations*, was published after his death by Nicholas Ferrar, patriarch of the religious community at Little Gidding where Herbert had been a frequent visitor. Herbert had sent Ferrar all his English poetry before he died, famously asking him to burn everything unless, and only unless, it could 'turn to the advantage of any dejected poor soul'. But Ferrar was impressed by the poems' virtuosic use of rhyme and wordplay, and saw them into publication. Their beauty is visual as well as formal: as *The Temple* proceeds through the architecture of a church, moving from 'The Church-Porch' towards 'The Altar', it passes by various other things, often depicted in lines shaped to look like the object itself. He was fascinated not only by the shapes, but also by the musicality of words; Aubrey intriguingly claims that Herbert 'had a very good hand on the Lute, and that he set his own Lyrics or sacred poems' to music. His emphasis on the ornate fabric of church buildings and the sensory richness of worship complemented the 'beauty of holiness' that was being proclaimed as an ideal by Archbishop Laud and his followers. While his playing with language was scorned by later critics, including, notoriously, Dryden (who mocked poets living in 'Acrostic Land'), *The Temple* anticipated the typographic innovations that would come into prominence centuries later with the likes of Stéphane Mallarmé, and the genre of concrete poetry that followed. While no new editions of *The Temple* appeared between 1709 and 1799, a period when Herbert was largely ignored, his reputation among poets was revived in the nineteenth century, and academic criticism took notice in the middle of the twentieth. His status today, as one of the greatest of all English religious poets, is secure among readers, authors and critics alike.

The Altar

A broken altar, Lord, thy servant rears,
Made of a heart, and cemented with tears:
Whose parts are as thy hand did frame;
No workman's tool hath touched the same.
A heart alone
Is such a stone,
As nothing but
Thy power doth cut.
Wherefore each part
Of my hard heart
Meets in this frame,
To praise thy Name:
That, if I chance to hold my peace,
These stones to praise thee may not cease.
O let thy blessed Sacrifice be mine,
And sanctify this Altar to be thine.

Easter

Rise heart; thy Lord is risen. Sing his praise
                    Without delays.
Who takes thee by the hand, that thou likewise
                    With him mayst rise:
That, as his death calcined thee to dust,
His life may make thee gold, and much more, just.

Awake, my lute, and struggle for thy part
                    With all thy art.
The cross taught all wood to resound his name,
                    Who bore the same.
His stretched sinews taught all strings, what key
Is best to celebrate this most high day.

Consort both heart and lute, and twist a song
                    Pleasant and long:
Or, since all music is but three parts vied
                    And multiplied,
O let thy blessed Spirit bear a part,
And make up our defects with his sweet art.

I got me flowers to straw thy way;
I got me boughs off many a tree:
But thou wast up by break of day,
And broughtst thy sweets along with thee.

The sun arising in the east,
Though he give light, & th'east perfume;
If they should offer to contest
With thy arising, they presume.

Can there be any day but this,
Though many suns to shine endeavour?
We count three hundred, but we miss:
There is but one, and that one ever.

'Easter Wings' from George Herbert, *The Temple*, 3rd edition (1634),
pp. 34–35.

Easter-Wings

Lord, who createdst man in wealth and store,
Though foolishly he lost the same,
Decaying more and more,
Till he became
Most poor:
With thee
O let me rise
As larks, harmoniously,
And sing this day thy victories:
Then shall the fall further the flight in me.

My tender age in sorrow did begin:
And still with sicknesses and shame
Thou didst so punish sin,
That I became
Most thin.
With thee
Let me combine
And feel this day thy victory:
For, if I imp my wing on thine,
Affliction shall advance the flight in me.

Prayer (I)

Prayer the church's banquet, angel's age,
  God's breath in man returning to his birth,
  The soul in paraphrase, heart in pilgrimage,
The Christian plummet sounding heaven and earth;
Engine against th'almighty, sinner's tower,
  Reversed thunder, Christ-side-piercing spear,
  The six-days world transposing in an hour,
A kind of tune, which all things hear and fear;
Softness, and peace, and joy, and love, and bliss,
  Exalted manna, gladness of the best,
  Heaven in ordinary, man well dressed,
The Milky Way, the bird of paradise,
  Church-bells beyond the stars heard, the soul's blood,
  The land of spices; something understood.

Love (I)

Immortal Love, author of this great frame,
  Sprung from that beauty which can never fade;
  How hath man parcelled out thy glorious name,
And thrown it on that dust which thou hast made,
While mortal love doth all the title gain!
  Which siding with invention, they together
  Bear all the sway, possessing heart and brain,
(Thy workmanship) and give thee share in neither.
Wit fancies beauty, beauty raiseth wit:
  The world is theirs; they two play out the game,
  Thou standing by: and though thy glorious name
Wrought our deliverance from th'infernal pit,
  Who sings thy praise? only a scarf or glove
  Doth warm our hands, and make them write of love.

Love (II)

Immortal Heat, O let thy greater flame
  Attract the lesser to it: let those fires,
  Which shall consume the world, first make it tame;
And kindle in our hearts such true desires,
As may consume our lusts, and make thee way.
  Then shall our hearts pant thee; then shall our brain
  All her invention on thine altar lay,
And there in hymns send back thy fire again:
Our eyes shall see thee, which before saw dust;
  Dust blown by wit, till that they both were blind:
  Thou shalt recover all thy goods in kind,
Who wert diseased by usurping lust:
  All knees shall bow to thee; all wits shall rise,
  And praise him who did make and mend our eyes.

Jordan (I)

Who says that fictions only and false hair
Become a verse? Is there in truth no beauty?
Is all good structure in a winding stair?
May no lines pass, except they do their duty
  Not to a true, but painted chair?

Is it no verse, except enchanted groves
And sudden arbours shadow coarse-spun lines?
Must purling streams refresh a lover's loves?
Must all be veiled, while he that reads, divines,
  Catching the sense at two removes?

Shepherds are honest people; let them sing:
Riddle who list, for me, and pull for prime:
I envy no man's nightingale or spring;
Nor let them punish me with loss of rhyme,
  Who plainly say, 'My God, My King'.

Church-Monuments

While that my soul repairs to her devotion,
Here I entomb my flesh, that it betimes
May take acquaintance of this heap of dust;
To which the blast of death's incessant motion,
Fed with the exhalation of our crimes,
Drives all at last. Therefore I gladly trust

My body to this school, that it may learn
To spell his elements, and find his birth
Written in dusty heraldry and lines;
Which dissolution sure doth best discern,
Comparing dust with dust, and earth with earth.
These laugh at jet and marble put for signs,

To sever the good fellowship of dust,
And spoil the meeting. What shall point out them,
When they shall bow, and kneel, and fall down flat
To kiss those heaps, which now they have in trust?
Dear flesh, while I do pray, learn here thy stem
And true descent; that when thou shalt grow fat,

And wanton in thy cravings, thou mayst know,
That flesh is but the glass, which holds the dust
That measures all our time; which also shall
Be crumbled into dust. Mark here below
How tame these ashes are, how free from lust,
That thou mayst fit thy self against thy fall.

The Windows

Lord, how can man preach thy eternal word?
      He is a brittle crazy glass:
Yet in thy temple thou dost him afford
        This glorious and transcendent place,
        To be a window, through thy grace.

But when thou dost anneal in glass thy story,
      Making thy life to shine within
The holy preacher's; then the light and glory
        More reverend grows, & more doth win:
        Which else shows waterish, bleak, and thin.

Doctrine and life, colours and light, in one
      When they combine and mingle, bring
A strong regard and awe: but speech alone
        Doth vanish like a flaring thing,
        And in the ear, not conscience ring.

Vanity (I)

      The fleet astronomer can bore,
And thread the spheres with his quick-piercing mind:
He views their stations, walks from door to door,
      Surveys, as if he had designed
To make a purchase there: he sees their dances,
        And knoweth long before
Both their full-eyed aspects, and secret glances.

      The nimble diver with his side
Cuts through the working waves, that he may fetch
His dearly-earned pearl, which God did hide
      On purpose from the ven'trous wretch;
That he might save his life, and also hers,
        Who with excessive pride
Her own destruction and his danger wears.

The subtle chymick[43] can divest
And strip the creature naked, till he find
The callow principles within their nest:
    There he imparts to them his mind,
Admitted to their bed-chamber, before
      They appear trim and dressed
To ordinary suitors at the door.

    What hath not man sought out and found,
But his dear God? who yet his glorious law
Embosoms in us, mellowing the ground
    With showers and frosts, with love and awe,
So that we need not say, 'where's this command?'.
    Poor man, thou searchest round
To find out death, but missest life at hand.

The Pearl. Matthew 13:45

I know the ways of learning; both the head
And pipes that feed the press, and make it run;
What reason hath from nature borrowed,
Or of itself, like a good housewife, spun
In laws and policy; what the stars conspire,
What willing nature speaks, what forced by fire;
Both th'old discoveries, and the new-found seas,
The stock and surplus, cause and history:
All these stand open, or I have the keys:
    Yet I love thee.

I know the ways of honour, what maintains
The quick returns of courtesy and wit:
In vies of favours whether party gains,
When glory swells the heart, and mouldeth it
To all expressions both of hand and eye,
Which on the world a true-love-knot may tie,
And bear the bundle, wheresoe'er it goes:
How many drams of spirit there must be
To sell my life unto my friends or foes:
    Yet I love thee.

I know the ways of pleasure, the sweet strains,
The lullings and the relishes of it;
The propositions of hot blood and brains;
What mirth and music mean; what love and wit
Have done these twenty hundred years, and more:
I know the projects of unbridled store:
My stuff is flesh, not brass; my senses live,
And grumble oft, that they have more in me
Than he that curbs them, being but one to five:
       Yet I love thee.

I know all these, and have them in my hand:
Therefore not seeled, but with open eyes
I fly to thee, and fully understand
Both the main sale, and the commodities;
And at what rate and price I have thy love;
With all the circumstances that may move:
Yet through these labyrinths, not my grovelling wit,
But thy silk twist let down from heaven to me,
Did both conduct and teach me, how by it
       To climb to thee.

Life

I made a posy, while the day ran by:
Here will I smell my remnant out, and tie
       My life within this band.
But time did beckon to the flowers, and they
By noon most cunningly did steal away,
       And withered in my hand.

My hand was next to them, and then my heart:
I took, without more thinking, in good part
       Time's gentle admonition:
Who did so sweetly death's sad taste convey,
Making my mind to smell my fatal day;
       Yet sugaring the suspicion.

Farewell dear flowers, sweetly your time ye spent,
Fit, while ye lived, for smell or ornament,
        And after death for cures.
I follow straight without complaints or grief,
Since if my scent be good, I care not if
        It be as short as yours.

Jordan (II)

When first my lines of heavenly joys made mention,
Such was their lustre, they did so excel,
That I sought out quaint words, and trim invention;
My thoughts began to burnish, sprout, and swell,
Curling with metaphors a plain intention,
Decking the sense, as if it were to sell.

Thousands of notions in my brain did run,
Offering their service, if I were not sped:
I often blotted what I had begun;
This was not quick enough, and that was dead.
Nothing could seem too rich to clothe the sun,
Much less those joys which trample on his head.

As flames do work and wind, when they ascend,
So did I weave my self into the sense.
But while I bustled, I might hear a friend
Whisper, 'How wide is all this long pretence!
There is in love a sweetness ready penn'd:
Copy out only that, and save expense'.

Dullness

Why do I languish thus, drooping and dull,
　　As if I were all earth?
O give me quickness, that I may with mirth
　　Praise thee brim-full!

The wanton lover in a curious strain
　　Can praise his fairest fair;
And with quaint metaphors her curled hair
　　Curl o'er again.

Thou art my loveliness, my life, my light,
　　Beauty alone to me:
Thy bloody death and undeserved, makes thee
　　Pure red and white.

When all perfections as but one appear,
　　That those thy form doth show,
The very dust, where thou dost tread and go,
　　Makes beauties here.

Where are my lines then? my approaches? views?
　　Where are my window-songs?
Lovers are still pretending, and e'en wrongs
　　Sharpen their Muse:

But I am lost in flesh, whose sugared lies
　　Still mock me, and grow bold:
Sure thou didst put a mind there, if I could
　　Find where it lies.

Lord, clear thy gift, that with a constant wit
　　I may but look towards thee:
Look only; for to love thee, who can be,
　　What angel fit?

Paradise

I bless thee, Lord, because I GROW
Among thy trees, which in a ROW
To thee both fruit and order OW.

What open force, or hidden CHARM
Can blast my fruit, or bring me HARM,
While the enclosure is thine ARM?

Enclose me still for fear I START.
Be to me rather sharp and TART,
Than let me want thy hand and ART.

When thou dost greater judgements SPARE,
And with thy knife but prune and PARE,
Ev'n fruitful trees more fruitful ARE.

Such sharpness shows the sweetest FREND:
Such cuttings rather heal than REND:
And such beginnings touch their END.

The Pulley

When God at first made man,
Having a glass of blessings standing by;
Let us (said he) pour on him all we can:
Let the world's riches, which dispersed lie,
        Contract into a span.

So strength first made a way;
Then beauty flowed, then wisdom, honour, pleasure:
When almost all was out, God made a stay,
Perceiving that alone of all his treasure
        Rest in the bottom lay.

For if I should (said he)
Bestow this jewel also on my creature,
He would adore my gifts in stead of me,
And rest in Nature, not the God of Nature:
        So both should losers be.

Yet let him keep the rest,
But keep them with repining restlessness:
Let him be rich and weary, that at least,
If goodness lead him not, yet weariness
        May toss him to my breast.

The Odour. 2 Corinthians 2:15

How sweetly doth *My Master* sound! *My Master*!
        As ambergris leaves a rich scent
                Unto the taster:
        So do these words a sweet content,
An oriental fragrancy, *My Master*.

With these all day I do perfume my mind,
        My mind ev'n thrust into them both:
                That I might find
        What cordials make this curious broth,
This broth of smells, that feeds and fats my mind.

My Master, shall I speak? O that to thee
        My servant were a little so,
                As flesh may be;
        That these two words might creep and grow
To some degree of spiciness to thee!

Then should the pomander, which was before
        A speaking sweet, mend by reflection,
                And tell me more:
        For pardon of my imperfection
Would warm and work it sweeter than before.

For when *My Master*, which alone is sweet,
        And ev'n in my unworthiness pleasing,
                Shall call and meet,
        My servant, as thee not displeasing,
That call is but the breathing of the sweet.

This breathing would with gains by sweetening me
(As sweet things traffic when they meet)
Return to thee.
And so this new commerce and sweet
Should all my life employ and busy me.

The Elixir

Teach me, my God and King,
In all things thee to see,
And what I do in any thing,
To do it as for thee:

Not rudely, as a beast,
To run into an action;
But still to make thee prepossessed,
And give it his perfection.

A man that looks on glass,
On it may stay his eye;
Or if he pleaseth, through it pass,
And then the heaven espy.

All may of thee partake:
Nothing can be so mean,
Which with his tincture (for thy sake)
Will not grow bright and clean.

A servant with this clause
Makes drudgery divine:
Who sweeps a room, as for thy laws,
Makes that and th'action fine.

This is the famous stone
That turneth all to gold:
For that which God doth touch and own
Cannot for less be told.

Love (III)

Love bade me welcome: yet my soul drew back,
    Guilty of dust and sin.
But quick-eyed Love, observing me grow slack
    From my first entrance in,
Drew nearer to me, sweetly questioning,
    If I lacked any thing.

A guest, I answered, worthy to be here:
    Love said, 'You shall be he'.
I the unkind, ungrateful? 'Ah my dear,
    I cannot look on thee'.
Love took my hand, and smiling did reply,
    'Who made the eyes but I?'.

'Truth Lord, but I have marred them: let my shame
    Go where it doth deserve'.
'And know you not', says Love, 'who bore the blame?';
    'My dear, then I will serve'.
'You must sit down', says Love, 'and taste my meat':
    So I did sit and eat.

THOMAS RANDOLPH
1605–35

Thomas Randolph's literary ambitions began early, for John Aubrey attests to his having written a 'History of the Incarnation of our Saviour' at the tender age of nine, no less. Aubrey noted Randolph's precocity while lamenting his unfortunate appearance, with 'flaggy' white-blonde hair and 'a pale ill complexion and pockpitten'. This ghostly youth quickly impressed his elders, entering Westminster as a King's Scholar where, by the time he was ten, he was being asked to extemporise Latin verses for the school's formal dinners. Established as Westminster's most brilliant student and Head of School, he went up to Trinity aged eighteen. There he continued to write Latin verses, contributing elegies and commendatory poems to various University anthologies, but also turned to writing for the stage. His first play, *Aristippus, or the Jovial Philosopher*, was an adaptation of Aristophanes' *Plutus*, performed before the Fellows of the College in 1626. He revived the dormant tradition of Salting, where witty speeches were made by the older undergraduates to welcome the freshers into college life – a tradition that has long since died, but not before a young John Milton continued it at Christ's, one year after Randolph.

When Randolph graduated, all available Fellowships had been filled, but as a mark of the esteem in which he was held, the Master, Leonard Mawe, organised for him a Fellowship by royal mandate. Word of Randolph's comic skill spread to London, and he soon made the acquaintance of Ben Jonson, who adopted him as one of his literary 'sons', and may have helped establish him on the London scene where several of his plays were produced. Randolph earned some measure of royal patronage, too, having *The Jealous Lovers* performed before Charles I in 1632, and supposedly getting the King's support to regain his Trinity Fellowship after, for reasons that remain obscure, it was taken away. Throughout these years Randolph continued to write poems, mainly Latin verses for occasions, but also English love poems, songs, and pastorals. Though these were less well-known than his plays at the time, they were equally well-regarded. He was set to follow Jonson as one of the most significant poets in the land when he unexpectedly died, probably from smallpox and the effects of a dissolute lifestyle, aged only twenty-nine. Randolph's poetry was collected and published posthumously three years later, quickly running through several editions. His star, however, has since been somewhat eclipsed, mainly by the subsequent rise and enduring reputations of Milton, Marvell and Dryden.

An Elegy upon the Lady Venetia Digby

Death, who'ld not change prerogatives with thee,
That dost such rapes, yet mayst not questioned be?
Here cease thy wanton lust, be satisfied,
Hope not a second, and so fair a bride.
Where was her Mars, whose valiant arms did hold
This Venus once, that thou durst be so bold?
By thy too nimble theft, I know 'twas fear,
Lest he should come, that would have rescued her.
Monster confess, didst thou not blushing stand,
And thy pale cheek turn red to touch her hand?
Did she not lightning-like strike sudden heat
Through thy cold limbs, and thaw thy frost to sweat?
Well since thou hast her, use her gently, Death,
And in requital of such precious breath
Watch sentinel to guard her, do not see
The worms thy rivals, for the gods will be.
Remember Paris, for whose pettier sin,
The Trojan gates let the stout Grecians in;
So when time ceases (whose unthrifty hand
Has now almost consumed his stock of sand),
Myriads of angels shall in armies come,
And fetch (proud ravisher) their Helen home.
And to revenge this rape, thy other store
Thou shalt resign too, and shalt steal no more.
Till then fair ladies (for you now are fair,
But till her death I feared your just despair),
Fetch all the spices that Arabia yields,
Distil the choicest flowers of the fields:
And when in one their best perfections meet
Embalm her course, that she may make them sweet.
Whilst for an Epitaph upon her stone
I cannot write, but I must weep her one.

Epitaph

Beauty itself lies here, in whom alone,
Each part enjoyed the same perfection.
In some the eyes we praise; in some the hair;
In her the lips; in her the cheeks are fair;
That nymph's fine feet, her hands we beauteous call,
But in this form we praise no part, but all.
The ages past have many beauties shown,

And I more plenty in our time have known;
But in the age to come I look for none,
Nature despairs, because her pattern's gone.

Upon the Loss of His Little Finger

Arithmetic nine digits, and no more,
Admits of; then I still have all my store.
For what mischance hath ta'en from my left hand,
It seems did only for a cipher stand.
But this I'll say for thee, departed joint,
Thou wert not given to steal, nor pick, nor point
At any in disgrace; but thou didst go
Untimely to thy death only to show
The other members what they once must do:
Hand, arm, leg, thigh, and all must follow too.
Oft didst thou scan my verse, where, if I miss
Henceforth, I will impute the cause to this.
A finger's loss (I speak it not in sport)
Will make a verse a foot too short.
Farewell, dear finger: much I grieve to see
How soon mischance hath made a hand of thee.

Upon His Picture

When age hath made me what I am not now;
And every wrinkle tells me where the plough
Of time hath furrowed; when an ice shall flow
Through every vein, and all my head wear snow:
When death displays his coldness in my cheek,
And I, myself in my own picture seek.
Not finding what I am, but what I was,
In doubt which to believe, this, or my glass:
Yet though I alter, this remains the same
As it was drawn, retains the primitive frame,
And first complexion; here will still be seen
Blood on the cheek, and down upon the chin.
Here the smooth brow will stay, the lively eye,

The ruddy lip, and hair of youthful dye.
Behold what frailty we in man may see,
Whose shadow is less given to change than he.

Ad Amicum Litigantem [44]

Would you commence a poet, sir, and be
A graduate in the threadbare mystery?
The Ox's ford will no man thither bring,
Where the horse-hoof raised the Pegasian spring;
Nor will the bridge through which low Cam doth run,
Direct you to the banks of Helicon.
If in that art you mean to take degrees,
Bedlam's the best of universities.
There study it, and when you would no more
A poet be, go drink some hellebore;
Which drug when I had tasted, soon I left
The bare Parnassus, and the barren cleft;
And can no more one of their nation be,
Because recovered of my lunacy.
But you may then succeed me in my place
Of poet, no pretence to make your grace
Denied you, for you go to law, 'tis said;
And then 'tis taken for granted you are mad.

In Praise of Women in General

He is a parricide to his mother's name,
And with an impious hand murders her fame,
That wrongs the praise of women: that dares write
Libels on saints, or with foul ink requite
The milk they lent us. Better sex, command
To your defence my more religious hand
At sword or pen. Yours was the nobler birth;
For you of man were made, man but of earth,
The son of dust; and though your sin did breed
His fall, again you raised him in your seed.
Adam in's sleep a gainful loss sustained,

That for one rib a better self regained;
Who had he not your blest creation seen,
An anchorite in paradise had been.
Why in this work did the creation rest,
But that eternal providence thought you best
Of all his six days' labour: beasts should do
Homage to man, but man should wait on you.
You are of comelier sight, of daintier touch,
A tender flesh, a colour bright, and such
As Parians[45] see in marble; skin more fair,
More glorious head, and far more glorious hair;
Eyes full of grace and quickness; purer roses
Blush in your cheeks; a milder white composes
Your stately fronts; your breath, more sweet than his,
Breathes spice, and nectar drops at every kiss.
Your skins are smooth; bristles on theirs do grow,
Like quills of porcupines; rough wool doth flow
O'er all their faces; you approach more near
The form of angels, they like beasts appear.
If then in bodies, where the souls do dwell,
You better us, do then our souls excel?
No; we in souls equal perfection see:
There can in them nor male nor female be.
Boast we of knowledge, you have more than we:
You were the first ventured to pluck the tree,
And that more rhetoric in your tongues doth lie,
Let him dispute against, that dares deny
Your least commands, and not persuaded be
With Samson's strength and David's piety
To be your willing captives; virtue, sure,
Were blind as fortune, should she choose the poor
Rough cottage, man, to live in, and despise
To dwell in you – the statelier edifice.
Thus you are proved the better sex, and we
Must all repent that in our pedigree
We choose the father's name, where should we take
The mother's – a more honoured blood, 'twould make
Our generation sure and certain be,
And I'd believe some faith in heraldry!
Thus, perfect creatures, if detraction rise
Against your sex, dispute but with your eyes,
Your hand, your lip, your brow: there will be sent

So subtle and so strong an argument
Will teach the stoic his affection too,
And call the cynic from his tub to woo.
Thus mustering up your beauteous troops, go on:
The fairest is the valiant Amazon.

SIR JOHN SUCKLING
1609–42

John Suckling was born into a Royalist family, his father an MP who would later become the Comptroller of the King's Household. The young Suckling may well have attended Westminster – this is John Aubrey's guess – but we do not know for sure; certainly he went up to Trinity aged fourteen or so, although he seems to have left without completing a degree. Suckling had his inheritance withheld by order of his father's will until he was twenty-five. He tried a variety of occupations in the meantime, from a brief spell at Gray's Inn to cavalry enlistment in Belgium, but none of them stuck. He was well-known for his gambling, which was his principal employment: his prodigality was so great that to cover his expenses he had to turn himself into the finest card-player in England. This he became, and invented the game of Cribbage to boot. He was knighted at Theobalds in 1630, and was always known as one of the greatest wits at court – as Aubrey puts it, he was 'incomparably ready at repartying'. He also reported that Suckling travelled for three or four years on the Continent following his time at Trinity, and 'returned into England an extraordinary accomplished Gent.', who 'grew famous at Court for his ready Sparkling wit, which was envied'. This sparkling wit is amply apparent in Suckling's poetry, but, whether due to envy or his undoubted talent for giving offence, it also led him into a series of unseemly scuffles and brawls. Fortunately for him, these escapades were coming to be practically expected of a 'Cavalier' poet.

The earliest known works by Suckling are religious poems, written when he was around fifteen. He would continue to write poetry at a steady rate, and produced four plays as well, but it was towards the end of his life that he came into his own. His most famous poem, 'The Wits', presents an imagined contest between poets including Jonson and Davenant, presided over by Apollo. It was written in the same year (1637) as his treatise, *An Account of Religion by Reason*, and also his tragedy *Aglaura*, which seems to have been the first play on the English stage to use extensive, decorative scenery. Suckling continued to write smooth and elegant verse, in forms ranging from satire to pastoral, which circulated widely in manuscript, until his untimely death in Paris in his early thirties. Alexander Pope tells a good tale involving a servant who attacked Suckling with a rusty nail and left his wound to become infected; the reality is probably that Suckling, a staunch Royalist, committed suicide after fleeing England on account of his involvement in the First Army Plot.

Against Fruition

Stay here, fond youth, and ask no more; be wise:
Knowing too much long since lost paradise.
The virtuous joys thou hast, thou wouldst should still
Last in their pride; and wouldst not take it ill,
If rudely from sweet dreams (and for a toy)
Thou wert waked? He wakes himself, that does enjoy.

Fruition adds no new wealth, but destroys,
And while it pleaseth much the palate, cloys;
Who thinks he shall be happier for that,
As reasonably might hope he might grow fat
By eating to a surfeit; this once past,
What relishes? Even kisses lose their taste.

Urge not 'tis necessary: alas! we know
The homeliest thing which mankind does is so;
The world is of a vast extent, we see,
And must be peopled; children there must be;
So must bread too; but since they are enough
Born to the drudgery, what need we plough?

Women enjoyed (whate'er before they've been)
Are like romances read, or sights once seen:
Fruition's dull, and spoils the play much more
Than if one read or knew the plot before.
'Tis expectation makes a blessing dear;
Heaven were not heaven, if we knew what it were.

And as in prospects we are there pleased most,
Where something keeps the eye from being lost,
And leaves us room to guess; so here restraint
Holds up delight, that with excess would faint.
They who know all the wealth they have, are poor,
He's only rich that cannot tell his store.

[That none beguiled be by Time's quick flowing]

That none beguiled be by Time's quick flowing,
Lovers have in their hearts a clock still going;
  For though Time be nimble, his motions
              are quicker
              and thicker
    where Love hath his notions:

Hope is the main spring on which moves desire,
And these do the less wheels, fear, joy, inspire;
  The balance is thought, evermore
              clicking
            and striking,
    and ne'er giving o'er;

Occasion's the hand which still's moving round,
Till by it the critical hour may be found,
  And when that falls out, it will strike
              kisses,
            strange blisses,
    and what you best like.

A Summons to Town

Sir,
Whether these lines do find you out,
Putting or clearing of a doubt;
(Whether predestination,
Or reconciling three in one,
Or the unriddling how men die,
And live at once eternally,
Now take you up) know 'tis decreed
You straight bestride the college steed:
Leave Socinus[46] and the schoolmen,
(Which Jack Bond[47] swears do but fool men)
And come to town; 'tis fit you show
Your self abroad, that men may know
(Whate'er some learned men have guessed)
That oracles are not yet ceased:

There you shall find the wit, and wine
Flowing alike, and both divine;
Dishes, with names not known in books,
And less amongst the college-cooks,
With sauce so pregnant that you need
Not stay till hunger bids you feed.
The sweat of learned Jonson's brain,
And gentle Shakespeare's easier strain,
A hackney-coach conveys you to,
In spite of all that rain can do:
And for your eighteen pence you sit
The lord and judge of all fresh wit.
News in one day as much we've here
As serves all Windsor for a year,
And which the carrier brings to you,
After't has here been found not true.
Then think what Company's designed
To meet you here, men so refined,
Their very common talk at board,
Makes wise, or mad a young court-lord,
And makes him capable to be
Umpire in's father's company.
Where no disputes nor forced defence
Of a man's person for his sense
Take up the time, all strive to be
Masters of truth, as victory:
And where you come, I'd boldly swear
A synod might as easily err.

[Out upon it! I have loved]

1

Out upon it! I have loved
  Three whole days together;
And am like to love three more,
  If it prove fair weather.

2

Time shall moult away his wings,
  Ere he shall discover
In the whole wide world again
  Such a constant lover.

3

But a pox upon't, no praise
  Is due at all to me:
Love with me had made no stays,
  Had it any been but she.

4

Had it any been but she,
  And that very very face,
There had been at least ere this
  A dozen dozen in her place.

Farewell to Love

Well-shadowed landscape, fare-ye-well:
How I have loved you, none can tell,
        At least so well
    As he that now hates more
    Than e'er he loved before.

But my dear nothings, take your leave;
No longer must you me deceive,
        Since I perceive
    All the deceit, and know
    Whence the mistake did grow.

As he whose quicker eye doth trace
A false star shot to a marked place
        Does run apace,
    And thinking it to catch
    A jelly up does snatch:

So our dull souls, tasting delight
Far off, by sense, and appetite,
        Think that is right
    And real good, when yet
    'Tis but the counterfeit.

Oh, how I glory now that I
Have made this new discovery!
        Each wanton eye
    Enflamed before: no more
    Will I increase that score.

If I gaze now, 'tis but to see
What manner of death's-head 'twill be,
        When it is free
    From that fresh upper skin,
    The gazer's joy, and sin.

The gum and glistening which with art
And studied method in each part
    Hangs down the heart
   Looks (just) as if that day
   Snails there had crawled the hay.

The locks that curled o'er each ear be
Hang like two master-worms to me,
    That (as we see)
   Have tasted to the rest
   Two holes, where they liked best.

A quick corpse methinks I spy
In every woman; and mine eye,
    At passing by,
   Checks, and is troubled, just
   As if it rose from dust.

They mortify, not heighten me;
These of my sins the glasses be:
    And here I see
   How I have loved before.
   And so I love no more.

ABRAHAM COWLEY
1618–67

Abraham Cowley was entranced by poetry from the moment, before the age of ten, when he read, and then avidly re-read, his mother's copy of Spenser's *Faerie Queene*. He was only fifteen when his own first collection appeared, although *Poetical Blossoms* did only contain five poems; a second edition, and then a third, would enlarge the volume a little. Cowley asserted in later life that the narrative poems, 'Pyramus and Thisbe' and 'Constantius and Philetus', had been written at the ages of ten and twelve respectively. Whether or not this is strictly true, his intelligence was certainly precocious, and after completing his education at Westminster, he went up to Trinity. Within the year, his first play – a Latin comedy titled *Naufragium Joculare* – was performed before a university audience, and when the future Charles II passed through Cambridge four years later, another comedy, *The Guardian*, was staged for the Prince's entertainment. Cowley collected without trouble his BA, his MA and a minor Fellowship, but in 1643 he was thrown out of Trinity for his royalist allegiance, and headed west to St John's College, Oxford, where he was welcomed into royalist circles. He later followed Queen Henrietta Maria into exile on the continent, and became an all-round assistant, deciphering letters from King Charles and going on missions to various countries, his life under constant threat.

Cowley wrote poetry at a steady rate throughout his life. His most significant works were initially political ones: first he wrote two satirical poems, *The Puritan and the Papist* and *A Satire Against Separatists*, both of which circulated semi-unofficially. When the fighting broke out between King and Parliament, he began an epic poem called *The Civil War*, which celebrated the early royalist successes and lauded their cause. Given the way the war went, it is no surprise that he abandoned it. Later, on returning to England from the continent, he was unlucky enough to be arrested, in fact mistaken for someone else, and incarcerated. While in prison he prepared a collection of his verse thus far, *Poems* (1656), omitting his political works – probably his sympathies were still royalist, but he was trying to feign compliance with Cromwell's regime – but including most of his other verse, including *The Mistress*, a cycle of love poems already widely circulated and admired. Cowley's reputation rose and rose, and *Poems* went through fourteen

more printings after his death in 1667. He is remembered for being
the creator of the 'Pindaric ode', loosely derived from the fifth-century
Greek poet Pindar, and he would remain influential for many subse-
quent English authors including Milton, Dryden, Gray, Wordsworth
and Tennyson.

Upon Dr Harvey[48]

1

Coy Nature (which remained, though aged grown,
A beauteous virgin still, enjoyed by none,
    Nor seen unveiled by any one),
When Harvey's violent passion she did see,
Began to tremble, and to flee,
Took sanctuary like Daphne in a tree:
There Daphne's lover stopped, and thought it much
    The very leaves of her to touch,
But Harvey our Apollo, stopped not so,
Into the bark, and root he after her did go:
    No smallest fibres of a plant,
For which the eye-beams point doth sharpness want,
    His passage after her withstood.
What should she do? through all the moving wood
Of lives endowed with sense she took her flight,
Harvey pursues, and keeps her still in sight.
But as the deer long-hunted takes a flood,
She leaped at last into the winding streams of blood;
Of man's Meander all the purple reaches made,
    Till at the heart she stayed,
    Where turning head, and at a bay,
Thus, by well-purged ears, was she o'erheard to say.

2

Here sure shall I be safe (said she)
None will be able sure to see
    This my retreat, but only He
    Who made both it and me.
The heart of man, what art can e'er reveal?
    A wall impervious between
    Divides the very parts within,
And doth the heart of man even from its self conceal.
    She spoke, but ere she was aware,
    Harvey was with her there,
And held this slippery Proteus in a chain,
Till all her mighty mysteries she descried,
Which from his wit the attempt before to hide
Was the first thing that Nature did in vain.

3

He the young practice of new life did see,
  Whilst to conceal its toilsome Poverty,
It for a living wrought, both hard, and privately.
    Before the liver understood
    The noble scarlet dye of blood,
    Before one drop was by it made,
Or brought into it, to set up the trade;
Before the untaught heart began to beat
The tuneful march to vital heat,
From all the souls that living buildings rear,
Whether implied for earth, or sea, or air,
Whether it in the womb or egg be wrought,
A strict account to him is hourly brought,
  How the great fabric does proceed,
What time and what materials it does need.
He so exactly does the work survey,
As if he hired the workers by the day.

4

Thus Harvey sought for truth in truth's own book
  The creatures, which by God himself was writ;
    And wisely thought 'twas fit,
Not to read comments only upon it,
But on the original itself to look.
Methinks in art's great circle others stand
  Locked up together, hand in hand,
  Every one leads as he is led,
  The same bare path they tread,
A dance like fairies a fantastic round,
But neither change their motion, nor their ground:
Had Harvey to this road confined his wit,
His noble circle of the blood, had been untrodden yet.
Great Doctor! the art of Curing's cured by thee,
  We now thy patient physic see,
From all inveterate diseases free,
  Purged of old errors by thy care,
New dieted, put forth to clearer air,
  It now will strong and healthful prove,
Itself before lethargic lay, and could not move.

5

These useful secrets to his pen we owe,
And thousands more 'twas ready to bestow;
Of which a barbarous war's unlearned rage
　　Has robbed the ruined age;
O cruel loss! as if the Golden Fleece,
　With so much cost, and labour bought,
And from afar by a great hero brought
　Had sunk even in the Ports of Greece.
O cursed war! who can forgive thee this?
　　Houses and towns may rise again,
　　And ten times easier it is
To rebuild Paul's, than any work of his.
That mighty task none but himself can do,
　　Nay, scarce himself too now,
For though his wit the force of age withstand,
His body alas! and Time it must command,
And Nature now, so long by him surpassed,
Will sure have her revenge on him at last.

The Grasshopper

Happy Insect, what can be
In happiness compared to thee?
Fed with nourishment divine,
The dewy morning's gentle wine!
Nature waits upon thee still,
And thy verdant cup does fill,
'Tis filled where ever thou dost tread,
Nature self's thy Ganymede.
Thou dost drink, and dance, and sing;
Happier than the happiest king!
All the fields which thou dost see,
All the plants belong to thee,
All that summer hours produce,
Fertile made with early juice.
Man for thee does sow and plough;
Farmer he, and landlord thou!
Thou dost innocently joy;
Nor does thy luxury destroy;

The shepherd gladly heareth thee,
More harmonious than he.
Thee country hinds with gladness hear,
Prophet of the ripened year!
Thee Phoebus loves, and does inspire;
Phoebus is himself thy sire.
To thee of all things upon earth,
Life is no longer than thy mirth.
Happy insect, happy thou,
Dost neither age, nor winter know.
But when thou'st drunk, and danced, and sung
Thy fill, the flowery leaves among
(Voluptuous, and wise with all,
Epicurean animal!),
Sated with thy summer feast,
Thou retir'st to endless rest.

Against Fruition

No; thou'rt a fool, I'll swear, if e'er thou grant:
Much of my veneration thou must want,
When once thy kindness puts my ignorance out;
For a learn'd age is always least devout.
Keep still thy distance; for at once to me
Goddess and woman too, thou canst not be;
Thou'rt queen of all that sees thee; and as such
Must neither tyrannize, nor yield too much;
Such freedoms give as may admit command,
But keep the forts and magazines in thine hand.
Thou'rt yet a whole world to me, and dost fill
My large ambition; but 'tis dangerous still,
Lest I like the Pellaean Prince[49] should be,
And weep for other worlds having conquered thee;
When love has taken all thou hast away,
His strength by too much riches will decay.
Thou in my fancy dost much higher stand,
Than women can be placed by nature's hand;
And I must needs, I'm sure, a loser be,
To change thee, as thou'rt there, for very thee.
Thy sweetness is so much within me placed,

That shouldst thou nectar give, 'twould spoil the taste.
Beauty at first moves wonder, and delight;
'Tis nature's juggling trick to cheat the sight,
We admire it, whilst unknown, but after more
Admire our selves, for liking it before.
Love, like a greedy hawk, if we give way,
Does over-gorge himself, with his own prey;
Of very hopes a surfeit he'll sustain,
Unless by fears he cast them up again:
His spirit and sweetness dangers keep alone;
If once he lose his sting, he grows a drone.

ANDREW MARVELL
1621–78

Andrew Marvell was even more precocious than some of his aforementioned predecessors. The son of a Yorkshire clergyman, he was brought up and schooled in Hull before matriculating at Trinity three months before his thirteenth birthday. He would thus need to spend five years there, two more than the usual, before receiving his BA. The only poems known to date from this period are a few Greek verses and a Latin ode on the birth of the Princess Anne. This flirtation with royalism might seem unexpected in the future Cromwell supporter, as might his brief teenage dalliance with Catholicism; but throughout his life Marvell would wisely keep his exact political and religious views ambiguous enough to survive the personal dangers of the Civil War and the Restoration.

When he was twenty, his father drowned in the Humber, leaving a small inheritance which freed his son from the usual route from clever undergraduate to Fellow of Trinity. Marvell seems to have travelled abroad as a tutor to boys of noble birth, though our only evidence for his movements is Milton's assertion that he spent four years in Holland, France, Italy and Spain. This meant that he sidestepped the entirety of the First Civil War, a happy coincidence which he later explained, somewhat unconvincingly, by proposing that 'the Cause was too good to have been fought for'. He was back in London by 1647, and published his first verses, which were cannily temperate elegies for slain royalists. However, with the execution of Charles I in 1649, and the establishment of the Commonwealth, his views silently metamorphosed, and his great political poem, *An Horatian Ode upon Cromwell's Return from Ireland*, shows a more balanced, complicated view on the state of the nation.

With the Commonwealth firmly entrenched, Lord Fairfax, the commander of the Parliamentary army, could retire, and Marvell accompanied him back to his estates in Yorkshire, where he was employed as tutor to Fairfax's daughter. He tempered his political verse at this time, writing English and Latin poems that reflect on English pastoral landscapes and on the political turmoil that had ravaged them. The longest and best-known of these is *Upon Appleton House*, written in 1651. Before long, however, Marvell returned to London to join Cromwell's civil service, initially hoping only to assist the now blind Milton, but instead becoming a secretary of Latin himself, as well as an MP for Hull. Upon the Restoration in 1660, he was able to claim, again with quick wits, that he had only been a governmental functionary, which not only exculpated him, but enabled him to save Milton's life from royalist retaliation as well.

In later life, Marvell increasingly turned to theological disputes. The work which brought him greatest contemporary renown was *The Rehearsal Transpros'd* (1672), a tract which attacked Samuel Parker, the zealous Bishop of Oxford. He became more anti-Catholic with old age, perhaps wary of Charles II's leanings in that direction, but he died unexpectedly in 1678 and so fortuitously avoided the ascension, seven years later, of the openly Catholic James II. In his own lifetime his prose satires and religious pamphlets were much better known than his verse. It was only three years after his death that a collection of his shorter occasional poems was published, from papers fortuitously kept by his housekeeper. These expanded the scope of his work and reputation into the territories of the verse dialogue, the pastoral, love poetry and Latin epigrams, on which his reputation as one of the great poets of all times now rests.

To His Coy Mistress

Had we but world enough, and time,
This coyness, Lady, were no crime.
We would sit down, and think which way
To walk, and pass our long love's day.
Thou by the Indian Ganges' side
Should'st rubies find: I by the tide
Of Humber would complain. I would
Love you ten years before the Flood:
And you should if you please refuse
Till the conversion of the Jews.
My vegetable love should grow
Vaster then empires, and more slow.
An hundred years should go to praise
Thine eyes, and on thy forehead gaze.
Two hundred to adore each breast:
But thirty thousand to the rest.
An age at least to every part,
And the last age should show your heart.
For, Lady, you deserve this state;
Nor would I love at lower rate.
  But at my back I always hear
Time's winged chariot hurrying near:
And yonder all before us lie
Deserts of vast eternity.
Thy beauty shall no more be found;
Nor, in thy marble vault, shall sound
My echoing song: then worms shall try
That long preserved virginity:
And your quaint honour turn to dust;
And into ashes all my lust.
The grave's a fine and private place,
But none I think do there embrace.
  Now therefore, while the youthful hew
Sits on thy skin like morning dew,
And while thy willing soul transpires
At every pore with instant fires,
Now let us sport us while we may;
And now, like amorous birds of prey,
Rather at once our time devour,
Than languish in his slow-chapped power.

Let us roll all our strength, and all
Our sweetness, up into one ball:
And tear our pleasures with rough strife,
Through the iron gates of life.
Thus, though we cannot make our sun
Stand still, yet we will make him run.

An Horatian Ode upon Cromwell's Return from Ireland

The forward Youth that would appear
Must now forsake his Muses dear,
  Nor in the shadows sing
  His numbers languishing.
'Tis time to leave the Books in dust,
And oil the unused armour's rust:
  Removing from the wall
  The corslet[50] of the hall.
So restless Cromwell could not cease
In the inglorious arts of peace,
  But through adventurous war
  Urged his active star.
And, like the three-forked lightning, first
Breaking the clouds where it was nursed,
  Did through his own side
  His fiery way divide.
For 'tis all one to courage high
The emulous or enemy;
  And with such to enclose
  Is more than to oppose.
Then burning through the air he went,
And palaces and temples rent:
  And Caesar's head at last
  Did through his laurels blast.
'Tis madness to resist or blame
The force of angry heaven's flame:
  And, if we would speak true,
  Much to the man is due.
Who, from his private gardens, where
He lived reserved and austere,
  As if his highest plot

To plant the bergamot,
Could by industrious valour climb
To ruin the great work of time,
  And cast the kingdom old
  Into another mould.
Though justice against fate complain,
And plead the ancient rights in vain:
  But those do hold or break
  As men are strong or weak.
Nature that hateth emptiness,
Allows of penetration less:
  And therefore must make room
  Where greater spirits come.
What field of all the civil wars,
Where his were not the deepest scars?
  And Hampton[51] shows what part
  He had of wiser art.
Where, twining subtle fears with hope,
He wove a net of such a scope,
  That Charles himself might chase
  To Caresbrook's[52] narrow case.
That thence the royal actor born
The tragic scaffold might adorn:
  While round the armed bands
  Did clap their bloody hands.
He nothing common did or mean
Upon that memorable scene:
  But with his keener eye
  The axe's edge did try:
Nor called the gods with vulgar spite
To vindicate his helpless right,
  But bowed his comely head,
  Down as upon a bed.
This was that memorable hour
Which first assured the forced power.
  So when they did design
  The capitol's first line,
A bleeding head where they begun,
Did fright the architects to run;
  And yet in that the state
  Foresaw its happy fate.
And now the Irish are ashamed

To see themselves in one year tamed:
  So much one man can do,
  That does both act and know.
They can affirm his praises best,
And have, though overcome, confessed
  How good he is, how just,
  And fit for highest trust:
Nor yet grown stiffer with command,
But still in the Republic's hand:
  How fit he is to sway
  That can so well obey.
He to the Commons' feet presents
A kingdom, for his first year's rents:
  And, what he may, forbears
  His fame to make it theirs:
And has his sword and spoils ungirt,
To lay them at the public's skirt.
  So when the falcon high
  Falls heavy from the sky,
She, having killed, no more does search,
But on the next green bough to perch;
  Where, when he first does lure,
  The falconer has her sure.
What may not then our isle presume
While victory his crest does plume!
  What may not others fear
  If thus he crown each year!
A Caesar he ere long to Gaul,
To Italy an Hannibal,
  And to all states not free
  Shall clymacteric[53] be.
The Pict no shelter now shall find
Within his party-coloured mind;
  But from this valour sad
  Shrink underneath the plaid:
Happy if in the tufted brake
The English hunter him mistake;
  Nor lay his hounds in near
  The Caledonian deer.
But thou the wars' and Fortune's Son
March indefatigably on;
  And for the last effect

Still keep thy sword erect:
Besides the force it has to fright
The spirits of the shady night,
  The same arts that did gain
  A power must it maintain.

The Garden

How vainly men themselves amaze
To win the palm, the oak, or bays;
And their uncessant Labours see
Crowned from some single herb or tree.
Whose short and narrow verged Shade
Does prudently their toils upbraid;
While all flowers and all trees do close
To weave the garlands of repose.

Fair quiet, have I found thee here,
And innocence thy sister dear!
Mistaken long, I sought you then
In busy companies of men.
Your sacred plants, if here below,
Only among the plants will grow.
Society is all but rude,
To this delicious solitude.

No white nor red was ever seen
So amorous as this lovely green.
Fond lovers, cruel as their flame,
Cut in these trees their mistress's name.
Little, alas, they know, or heed,
How far these beauties hers exceed!
Fair trees! wheres'e'er your barks I wound,
No name shall but your own be found.

When we have run our passion's heat,
Love hither makes his best retreat.
The gods, that mortal beauty chase,
Still in a tree did end their race.
Apollo hunted Daphne so,

Only that she might laurel grow.
And Pan did after Syrinx speed,
Not as a nymph, but for a reed.

What wondrous life in this I lead!
Ripe apples drop about my head;
The luscious clusters of the vine
Upon my mouth do crush their wine;
The nectarine, and curious peach,
Into my hands themselves do reach;
Stumbling on melons, as I pass,
Ensnared with flowers, I fall on grass.

Meanwhile the mind, from pleasure less,
Withdraws into its happiness:
The mind, that ocean where each kind
Does straight its own resemblance find;
Yet it creates, transcending these,
Far other worlds, and other seas;
Annihilating all that's made
To a green thought in a green shade.

Here at the fountain's sliding foot,
Or at some fruit-tree's mossy root,
Casting the body's vest aside,
My soul into the boughs does glide:
There like a bird it sits, and sings,
Then whets, and combs its silver wings;
And, till prepared for longer flight,
Waves in its plumes the various light.

Such was that happy garden-state,
While man there walked without a mate:
After a place so pure, and sweet,
What other help could yet be meet!
But 'twas beyond a mortal's share
To wander solitary there:
Two paradises 'twere in one
To live in paradise alone.

How well the skilful gardener drew
Of flowers and herbs this dial new;
Where from above the milder sun
Does through a fragrant zodiac run;
And, as it works, the industrious bee
Computes its time as well as we.
How could such sweet and wholesome Hours
Be reckoned but with herbs and flowers!

The Mower Against Gardens

Luxurious man, to bring his vice in use,
  Did after him the world seduce:
And from the fields the flowers and plants allure,
  Where nature was most plain and pure.
He first enclosed within the garden's square
  A dead and standing pool of air:
And a more luscious earth for them did knead,
  Which stupefied them while it fed.
The pink grew then as double as his mind;
  The nutriment did change the kind.
With strange perfumes he did the roses taint.
  And flowers themselves were taught to paint.
The tulip, white, did for complexion seek;
  And learned to interline its cheek:
Its onion root they then so high did hold,
  That one was for a meadow sold.
Another world was searched, through oceans new,
  To find the marvel of Peru.[54]
And yet these rarities might be allowed,
  To man, that sovereign thing and proud;
Had he not dealt between the bark and tree,
  Forbidden mixtures there to see.
No plant now knew the stock from which it came;
  He grafts upon the wild the tame:
That the uncertain and adulterate fruit
  Might put the palate in dispute.
His green seraglio has its eunuchs too;
  Lest any tyrant him outdo.
And in the cherry he does nature vex,

To procreate without a sex.
'Tis all enforced; the fountain and the grot;
  While the sweet fields do lie forgot:
Where willing nature does to all dispense
  A wild and fragrant innocence:
And fauns and fairies do the meadows till,
  More by their presence than their skill.
Their statues polished by some ancient hand,
  May to adorn the gardens stand:
But howsoe'er the figures do excel,
  The gods themselves with us do dwell.

Bermudas

Where the remote Bermudas ride
In th'ocean's bosom unespied,
From a small boat, that rowed along,
The listening winds received this song.
  'What should we do but sing his praise
That led us through the watery maze,
Unto an isle so long unknown,
And yet far kinder than our own?
Where he the huge sea monsters wracks,
That lift the deep upon their backs.
He lands us on a grassy stage;
Safe from the storms, and prelate's rage.
He gave us this eternal spring,
Which here enamels every thing;
And sends the fowls to us in care,
On daily visits through the air.
He hangs in shades the orange bright,
Like golden lamps in a green night,
And does in the pomegranates close,
Jewels more rich than Ormus[55] shows.
He makes the figs our mouths to meet;
And throws the melons at our feet.
But apples, plants of such a price,
No tree could ever bear them twice.
With cedars, chosen by his hand,
From Lebanon, he stores the land.

And makes the hollow seas, that roar,
Proclaim the ambergris on shore.
He cast (of which we rather boast)
The gospel's pearl upon our coast,
And in these rocks for us did frame
A temple, where to sound his name.
Oh let our voice his praise exalt,
Till it arrive at heaven's vault:
Which thence (perhaps) rebounding, may
Echo beyond the Mexique Bay'.
Thus sung they, in the English boat,
An holy and a cheerful note,
And all the way, to guide their chime,
With falling oars they kept the time.

On Mr Milton's Paradise Lost

When I beheld the poet blind, yet bold,
In slender book his vast design unfold,
Messiah crowned, God's reconciled decree,
Rebelling angels, the forbidden tree,
Heaven, hell, Earth, chaos, all; the argument
Held me a while misdoubting his intent,
That he would ruin (for I saw him strong)
The sacred truths to fable and old song,
(So Sampson groped the temple's posts in spite)
The world o'erwhelming to revenge his sight.
  Yet as I read, soon growing less severe,
I liked his project, the success did fear;
Through that wide field how he his way should find
O'er which lame faith leads understanding blind;
Lest he perplexed the things he would explain,
And what was easy he should render vain.
  Or if a work so infinite he spanned,
Jealous I was that some less skilful hand
(Such as disquiet always what is well,
And by ill imitating would excel)
Might hence presume the whole creation's day
To change in scenes, and show it in a play.
  Pardon me, mighty poet, nor despise

My causeless, yet not impious, surmise.
But I am now convinced, and none will dare
Within thy labours to pretend a share.
Thou hast not missed one thought that could be fit,
And all that was improper dost omit:
So that no room is here for writers left,
But to detect their ignorance or theft.
  That majesty which through thy work doth reign
Draws the devout, deterring the profane.
And things divine thou treatst of in such state
As them preserves, and thee inviolate.
At once delight and horror on us seize,
Thou singst with so much gravity and ease;
And above human flight dost soar aloft,
With plume so strong, so equal, and so soft.
The bird named from that paradise you sing
So never flags, but always keeps on wing.
  Where couldst thou words of such a compass find?
Whence furnish such a vast expense of mind?
Just heaven thee, like Tiresias, to requite,
Rewards with prophecy thy loss of sight.
  Well mightst thou scorn thy readers to allure
With tinkling rhyme, of thy own sense secure;
While the town-bays[56] writes all the while and spells,
And like a pack-horse tires without his bells.
Their fancies like our bushy points appear,
The poets tag them; we for fashion wear.
I too transported by the mode offend,
And while I meant to praise thee, must commend.
Thy verse created like thy theme sublime,
In number, weight, and measure, needs not rhyme.

from *Upon Appleton House, to my Lord Fairfax* [lines 1–72]

Within this sober frame expect
Work of no foreign architect;
That unto caves the quarries drew,
And forests did to pastures hew;
Who of his great design in pain
Did for a model vault his brain,
Whose columns should so high be raised
To arch the brows that on them gazed.

Why should of all things man unruled
Such unproportioned dwellings build?
The beasts are by their dens expressed:
And birds contrive an equal nest;
The low roofed tortoises do dwell
In cases fit of tortoise-shell:
No creature loves an empty space;
Their bodies measure out their place.

But he, superfluously spread,
Demands more room alive than dead.
And in his hollow palace goes
Where winds as he themselves may lose.
What need of all this marble crust
T'impark the wanton mote of dust,
That thinks by breadth the world t'unite
Though the first builders failed in height?

But all things are composed here
Like nature, orderly and near:
In which we the dimensions find
Of that more sober age and mind,
When larger sized men did stoop
To enter at a narrow loop;
As practising, in doors so strait,
To strain themselves through heaven's gate.

And surely when the after age
Shall hither come in pilgrimage,
These sacred places to adore,
By Vere and Fairfax trod before,

Men will dispute how their extent
Within such dwarfish confines went:
And some will smile at this, as well
As Romulus his bee-like cell.

Humility alone designs
Those short but admirable lines,
By which, ungirt and unconstrained,
Things greater are in less contained.
Let others vainly strive t'immure
The circle in the quadrature!
These holy mathematics can
In every figure equal man.

Yet thus the laden house does sweat,
And scarce endures the master great:
But where he comes the swelling hall
Stirs, and the square grows spherical;
More by his magnitude distressed,
Than he is by its straitness pressed:
And too officiously it slights
That in itself which him delights.

So honour better lowness bears,
Than that unwonted greatness wears.
Height with a certain grace does bend,
But low things clownishly ascend.
And yet what needs there here excuse,
Where every thing does answer use?
Where neatness nothing can condemn,
Nor pride invent what to contemn?

A stately frontispiece of poor
Adorns without the open door:
Nor less the rooms within commends
Daily new furniture of friends.
The house was built upon the place
Only as for a mark of grace;
And for an inn to entertain
Its lord a while, but not remain.

Mr IOHN DRYDEN
Anno . 1698 . Ætat: 67 .

John Dryden aged 67, by Godfrey Kneller, frontispiece to the third volume of his translation of *The Works of Virgil* (1719).

JOHN DRYDEN
1631–1700

John Dryden had a tireless virtuosity. The variety of his work was immense, including plays, historiographical works, verse satires, religious poetry and translations from multiple languages. In Samuel Johnson's fulsome praise, he was the 'father of English criticism', authoring, among other critical works, the essay *Of Dramatic Poesie*. He transformed English versification and was an original theorist of translation.

Dryden was born in Northamptonshire to Erasmus Dryden and his wife Mary, in a background that was steadfastly Puritan. In 1644, the thirteen-year-old John was sent to Westminster School as a King's Scholar, where he received the saturation in classical writing which would inspire his own poetry, and which he would later translate. From the beginning he was precocious enough: he once translated Persius' third satire as a way of passing a Thursday evening, and it was at Westminster in 1649 that his first poem was published. He went up to Trinity in 1650, at a time when the Puritan streak was strong in the college, and distinguished himself academically, graduating in the top list in 1652. There was however some misdemeanour, recorded by the College as Dryden's 'disobedience to the vicemaster & his contumacy in taking of his punishment'. It remains unclear how he transgressed, though Thomas Shadwell (no friend to Dryden) would later describe a dispute with a nobleman. A peer of Dryden's at Cambridge, Robert Creighton, thought that his 'head was too roving and active, or what else you'll call it, to confine himself to a College Life'.

By 1657 Dryden was employed in Cromwell's government. The following year, at Cromwell's funeral procession he walked with Milton and Marvell as secretaries of the French and Latin tongues. His service beside Milton is intriguing, given the influence the older poet would have on him. Dryden himself marked Cromwell's death with what is generally regarded as his first significant poem, the *Heroic Stanzas*, a somewhat reserved appreciation. With the restoration of the monarchy in 1660, he settled into a literary career, cheering the return of the king with the poem *Astraea redux* ('Justice brought back').

In 1663, Dryden's first play, *The Wild Gallant*, was staged at the

Theatre Royal. After the plague of 1665 forced the closure of the theatres, he left London for Wiltshire, where he wrote (among other things) *Of Dramatic Poesie*, and the long poem *Annus Mirabilis*. His stock was rising, and in 1668 he was given a contract with the King's Company to write three plays a year in return for a share of profits. He became Poet Laureate later that year, and Historiographer Royal in 1670.

Dryden's commitment to writing for the theatre was largely due to financial need. Most notably, he wrote heroic drama in rhyming couplets, comedies such as *Marriage à-la-Mode* (1671) and adaptations of Shakespeare, including *All for Love, or, The World Well Lost* (1677), a re-writing of *Antony and Cleopatra* which was by far the preferred version throughout the next century. Likewise, when he composed a dramatic adaptation of Milton's *Paradise Lost*, entitled *The State of Innocence: An Opera*, it easily outsold the poem on which it was based. By the time he wrote *Aureng-Zebe* (1675), his last rhymed play, he claimed that he wanted to quit the theatre. However, he would continue to write for the stage until his last work, the tragi-comedy *Love Triumphant* (1694). Alongside his theatrical writing, Dryden's poetry flourished. His long-term altercation with Thomas Shadwell led to a prominent venture into satire. *Mac Flecknoe* (1676) had an important influence on later mock-heroic poetry in its imagining of a poetic kingdom of dullness and, in 1681, he published *Absalom and Achitophel*, his celebrated satire based on the exclusion crisis.

In 1685 Dryden converted to Catholicism, which – given the accession of the openly Catholic James II – was widely read as a politic manoeuvre. He had previously composed polemically religious writing in *Religio Laici* (1682) and, following his conversion, he returned to theological matters with his overtly Catholic *The Hind and the Panther* (1687), an allegory of the Roman and English Churches. After the Revolution of 1688, however, he found himself out of fashion and out of his laureateship, as William and Mary reinstated Protestantism as the official faith. He went on to produce the monumental *Works of Virgil* (1697) and the anthology *Fables Ancient and Modern* (1700) featuring works by Homer, Ovid, Boccaccio and Chaucer. Dryden described translation as a form of 'transfusion', giving life to older works. But in the late 1690s his own health was failing and he died in London, aged sixty-eight. He was first laid to rest in St Anne's, Soho, but only a few days later he found his place in Westminster Abbey, re-buried in Chaucer's grave.

Prologue to the University of Oxford (1676)

Though actors cannot much of learning boast,
Of all who want it, we admire it most:
We love the praises of a learned pit,
As we remotely are allied to wit.
We speak our poet's wit, and trade in ore,
Like those who touch upon the golden shore;
Betwixt our judges can distinction make,
Discern how much and why our poems take;
Mark if the fools, or men of sense, rejoice;
Whether th'applause be only sound or voice.
When our fop gallants, or our city folly
Clap over-loud, it makes us melancholy:
We doubt that scene which does their wonder raise,
And for their ignorance contemn their praise.
Judge then, if we who act and they who write
Should not be proud of giving you delight.
London likes grossly; but this nicer pit
Examines, fathoms, all the depths of wit;
The ready finger lays on every blot;
Knows what should justly please, and what should not.
Nature her self lies open to your view,
You judge by her what draft of her is true,
Where outlines false, and colours seem too faint,
Where bunglers daub, and where true poets paint.
But by the sacred genius of this place,
By every Muse, by each domestic Grace,
Be kind to wit, which but endeavours well,
And, where you judge, presumes not to excel.
Our poets hither for adoption come,
As nations sued to be made free of Rome:
Not in the suffragating tribes to stand,
But in your utmost, last, provincial band.
If his ambition may those hopes pursue,
Who with religion loves your arts and you,
Oxford to him a dearer name shall be,
Than his own mother university.
Thebes did his green unknowing youth engage,
He chooses Athens in his riper age.

from *Mac Flecknoe* (lines 1–34)

All human things are subject to decay,
And, when Fate summons, monarchs must obey:
This Flecknoe found, who, like Augustus, young
Was called to empire, and had governed long:
In prose and verse was owned without dispute
Through all the realms of *Nonsense*, absolute.
This aged Prince now nourishing in peace,
And blest with issue of a large increase,
Worn out with business, did at length debate
To settle the succession of the state:
And pond'ring which of all his sons was fit
To reign, and wage immortal war with wit,
Cried, ''tis resolved; for Nature pleads that he
Should only rule who most resembles me:
Shadwell alone my perfect image bears,
Mature in dullness from his tender years.
Shadwell alone, of all my sons, is he
Who stands confirmed in full stupidity.
The rest to some faint meaning make pretence,
But Shadwell never deviates into sense.
Some beams of wit on other souls may fall,
Strike through and make a lucid interval;
But Shadwell's genuine night admits no ray,
His rising fogs prevail upon the day:
Besides his goodly fabric fills the eye,
And seems designed for thoughtless majesty:
Thoughtless as monarch oaks that shade the plain,
And, spread in solemn state, supinely reign.
Heywood and Shirley were but types of thee,
Thou last great prophet of tautology:
Even I, a dunce of more renown than they,
Was sent before but to prepare thy way;
And coarsely clad in Norwich drugget[57] came
To teach the nations in thy greater name.'

To the Memory of Mr Oldham

Farewell, too little and too lately known,
Whom I began to think and call my own;
For sure our souls were near allied, and thine
Cast in the same poetic mould with mine.
One common note on either lyre did strike,
And knaves and fools we both abhorred alike:
To the same goal did both our studies drive,
The last set out the soonest did arrive.
Thus Nisus fell upon the slippery place,
While his young friend performed and won the race.
O early ripe! to thy abundant store
What could advancing age have added more?
It might (what Nature never gives the young)
Have taught the numbers of thy native tongue.
But satire needs not those, and wit will shine
Through the harsh cadence of a rugged line:
A noble error, and but seldom made,
When poets are by too much force betrayed.
Thy generous fruits, though gathered ere their prime
Still showed a quickness; and maturing time
But mellows what we write to the dull sweets of rhyme.
Once more, hail and farewell; farewell thou young,
But ah too short, Marcellus of our tongue;
Thy brows with ivy, and with laurels bound;
But fate and gloomy night encompass thee around.

from *The Hind and the Panther* (Part I, lines 62–105)

What weight of ancient witness can prevail
If private reason hold the public scale?
But, gracious God, how well dost thou provide
For erring judgments an unerring guide?
Thy throne is darkness in th'abyss of light,
A blaze of glory that forbids the sight;
O teach me to believe Thee thus concealed,
And search no farther than thyself revealed;
But her[58] alone for my director take
Whom thou hast promised never to forsake!

My thoughtless youth was winged with vain desires,
My manhood, long misled by wand'ring fires,
Followed false lights; and when their glimpse was gone,
My pride struck out new sparkles of her own.
Such was I, such by nature still I am,
Be thine the glory, and be mine the shame.
Good life be now my task: my doubts are done,
(What more could fright my faith, than Three in One?).
Can I believe eternal God could lie
Disguised in mortal mould and infancy?
That the great maker of the world could die?
And after that, trust my imperfect sense
Which calls in question his omnipotence?
Can I my reason to my faith compel,
And shall my sight, and touch, and taste rebel?
Superior faculties are set aside,
Shall their subservient organs be my guide?
Then let the moon usurp the rule of day,
And winking tapers show the sun his way;
For what my senses can themselves perceive
I need no revelation to believe.
Can they, who say the Host[59] should be descried
By sense, define a body glorified,
Impassible, and penetrating parts?
Let them declare by what mysterious arts
He shot that body through th'opposing might
Of bolts and bars impervious to the light,
And stood before his train confessed in open sight.
    For since thus wondrously he passed, 'tis plain
One single place two bodies did contain,
And sure the same omnipotence as well
Can make one body in more places dwell.
Let reason then at her own quarry fly,
But how can finite grasp infinity?

A Song for St Cecilia's Day, 1687

I

From harmony, from heav'nly harmony
    This universal frame began.
    When Nature underneath a heap
        Of jarring atoms lay,
    And could not heave her head,
The tuneful voice was heard from high,
        'Arise ye more than dead'.
Then cold, and hot, and moist, and dry,
In order to their stations leap,
        And music's pow'r obey.
From harmony, from heav'nly harmony
    This universal frame began:
        From harmony to harmony
Through all the compass of the notes it ran,
The diapason closing full in man.

II

What passion cannot music raise and quell!
        When Jubal struck the corded shell,
    His list'ning brethren stood around
    And wond'ring, on their faces fell
    To worship that celestial sound.
Less than a god they thought there could not dwell
        Within the hollow of that shell
        That spoke so sweetly and so well.
What passion cannot music raise and quell!

III

    The trumpet's loud clangor
        Excites us to arms
    With shrill notes of anger
        And mortal alarms.
    The double double double beat
        Of the thundring drum
Cries, 'hark the foes come;
Charge, charge, 'tis too late to retreat'.

IV

The soft complaining flute
In dying notes discovers
The woes of hopeless lovers,
Whose dirge is whispered by the warbling lute.

V

Sharp violins proclaim
Their jealous pangs, and desperation,
Fury, frantic indignation,
Depth of pains, and height of passion,
For the fair, disdainful dame.

VI

But oh! what art can teach,
What human voice can reach
The sacred organ's praise?
Notes inspiring holy love,
Notes that wing their heav'nly ways
To mend the choirs above.

VII

Orpheus could lead the savage race,
And trees unrooted left their place,
Sequacious of the lyre:
But bright Cecilia raised the wonder high'r,
When to her organ, vocal breath was giv'n.
An angel heard, and straight appeared
Mistaking earth for heaven.

Grand CHORUS

As from the pow'r of sacred lays
The spheres began to move,
And sung the great Creator's praise
To all the bless'd above;
So when the last and dreadful hour
This crumbling pageant shall devour,
The trumpet shall be heard on high,
The dead shall live, the living die,
And music shall untune the sky.

To My Dear Friend Mr Congreve, On His Comedy *called* The Double-Dealer

Well then, the promised hour is come at last;
The present age of wit obscures the past:
Strong were our sires; and as they fought they writ,
Conqu'ring with force of arms, and dint of wit;
Theirs was the giant race, before the flood;
And thus, when Charles returned, our empire stood.
Like Janus he the stubborn soil manured,
With rules of husbandry the rankness cured:
Tamed us to manners, when the stage was rude;
And boist'rous English wit, with art indued.
Our age was cultivated thus at length;
But what we gained in skill we lost in strength.
Our builders were with want of genius curst;
The second temple was not like the first:
Till you, the best Vitruvius, come at length;
Our beauties equal; but excel our strength.
Firm Doric pillars found your solid base:
The fair Corinthian crowns the higher space;
Thus all below is strength, and all above is grace.
In easy dialogue is Fletcher's praise:
He moved the mind, but had not power to raise.
Great Jonson did by strength of judgment please:
Yet doubling Fletcher's force, he wants his ease.
In differing talents both adorned their age;
One for the study, t'other for the stage.
But both to Congreve justly shall submit,
One matched in judgment, both o'er-matched in wit.
In him all beauties of this age we see;
Etherege his courtship, Southerne's purity;
The satire, wit, and strength of manly Wycherley.[60]
All this in blooming youth you have achieved;
Nor are your foiled contemporaries grieved;
So much the sweetness of your manners move,
We cannot envy you because we love.
Fabius might joy in Scipio, when he saw
A beardless consul made against the Law,
And join his suffrage to the votes of Rome,
Though he with Hannibal was overcome.
Thus old Romano bowed to Raphael's Fame;

And scholar to the youth he taught, became.
  Oh that your brows my laurel had sustained,
Well had I been deposed, if you had reigned!
The father had descended for the son;
For only you are lineal to the throne.
Thus when the state one Edward did depose;
A greater Edward in his room arose.
But now, not I, but poetry is cursed;
For Tom the Second reigns like Tom the First.[61]
But let 'em not mistake my patron's part;
Nor call his charity their own desert.
Yet this I prophesy; thou shalt be seen,
(Though with some short parenthesis between)
High on the throne of wit; and seated there,
Not mine (that's little) but thy laurel wear.
Thy first attempt an early promise made;
That early promise this has more than paid.
So bold, yet so judiciously you dare,
That your least praise, is to be regular.
Time, place, and action, may with pains be wrought,
But genius must be born; and never can be taught.
This is your portion, this your native store,
Heav'n that but once was prodigal before,
To Shakespeare gave as much; she could not give him more.
  Maintain your post: that's all the fame you need;
For 'tis impossible you should proceed.
Already I am worn with cares and age,
And just abandoning th'ungrateful stage:
Unprofitably kept at heaven's expense,
I live a rent-charge on his providence:
But you, whom ev'ry Muse and Grace adorn,
Whom I foresee to better fortune born,
Be kind to my remains; and oh defend,
Against your judgment your departed friend!
Let not the insulting foe my fame pursue;
But shade those laurels which descend to you:
And take for tribute what these lines express:
You merit more; nor could my love do less.

from *The Second Book of the Æneis* (lines 691–763)

Perhaps you may of Priam's fate enquire.
He, when he saw his regal town on fire,
His ruined palace, and his ent'ring foes,
On ev'ry side inevitable woes;
In arms, disused, invests his limbs decayed
Like them, with age; a late and useless aid.
His feeble shoulders scarce the weight sustain:
Loaded, not armed, he creeps along, with pain;
Despairing of success; ambitious to be slain!
Uncovered but by heav'n, there stood in view
An altar; near the hearth a laurel grew;
Doddered with age, whose boughs encompass round
The household Gods, and shade the holy ground.
Here Hecuba, with all her helpless train
Of dames, for shelter sought, but sought in vain.
Driv'n like a flock of doves along the sky,
Their images they hug, and to their altars fly.
The Queen, when she beheld her trembling Lord,
And hanging by his side a heavy sword,
'What rage', she cried, 'has seized my husband's mind;
What arms are these, and to what use designed?
These times want other aids: were Hector here,
Ev'n Hector now in vain, like Priam would appear.
With us, one common shelter thou shalt find,
Or in one common fate with us be joined.'
She said, and with a last salute embraced
The poor old man, and by the laurel placed.
Behold Polites, one of Priam's sons,
Pursued by Pyrrhus, there for safety runs.
Through swords, and foes, amazed and hurt, he flies
Through empty courts, and open galleries:
Him Pyrrhus, urging with his lance, pursues;
And often reaches, and his thrusts renews.
The youth transfixed, with lamentable cries
Expires, before his wretched parent's eyes:
Whom, gasping at his feet, when Priam saw,
The fear of death gave place to Nature's law.
And shaking more with anger, than with age,
'The Gods', said he, 'requite thy brutal rage:
As sure they will, barbarian, sure they must,

If there be Gods in heav'n, and Gods be just:
Who tak'st in wrongs an insolent delight;
With a son's death t'infect a father's sight.
Not he, whom thou and lying fame conspire
To call thee his; not he, thy vaunted sire,
Thus used my wretched age: the Gods he feared,
The laws of Nature and of nations heard.
He cheered my sorrows, and for sums of gold
The bloodless carcass of my Hector sold:
Pitied the woes a parent underwent,
And sent me back in safety from his tent.'
  This said, his feeble hand a javelin threw,
Which flutt'ring, seemed to loiter as it flew:
Just, and but barely, to the mark it held,
And faintly tinkled on the brazen shield.
   Then Pyrrhus thus: go thou from me to fate;
And to my father my foul deeds relate.
Now die. With that he dragged the trembling Sire,
Slidd'ring through clotter'd blood, and holy mire,
(The mingled paste his murdered son had made)
Hauled from beneath the violated shade;
And on the sacred pile, the royal victim laid.
His right hand held his bloody falchion bare;
His left he twisted in his hoary hair:
Then, with a speeding thrust, his heart he found:
The lukewarm blood came rushing through the wound,
And sanguine streams distained the sacred ground.
Thus Priam fell: and shared one common fate
With Troy in ashes, and his ruined state:
He, who the scepter of all Asia swayed,
Whom monarchs like domestic slaves obeyed.
On the bleak shore now lies th'abandoned king,
A headless carcass, and a nameless thing.[62]

from *The Fourth Book of the Æneis* (lines 216–81)

Now had they reached the hills, and stormed the seat
Of salvage[63] beasts, in dens, their last retreat;
The cry pursues the mountain goats; they bound
From rock to rock, and keep the craggy ground:
Quite otherwise the stags, a trembling train,
In herds unsingled, scour the dusty plain;
And a long chase, in open view, maintain.
The glad Ascanius, as his courser guides,
Spurs through the vale; and these and those outrides.
His horses' flanks and sides are forced to feel
The clanking lash, and goring of the steel.
Impatiently he views the feeble prey,
Wishing some nobler beast to cross his way:
And rather would the tusky boar attend,
Or see the tawny lion downward bend.
  Mean time, the gath'ring clouds obscure the skies;
From pole to pole the forky lightning flies;
The rattling thunders rowl; and Juno pours
A wintry deluge down; and sounding show'rs.
The company dispersed, to coverts ride,
And seek the homely cots, or mountain's hollow side.
The rapid rains, descending from the hills,
To rowling torrents raise the creeping rills.
The Queen and Prince, as love or fortune guides,
One common cavern in her bosom hides.
Then first the trembling earth the signal gave;
And flashing fires enlighten all the cave:
Hell from below, and Juno from above,
And howling nymphs, were conscious to their love.
From this ill omened hour, in time arose
Debate and death, and all succeeding woes.
  The Queen whom sense of honour could not move
No longer made a secret of her love;
But called it marriage, by that specious name,
To veil the crime and sanctify the shame.
  The loud report through Lybian cities goes;
Fame, the great ill, from small beginnings grows:
Swift from the first; and ev'ry moment brings
New vigour to her flights, new pinions to her wings.
Soon grows the pygmy to gigantic size;
Her feet on earth, her forehead in the skies:

Enraged against the Gods, revengeful earth
Produced her last of the Titanian birth.
Swift is her walk, more swift her winged haste:
A monstrous phantom, horrible and vast;
As many plumes as raise her lofty flight,
So many piercing eyes enlarge her sight:
Millions of opening mouths to fame belong;
And ev'ry mouth is furnished with a tongue:
And round with list'ning ears the flying plague is hung.
She fills the peaceful universe with cries;
No slumbers ever close her wakeful eyes.
By day from lofty tow'rs her head she shews;
And spreads through trembling crowds disastrous news:
With court informers haunts, and royal spies,
Things done relates, not done she feigns; and mingles truth with lies.
Talk is her business; and her chief delight
To tell of prodigies, and cause affright.
She fills the people's ears with Dido's name;
Who, lost to honour, and the sense of shame,
Admits into her throne and nuptial bed
A wand'ring guest, who from his country fled:
Whole days with him she passes in delights;
And wastes in luxury long winter nights:
Forgetful of her fame, and royal trust;
Dissolved in ease, abandoned to her lust.

from *Palamon and Arcite: or, the Knight's Tale from Chaucer.
In Three Books* (Book III, lines 800–53)

Farewell; but take me dying in your arms,
'Tis all I can enjoy of all your charms:
This hand I cannot but in death resign;
Ah, could I live! But while I live 'tis mine.
I feel my end approach, and thus embraced,
Am pleased to die; but hear me speak my last.
Ah! my sweet foe, for you, and you alone,
I broke my faith with injured Palamon.
But love the sense of right and wrong confounds,
Strong love and proud ambition have no bounds.
And much I doubt, should heav'n my life prolong,

I should return to justify my wrong:
For while my former flames remain within,
Repentance is but want of pow'r to sin.
With mortal hatred I pursued his life,
Nor he, nor you, were guilty of the strife;
Nor I, but as I loved: Yet all combined,
Your beauty, and my impotence of mind,
And his concurrent flame, that blew my fire;
For still our kindred souls had one desire.
He had a moment's right in point of time;
Had I seen first, then his had been the crime.
Fate made it mine, and justified his right;
Nor holds this earth a more deserving knight,
For virtue, valour, and for noble blood,
Truth, honour, all that is comprised in good;
So help me heav'n, in all the world is none
So worthy to be loved as Palamon.
He loves you too, with such a holy fire
As will not, cannot but with life expire:
Our vowed affections both have often tried,
Nor any love but yours could ours divide.
Then by my love's inviolable band,
By my long suff'ring, and my short command,
If e'er you plight your vows when I am gone,
Have pity on the faithful Palamon.
  This was his last; for death came on amain,
And exercised below, his iron reign;
Then upward, to the seat of life he goes;
Sense fled before him, what he touched he froze;
Yet could he not his closing eyes withdraw,
Though less and less of Emily he saw:
So, speechless, for a little space he lay;
Then grasped the hand he held, and sighed his soul away.
  But whither went his soul, let such relate
Who search the secrets of the future state:
Divines can say but what themselves believe;
Strong proofs they have, but not demonstrative:
For, were all plain, then all sides must agree,
And faith it self be lost in certainty.
To live uprightly then is sure the best,
To save ourselves, and not to damn the rest.
The Soul of Arcite went, where heathens go,
Who better live than we, though less they know.

CHARLES MONTAGU, EARL OF HALIFAX
1661–1715

Charles Montagu, later Lord Halifax, was one of the most powerful statesmen of post-Revolution England. He was born in Northamptonshire into the aristocracy and schooled at Westminster where he was soon known for his 'extempore epigrams'. He went to Trinity aged eighteen. Within only four years he was a Fellow, the college having conferred his BA and then received orders from Charles II to give him their next Fellowship whatever the circumstances. The King died two years later, and whether out of gratitude or a search for further favour, Montagu wrote a set of verses for a commemorative University collection. In what became characteristic of Montagu's career, he obtained the favour, being invited by an impressed Charles Sackville, Earl of Dorset, whom he met at Cambridge, to enter the London literary scene. Montagu supported the invasion of William and Mary three years later, and went on to compose his Epistle to the Earl of Dorset, celebrating William's triumph at the Battle of the Boyne. From this date on, he occupied increasingly high levels of state office, helping establish the Bank of England and becoming Chancellor of the Exchequer. He also served as President of the Royal Society. Montagu earned a reputation for political machinations, and narrowly escaped corruption charges – thanks to help from the House of Lords – on several occasions.

Montagu's poetry was, for the most part, typical of contemporary London life: witty and urbane, with (in his case) a tendency more to flattery than satire. This explains not only why he received plenty of praise in verse, and lavished it in turn, but also why, along with his Whig politics, the greatest satirists of the time, Swift and Pope, respectively dismissed and despised him. Some of his youthful work was well-liked, such as the parody of Dryden's *The Hind and the Panther* which he co-wrote with Matthew Prior, titled *The City Mouse and the Country Mouse*. His *Epistle to Dorset* was deemed exemplary in Whig literary circles and was much reprinted. Montagu was also the subject of one of Samuel Johnson's *Lives of the Most Eminent English Poets*. But his lasting achievement may be his patronage, in later life, of other poets; he supported, among others, Addison, Steele and Congreve. He continued to act as a literary patron, dispensing the largesse he extracted from political dealings, until his death in 1715.

from *An Epistle to the Right Honourable Charles,
Earl of Dorset and Middlesex, Lord Chamberlain of
His Majesty's Household*

But *William*'s genius takes a wider scope,
And gives the injured, in all kingdoms, hope:
Born to subdue insulting tyrants' rage,
The ornament, and terror, of the age;
The refuge, where afflicted nations find
Relief from those oppressors of mankind,
Whom laws restrain not, and no oaths can bind.
Him their deliv'rer Europe does confess,
All tongues extol, and all religions bless;
The Po, the Danube, Bœtis, and the Rhine,
United in his praise their wonder join:
While, in the public cause, he takes the field,
And sheltered nations fight behind his shield.
His foes themselves dare not applause refuse;
And shall such actions want a faithful Muse?
Poets have this to boast; without their aid,
The freshest laurels, nipped by malice, fade,
And virtue to oblivion is betrayed:
The proudest honours have a narrow date,
Unless they vindicate their names from fate.
But who is equal to sustain the part;
Dryden has numbers, but he wants a heart;
Enjoined a penance (which is too severe
For playing once the fool) to persevere.
Others, who knew the trade, have laid it down;
And, looking round, I find you stand alone.
How, Sir! can you, or any English Muse,
Our country's fame, our Monarch's arms, refuse?
'Tis not my want of gratitude, but skill,
Makes me decline what I can ne'er fulfill:
I cannot sing of conquests, as I ought,
And my breath fails to swell a lofty note.
I know my compass, and my Muse's size,
She loves to sport and play, but dares not rise;
Idly affects, in this familiar way,
In easy numbers loosely to convey,
What mutual friendship would at distance say.

Poets assume another tone and voice,
When victory's their theme, and arms their choice;
To follow heroes, in the chase of fame,
Asks force, and heat, and fancy, winged with flame.
What words can paint the royal warrior's face?
What colours can the figure boldly raise?
When, covered o'er with comely dust and smoke,
He pierced the foe, and thickest squadrons broke?
His bleeding arm, still painful with the sore,
Which, in his people's cause, the pious father bore:
Whom, clearing through the troops a glorious way,
Not the united force of France, and hell, could stay.

LEONARD WELSTED
1688–1747

Leonard Welsted was the son of a priest, but was orphaned at the age of six and brought up by relatives. Nevertheless he followed his father's path to Westminster, and entered as a Queen's Scholar; it was there that he began to write poetry. He then went to Trinity aged nineteen, but his university career was cut short within months on account of his clandestine marriage to Frances Purcell, the likewise orphaned daughter of the composer Henry Purcell. Domestic bliss did not last long: Welsted lost his wife within a few years, and their only daughter would also die, aged eighteen. He would mourn the latter tragedy in his 'Hymn to the Creator' (1727).

Almost all of Welsted's earlier poems act as attempts to obtain a patron. Generally competent, if ingratiating, these appeared at a steady rate for several years until he found success in 1714. His satire on Tory leader Richard Harley (*The Prophecy*) caught the attention of leading Whigs just as the Hanoverian succession ensured the Whiggish camp was the side to take. From then on, he contributed to the Whig periodicals *Town-Talk* and *The Free-Thinker*. Unfortunately, he then overreached himself by wading into the contemporary satirical fray, and taking aim at Pope not once but twice. Welsted published *Palaemon to Caelia, or The Triumvirate* in 1717, a parody of Pope, Gay and Arbuthnot's *Three Hours after Marriage*, then followed it seven years later with an uncomplimentary reference to Pope in the preface to his own *Epistles, Odes, &c.* Sufficiently roused, Pope ridiculed Welsted on several occasions including *Peri Bathous*, *The Dunciad* – 'Flow, Welsted, flow! like thine inspirer, Beer' – and the *Epistle to Arbuthnot*, casting him as talentless, laughable, and too obsequious to be taken seriously. Welsted attempted to return fire, with his *One Epistle to A. Pope*, but the damage was done, and he wrote little verse afterwards.

Characteristically, Pope's verdict contains a blend of truth and exaggeration, but it is the verdict that survives today, and Welsted is mainly remembered for his place in the *Dunciad*. Yet, Welsted could write leisurely, convivial verse that has a charm. His employment in the Ordnance Office from 1725 meant that he lived in the Tower of London, a home he details in the *Oikographia*. Domestic sociability also governs 'The Invitation' and *Summum Bonum, or, Wisest Philosophy*, his last poem. He died in the Tower of London and was survived, briefly, by his second wife, Anne.

The Invitation

Freeman, I treat tonight, and treat your friends:
If, happily, from care your thought unbends,
If Lucy rules not with her jealous sway,
I shall expect you at the close of day.
  I give you the rough wholesome grape, that grows
In Tuscan vales, or where the Tagus flows;
Or, if the Gallic vine delight you more,
Of Hermitage I boast a slender store.
This is my wealth: if you have better wine,
Make me your guest; if not, I claim you mine.
  Already is my little sideboard graced;
The glasses marshalled; the decanters placed:
The room is cool; the summer-hearth is gay
With greens and flowers, th'exub'rance of the May.
Indulge the bliss this cheerful season brings;
Omit minuter hopes, and joyless things;
Let fame and riches wait: this happy morn,
With Brunswick, peace and liberty were born![64]
'Tis fit, my friend, we consecrate to mirth
The day, which gave th'illustrious monarch birth:
When the sun sets, we'll break into delight,
And give to gay festivity the night.
  Of what avail is fortune unenjoyed?
Or what is life, in anxious hours employed?
Let the dull miser pine with niggard care,
And brood o'er gold, devoted to his heir:
While we in honest mirth send time away,
Regardless what severer sages say.
In cheerful minds unbidden joys arise,
And well-timed levities become the wise.
  What virtue does not generous wine impart?
It gives a winning frankness to the heart;
With sprightly hope the drooping spirits arms;
Awakens love, and brightens beauty's charms;
High, florid thoughts th'inspiring juices breed;
Spleen they dispel, and clear the brow of need.
  Expect superfluous splendour from the great;
Ragouts, and costly follies served in plate;
And ortolans, from distant regions brought.
In foreign arts of luxury untaught,

I give you only lamb from Uxbridge fields:
And add the choicest herb, the garden yields;
Silesian lettuce, with soft Lucca oil,
Delicious blessings, of a different soil!
   None do our band of fellowship compose,
But know the chasteness of the banquet-rose.
Belmour is ours; Loveless, with humour stored;
And careless Florio, if he keeps his word.
I should exceed your rule, were more allowed:
There's less of mirth, than tumult, in a crowd.
   Remember, time posts on with subtle haste:
Now, as I write, the numbered minutes waste.
Then, Freeman, let us seize the present hour,
And husband the swift moments in our pow'r.
Good-humour bring along, and banish care:
You know your friends; you know your bill of fare.

LAURENCE EUSDEN
1688–1730

Laurence Eusden is the second of Trinity's Poet Laureates. He was born in York, from where he moved south to Trinity aged sixteen. His progress was smooth: he became a Scholar of the College after a year, graduated with a BA after two more, and by twenty-four was a full Fellow. Trinity was in a state of some ferment, with the Master, Richard Bentley, the subject of a petition from the Fellowship to remove him; Bentley had arrived as an outside appointment in 1700, and immediately caused waves by cutting back on Fellows' privileges in order to fund the restoration of Trinity's buildings. Like fellow Trinity poet John Byrom, Eusden took the side of Bentley. He praised the Master's restoration of the College Chapel in the poem 'To the Rev. Dr. Bentley', in what was to be a lifelong trend of siding with the one in power.

Eusden was a Whig, and throughout his life he steadily produced commendatory verses to leading members of the party. By doing so, he earned the patronage of figures from Lord Halifax to the Duke of Newcastle; the latter was Lord Chamberlain, and would eventually make Eusden, aged only thirty, the country's youngest Poet Laureate (a distinction he still holds). In turn, Eusden earned the scorn of Thomas Cooke and Jonathan Swift, who parodied his relentless stream of adulation in *The Battle of the Poets* and 'Directions for a Birth-Day Song', respectively. Even more severe was Alexander Pope, who took repeated aim at him (among others) in *Peri Bathous*, the *Dunciad*, and the *Epistle to Dr. Arbuthnot*. Eusden steadfastly ignored all the derision, and never wrote a line of verse in response. Aside from his praise of patrons and aristocrats, he worked mainly on classical translations, from both Latin (Claudian) and Greek (Musaeus), and upon his death in 1730 in Coningsby, Lincolnshire, where he was Rector, he was also finishing a translation of the Italian works of Tasso.

To the Rev. Dr. Bentley, on the Opening of Trinity-College Chapel, Cambridge

Long have we, safe, Time's envious fury scorned,
By kings first founded, then by kings adorned;
If fainting e'er we feared a fatal close,
Some new Maecenas with new life arose.
Fretted by age we still the stronger grow,
And to our ruins all our beauties owe.
So Cassia roughly chafed the sweeter smells,
And silver more consumed in brightness more excels.
Raised on high columns the proud fabric stands,
Where Barrow praise from ev'ry tongue commands:
Where the vast treasures of the learn'd are shown;
No works more rich, more noble, than his own.
The Muses soon the stately seat admired,
And in full transports their glad sons inspired:
Their sons inspired sung loud, and all around
Echo redoubled back the cheerful sound;
Sweet was the song, when lays (if such they give)
Worth of cedar, shall in cedar live.
      This sumptuous pile showed the brave founder's mind,
But equal labours still remain behind.
God's sacred house too long neglected lies,
And from some other Joash wants supplies;
But none was found, till you resolved to show
How far exalted piety could go:
From little funds, so largely to design,
Yet to make all in full perfection shine,
Great is the glory, and the glory's thine.
      Of old a joy in ev'ry face was seen,
Flushed by the promise of a bounteous Queen:
She vowed a temple; but too soon her breath
Vanished, and sealed her pious vows in death.
Thus David drew the scheme, but not begun;
The dome was builded by his wiser son.
Not so we fared. Tho' by Eliza loved,
Her sister's thoughts were lost, but not disproved.[65]
Till now we mourned our fate, but mourn no more;
Chased are the mists, which dulled the light before.
New golden censers on new altars blaze,
New music sounds the great Creator's praise.

Angels again from heav'n might list'ning stray,
Did but another sweet Cecilia play.
Here, long concealed we view the living paint;
Admire the picture, not adore the saint.
There, cherubs with stretched wings deceive the sight,
And bending forwards seem prepared for flight;
While flow'rs in pleasing folds adorn each side,
Some droop their sickly heads, some wanton in their pride,
Much more we see, and silent with surprise,
Recall times past, and scarce believe our eyes;
How gloomy once these hallowed mansions were,
But now, how wondrous lovely, how divinely fair!
So quickly, where the fragrant dust was spread,
Riseth the phoenix from his spicy bed:
Or such the change the witty poets feigned,
When hoary Aeson his young bloom regained.
He but regained what was before his own,
While here are beauties seen, till now unknown.
　　　　If it so charms, how can we ever show
Thy matchless worth, to whom those charms we owe?
Our vain essays our weakness may proclaim,
But not enlarge the circle of thy fame.
Praises from some delusive may appear;
When foes extol, we need no flatt'ries fear.
The stubborn atheist a fierce shock has felt;
Steeled though he was, he now begins to melt:
Since thus he sees all prejudice removed,
Thy acts confess the God thy learning proved.

JOHN BYROM
1692–1763

John Byrom achieved significant acclaim during his lifetime. Born into a rich merchant's family in Manchester, he attended schools in Chester and London before going up to Trinity at the age of sixteen. He was elected a scholar in the following year, and became a Fellow soon after; but when he refused to take holy orders – as was then *de rigueur* – his Fellowship was revoked. He briefly travelled to Montpellier in an abortive attempt to study medicine, but returned to Cambridge, where he remained on and off for several years. While at and around Trinity, Byrom became part of the circle of the Master, Richard Bentley, siding with him in his long-running dispute with the Fellowship. Byrom's feelings showed not only in a supportive (and anonymous) pamphlet, but also in a pastoral poem inspired by Bentley's young daughter Joanna, 'Colin and Phoebe', which appeared in *The Spectator*.

Byrom's most significant work at Trinity was the invention of a system of shorthand, which would in 1724 earn him election to the Royal Society. The system was immensely successful, gaining popularity among the gentry and men of letters, and he earned his living by teaching it to pupils in Cambridge, Oxford, and London. Byrom's shorthand was only superseded in the nineteenth century, by which time it was being officially used at the Universities of Oxford and Cambridge, as well as the House of Lords. While working as a tutor, he also continued to write poems, mainly satirical or religious verse. Though little of this is much read today, one of his surviving coinages is the phrase 'Tweedledum and Tweedledee', from his 'Epigram on the Feuds between Handel and Bononcini'.

John Wesley, who himself used Byrom's shorthand, compared the poet's wit and skill to Swift's. The real talent that Byrom had for pithy couplets is borne out by the fact that some of his lines were later attributed not only to Swift himself but also to Pope. Many of Byrom's more serious poems were written for hymn-books, and the work for which he is now best-known is his hymn 'Christians awake, salute the happy morn'. This, first titled 'Christmas Day for Dolly', was a present for his daughter, after she asked him for 'a poem' for

Christmas. Byrom continued to engage in satirical writing and gentle controversialism until he died aged seventy-one, leaving behind a number of other poems collected and published in Manchester ten years later.

Epigram on the Feuds between Handel and Bononcini

Some say, compared to Bononcini,
That Mynheer Handel's but a ninny;
Others aver, that he to Handel
Is scarcely fit to hold a candle.
Strange that all this difference should be,
'Twixt Tweedle-dum and Tweedle-dee!

Hymn for Christmas Day

Christians awake, salute the happy morn,
Whereon the Saviour of the world was born;
Rise, to adore the mystery of love,
Which hosts of angels chanted from above:
With them the joyful tidings first begun
Of God incarnate, and the Virgin's son:
Then to the watchful shepherds it was told,
Who heard the angelic herald's voice – 'Behold!
I bring good tidings of a Saviour's birth
To you, and all the nations upon earth;
This day hath God fulfilled his promised word;
This day is born a Saviour, Christ, the Lord:
In David's city, shepherds, ye shall find
The long foretold Redeemer of mankind;
Wrapt up in swaddling clothes, the babe divine
Lies in a manger; this shall be your sign'.
He spake, and straightway the celestial choir,
In hymns of joy, unknown before, conspire:
The praises of redeeming love they sung,
And heaven's whole orb with halleluhjahs rung:
God's highest glory was their anthem still;
Peace upon earth, and mutual good-will.
To Bethlehem straight th'enlightened shepherds ran,
To see the wonder God had wrought for man;
And found, with Joseph and the blessed maid,
Her son, the Saviour, in a manger laid.
Amazed, the wondrous story they proclaim;
The first apostles of his infant fame:
While Mary keeps, and ponders in her heart,

The heav'nly vision, which the swains impart;
They to their flocks, still praising God, return,
And their glad hearts within their bosoms burn.
Let us, like these good shepherds then, employ
Our grateful voices to proclaim the joy:
Like Mary, let us ponder in our mind
God's wondrous love in saving lost mankind;
Artless, and watchful, as these favoured swains,
While virgin meekness in the heart remains:
Trace we the babe, who has retrieved our loss,
From his poor manger to his bitter cross;
Treading his steps, assisted by his grace,
Till man's first heav'nly state again takes place:
Then may we hope, th'angelic thrones among,
To sing, redeemed, a glad triumphal song;
He that was born, upon this joyful day,
Around us all, his glory shall display;
Saved by his love, incessant we shall sing
Of angels, and of angel-men, the King.

On the Origin of Evil

Evil, if rightly understood,
Is but the skeleton of good,
Divested of its flesh and blood.

While it remains, without divorce
Within its hidden, secret source,
It is the good's own strength and force.

As bone has the supporting share,
In human form divinely fair,
Although an evil when laid bare;

As light and air are fed by fire,
A shining good, while all conspire,
But (separate) dark, raging ire;

As hope and love arise from faith,
Which then admits no ill, nor hath,
But, if alone, it would be wrath;

Or any instance thought upon
In which the evil can be none,
Till unity of good is gone;

So, by abuse of thought and skill,
The greatest good, to wit, *free-will*,
Becomes the *origin* of ill.

Thus when rebellious angels fell,
The very heav'n, where good ones dwell,
Became th'apostate spirits' hell.

Seeking, against eternal right,
A force without a love and light,
They found and felt its evil might.

Thus Adam biting at their bait,
Of good and evil when he ate,
Died to his first thrice happy state;

Fell to the evils of this ball,
Which, in harmonious union all,
Were Paradise before his fall.

And when the life of Christ in men
Revives its *faded* image, then,
Will all be Paradise again.

ROBERT LLOYD
1733–64

Robert Lloyd's life was a short and unfulfilled one. Dedicated to following a literary career, he died in debtors' prison at the age of thirty-one. Robert followed his father Pierson, a priest and schoolmaster, in attending both Westminster School and Trinity College. He seemed well-set to emulate his father's livelihood too, being successively Captain of School, head of those proceeding to Trinity, and graduating with a BA in 1755. Two further years passed, in which Pierson expected Robert to pursue a college Fellowship and head towards the Church. But he did not, and, in 1757, he instead returned to London, upon which his father secured Robert the position of usher at Westminster. And yet the younger Lloyd hated the grind of teaching Latin versification to schoolboys and he was soon to excoriate school and college life, and educators in particular, in a poem published in the *St James's Magazine*, and included here. In 1760 he quit and devoted his life to writing.

Robert's passion for literature had begun early. A shared taste for satire and burlesque had brought Lloyd together with William Cowper and five other Westminster boys to form the 'Nonsense Club'. Only two products survive, both by Lloyd and George Colman in collaboration: a series of poems parodying William Mason's verse (1756), and another meting out the same treatment to Thomas Gray's Pindaric odes (1757). Both Lloyd and Colman wanted to gain the favour of David Garrick and get into writing for Drury Lane. Lloyd wrote a long poem titled *The Actor* (1760), a thinly disguised hymn to Garrick. Like Colman, whose dramatic writing quickly proved successful, Lloyd was doing well, winning Garrick's approval.

In 1761 he became a poetry editor at *The Library*, with the satirist Charles Churchill, an old school friend with whom he shared literary interests and an imprudent lifestyle. Lloyd then became poetry reviewer for the *Monthly Review*, but for only six months. The following year *The Library* itself ceased publication and Lloyd tried to prop up his income with a book of his poems, *Poems by Robert Lloyd, A.M.* The subscriber-list, aided by his father's connections, was extraordinary: two bishops, fifty peers, and countless Fellows at Oxford and Cambridge colleges, then artistic and literary figures from Garrick to Hogarth, Johnson to

Sterne. Despite increasing difficulties in balancing his working life with poetic output, he continued to produce translations, mostly anonymous, including the first book of Voltaire's *Henriade*. After the failure in 1764 of a new venture, the *St James's Magazine*, he was arrested and thrown into the Fleet for debt. Towards the end of the year, his fortunes were beginning to turn: his comic opera, *The Capricious Lovers*, produced at Drury Lane, received highly positive reviews. It was cruel, then, that on the 15th December, still in debtors' prison and engaged to Churchill's sister, Patience, he caught a fever and died.

The Cit's Country Box

Vos sapere & solos aio bene vivere, quorum,
Conspicitur nitidis fundata pecunia villis.
HORACE[66]

The wealthy Cit, grown old in trade,
Now wishes for the rural shade,
And buckles to his one-horse chair,
Old Dobbin, or the foundered mare;
While wedged in closely by his side,
Sits Madam, his unwieldy bride,
With Jacky on a stool before 'em,
And out they jog in due decorum.
Scarce past the turnpike half a mile,
How all the country seems to smile!
And as they slowly jog together,
The Cit commends the road and weather;
While Madam dotes upon the trees,
And longs for ev'ry house she sees,
Admires its views, its situation,
And thus she opens her oration.
  'What signify the loads of wealth,
Without that richest jewel, health?
Excuse the fondness of a wife,
Who dotes upon your precious life!
Such easeless toil, such constant care,
Is more than human strength can bear.
One may observe it in your face –
Indeed, my dear, you break apace:
And nothing can your health repair,
But exercise, and country air.
Sir Traffic has a house, you know,
About a mile from Cheney-Row:
He's a *good* man, indeed 'tis true,
But not so *warm*, my dear, as you:
And folks are always apt to sneer –
One would not be out-done, my dear!'
  Sir Traffic's name so well applied
Awaked his brother merchant's pride;
And Thrifty, who had all his life
Paid utmost deference to his wife,

Confessed her arguments had reason,
And by th'approaching summer season,
Draws a few hundreds from the stocks,
And purchases his country box.

   Some three or four mile out of town
(An hour's ride will bring you down),
He fixes on his choice abode,
Not half a furlong from the road:
And so convenient does it lay,
The stages pass it ev'ry day:
And then so snug, so mighty pretty,
To have an house so near the city!
Take but your places at the Boar,
You're set down at the very door.

   Well then, suppose them fixed at last,
White-washing, painting, scrubbing past,
Hugging themselves in ease and clover,
With all the fuss of moving over;
Lo, a new heap of whims are bred!
And wanton in my lady's head.

   'Well to be sure, it must be owned,
It is a charming spot of ground;
So sweet a distance for a ride,
And all about so *countrified!*
'Twould come to but a trifling price
To make it quite a paradise;
I cannot bear those nasty rails,
Those ugly broken mouldy pales:
Suppose, my dear, instead of these,
We build a railing, all Chinese.
Although one hates to be exposed,
'Tis dismal to be thus inclosed;
One hardly any object sees –
I wish you'd fell those odious trees.
Objects continual passing by
Were something to amuse the eye,
But to be pent within the walls –
One might as well be at St. Paul's.
Our house beholders would adore,
Was there a level lawn before,
Nothing its views to incommode,
But quite laid open to the road;

While ev'ry trav'ler in amaze,
Should on our little mansion gaze,
And pointing to the choice retreat,
Cry, "That's Sir Thrifty's country seat".'
    No doubt her arguments prevail,
For Madam's *TASTE* can never fail.
    Blest age! when all men may procure,
The title of a connoisseur;
When noble and ignoble herd,
Are governed by a single word;
Though, like the royal German dames,
It bears an hundred Christian names;
As Genius, Fancy, Judgment, Goût,
Whim, Caprice, Je-ne-sais-quoi, Virtù:
Which appellations all describe
Taste, and the modern *tasteful* tribe.
Now bricklay'rs, carpenters, and joiners,
With Chinese artists, and designers,
Produce their schemes of alteration,
To work this wond'rous reformation.
The useful dome, which secret stood,
Embosomed in the yew-tree's wood,
The trav'ler with amazement sees
A temple, Gothic, or Chinese,
With many a bell, and tawdry rag on,
And crested with a sprawling dragon;
A wooden arch is bent astride
A ditch of water, four foot wide,
With angles, curves, and zigzag lines,
From Halfpenny's exact designs.
In front, a level lawn is seen,
Without a shrub upon the green,
Where Taste would want its first great law,
But for the skulking, sly *ha-ha*,
By whose miraculous assistance,
You gain a prospect two fields' distance.
And now from Hyde-Park Corner come
The Gods of Athens, and of Rome.
Here squabby Cupids take their places,
With Venus, and the clumsy Graces:
Apollo there, with aim so clever,
Stretches his leaden bow for ever;

And there, without the pow'r to fly,
Stands fixed a tip-toe Mercury.
    The villa thus completely graced,
All own, that Thrifty has a Taste;
And Madam's female friends, and cousins,
With common-council-men, by dozens,
Flock ev'ry Sunday to the seat,
To stare about them, and to eat.

from *A Familiar Epistle, to J. B. Esq*

            To cheat *this* World, the hardest task
Is to be constant to our mask.
Externals make direct impressions
And masks are worn by all professions.
            What need to dwell on topics stale?
Of parsons drunk with wine or ale?
Of lawyers, who, with face of brass,
For learned rhetoricians pass?
Of scientific doctors big,
Hid in the penthouse of their wig?
Whose conversation hardly goes
Beyond half words, and hums! and oh's:
Of Scholars, of superior *taste*,
Who cork it up for fear of waste,
Nor bring one bottle from their shelves,
But keep it always for themselves?
            Wretches like these, my soul disdains,
And doubts their hearts as well as brains.
Suppose a neighbour should desire
To light a candle at your fire,
Would it deprive your flame of light
Because another profits by 't?
            But youth must often pay its court
To these *great* scholars, *by report*,
Who live on hoarded reputation,
Which dares no risk of conversation,
And boast within a store of knowledge,
Sufficient, bless us! for a college,
But take a prudent care, no doubt,

That not a grain shall straggle out,
And are of wit too nice and fine,
To throw their pearl and gold to *swine*:
And therefore, to prevent deceit,
Think every man a *hog* they meet.
      These may perhaps as scholars shine
Who hang *themselves* out for a *sign*.
What signifies a lion's skin,
If it conceals an ass within?
If thou 'rt a lion, prithee roar.
If ass – bray once, and stalk no more.
Silence is folly in disguise;
With so much wisdom bottled up,
Uncork, and give your friends a sup.

GEORGE GORDON, LORD BYRON
1788–1824

Though he was the sixth to carry the title, there is surely only one Lord Byron: celebrity, carouser, melancholic, freedom fighter, and poet, George Gordon Noel Byron was born in January 1788 in London. The infant Byron's first appearance in the world was (to some at least) magically auspicious – and the occasion, moreover, for some celebrity merchandising. He was born with the inner foetal membrane (the 'caul') still over his head and this first, somewhat grisly Byron relic was sold as a putatively magical preventative against drowning to Royal Navy captain James Hanson, the brother of Byron's guardian, John Hanson. Captain Hanson's ship was duly wrecked some twelve years later, Hanson drowning with the vast majority of his crew.

Byron's own tempestuous life and poetry lends the adjective 'Byronic' its dark, glamorous force. Throughout his life he was embroiled in a number of scandals and he died of an infection at Missolonghi in Greece, where he had joined the cause of Greek independence from the Ottoman empire (his poignant, fittingly maudlin last poem, written in Missolonghi on his thirty-sixth birthday, is included here). Byron entered Trinity, more or less against his wishes, in 1805: he had wanted to go to Oxford ('there were no rooms vacant at Christchurch', he complained) where most of his friends from Harrow School had gone. His time at Trinity involved little – *very* little – study, much carousing, and enormous expenditure. Pleased with his '*Super*excellent rooms' – most likely on I staircase in Nevile's Court – Byron quickly ran through his exceedingly generous annual allowance of £500 by decorating his accommodation, gambling, ordering prodigious quantities of 'Wine, Port – Sherry – Claret, & Madeira', and, of course, by acquiring a pet bear. (It is highly unlikely, by the way, that Byron kept the bear in College and unlikelier still that he bathed it in the fountain; he probably kept it, along with his horse Oateater, at the Ram Yard, near the Round Church on Bridge Street.) During his time at Trinity Byron also became infatuated with a young choirboy, John Edleston, though he insisted, not without equivocation, that his 'love and passion' for Edleston was 'violent, though *pure*'. Despite this passionate relationship, and the numerous privileges he enjoyed as a nobleman, as well as the opportunities Cambridge afforded for making the acquaintance of 'a large assortment of jockies, gamblers, boxers, authors, parsons, and poets', Byron thought little of his time at Trinity – which was itself rather little time: he managed to extract a degree from the University without having spent the requisite number of terms in residence. He declared, at any rate, that 'I certainly do not feel that predilection for Mathematics, which may pervade the inclinations of men destined for a clerical, or collegiate life', and we get some sense of his view of the College curriculum from his poem 'Granta, a Medley', printed here.

With the publication of the first two cantos of *Childe Harold's Pilgrimage* (1812), Byron became instantly famous, lionised by fashionable and literary society. Childe Harold, it is often said, is the inaugural Byronic hero, though that (dubious) honour surely goes to Byron himself. It was around this time, incidentally, that he conducted one of many scandalous and well-publicised affairs with married women, and it was Lady Caroline Lamb ('Caro' to Byron) who left to posterity the description of Byron as 'mad, bad, and dangerous to know'. Following the success of the initial cantos of *Childe Harold*, Byron would leave England for good, as a consequence, in part, of his disastrous marriage to Annabella Milbanke. In Geneva he met another English poet, Percy Shelley, soon to be permanently exiled himself, who had eloped from England with Mary, the daughter of the radical political thinkers William Godwin and Mary Wollstonecraft. It was in Geneva that Byron took part in one of the great, legendary literary games of the nineteenth century: the competition to write a ghost story that produced Mary Shelley's *Frankenstein*. Though he abandoned his own attempt, he continued to write poetry, including the poems in *The Prisoner of Chillon* volume. 'Darkness' and 'Prometheus', included here, are brooding masterpieces, at turns misanthropic and revolutionary. Though both poems are steeped in the political tumult of their times, they have had a long afterlife – the former, for instance, seeming to some during the most dangerous days of the Cold War a dreadful foreshadowing of the coming nuclear winter.

In addition to these darkly visionary poems, Byron was also one of the great amatory poets, as the short lyrics included here attest, and one of the very greatest of comic poets. His epic *Don Juan* deployed to scintillating and sometimes devastating effect both the Italian *ottava rima* stanza and the frequently outlandish rhymes of Samuel Butler's *Hudibras* or of *The Dunciad* and *The Rape of the Lock* by Alexander Pope, an admired poetic forebear. Nevertheless, *Don Juan* did not enjoy the immediate success of *Childe Harold*, despite its being, as Anne Barton has remarked in her influential reading of it, the poem in which Byron's beguiling poetic personality is 'most fully present'. Subsequent critical opinion, however, has often viewed *Don Juan* as his masterpiece. Though Byron is at his sharpest, most merciless, and hilariously satirical in *Don Juan*, we would miss something important about it were we to read it *merely* as a comic poem. As William Hazlitt pointed out in defence of this great epic, 'In real life the most ludicrous incidents border on the most affecting and shocking.' Ludicrous, affecting, shocking – and much more besides – Byron remains one of the most various, virtuoso, and brilliant poets that English literature can boast.

Granta, a Medley

1

Oh! could Le Sage's demon's gift,[67]
　Be realized at my desire;
This night my trembling form he'd lift,
　To place it on St. Mary's spire.

2

Then would, unroofed, old Granta's halls
　Pedantic inmates full display;
Fellows, who dream on lawn, or stalls,
　The price of venal votes to pay.

3

Then would I view each rival wight,
　Petty and Palmerston survey;[68]
Who canvass there, with all their might.
　Against the next elective day.

4

Lo! candidates and voters lie,
　All lulled in sleep, a goodly number!
A race renowned for piety,
　Whose conscience won't disturb their slumber.

5

Lord Hawke indeed, may not demur,[69]
　Fellows are sage, reflecting, men;
They know preferment can occur,
　But very seldom, now and then.

6

They know, the Chancellor has got
　Some pretty livings, in disposal;
Each hopes, that one may be his lot,
　And, therefore, smiles on his proposal.

7

Now, from the soporific scene,
　I'll turn mine eye, as night grows later,
To view, unheeded, and unseen,
　The studious sons of Alma Mater.

8

There, in apartments small and damp
   The candidate for college prizes,
Sits poring by the midnight lamp,
   Goes late to bed, yet early rises.

9

He surely well deserves to gain them,
   With all the honours of his college,
Who, striving hardly to obtain them,
   Thus seeks unprofitable knowledge:

10

Who sacrifices hours of rest,
   To scan precisely metres Attic;
Or agitates his anxious breast,
   In solving problems mathematic.

11

Who reads false quantities in Sele,[70]
   Or puzzles o'er the deep triangle;
Deprived of many a wholesome meal,
   In barbarous Latin, doomed to wrangle.[71]

12

Renouncing every pleasing page,
   From authors of historic use;
Preferring to the lettered sage,
   The square of the hypotenuse.[72]

13

Still harmless are these occupations,
   That hurt none but the hapless student,
Compared with other recreations,
   Which bring together the impudent.

14

Whose daring revels shock the sight,
   When vice and infamy combine;
When drunkenness and dice unite,
   As every sense is steeped in wine.

15

Not so, the methodistic crew,
  Who plans of reformation lay;
In humble attitude they sue,
  And for the sins of others pray.

16

Forgetting that their pride of spirit,
  Their exultation in their trial;
Detracts, most largely, from the merit
  Of all their boasted self-denial.

17

'Tis morn, – from these I turn my sight,
  What scene is this, which meets the eye?
A numerous crowd, arrayed in white,[73]
  Across the green in numbers fly.

18

Loud rings, in air, the chapel bell;
  'Tis hushed; What sounds are these I hear?
The organ's soft celestial swell,
  Rolls deeply on the listening ear.

19

To this is joined the sacred song,
  The royal minstrel's hallowed strain;
Though he, who hears the music long,
  Will never wish to hear again.

20

Our choir would scarcely be excused,
  Even as a band of raw beginners;
All mercy, now, must be refused,
  To such a set of croaking sinners.

21

If David, when his toils were ended,
  Had heard these blockheads sing before him,
To us, his psalms had ne'er descended,
  In furious mood, he would have tore 'em.

22

The luckless Israelites, when taken,
  By some inhuman tyrant's order,
Were asked to sing, by joy forsaken,
  On Babylonian river's border.

23

Oh! had they sung in notes like these,
  Inspired by stratagem, or fear;
They might have set their hearts at ease,
  The devil a soul had stayed to hear.

24

But, if I scribble longer now,
  The deuce a soul will stay to read;
My pen is blunt, my ink is low,
  'Tis almost time to stop, indeed.

25

Therefore, farewell, old GRANTA's spires,
  No more, like Cleofas, I fly,
No more thy theme my muse inspires,
  The reader's tired and so am I.

[She walks in beauty, like the night]

1

She walks in beauty, like the night
  Of cloudless climes and starry skies;
And all that's best of dark and bright
  Meet in her aspect and her eyes:
Thus mellowed to that tender light
  Which heaven to gaudy day denies.

2

One shade the more, one ray the less,
  Had half-impaired the nameless grace
Which waves in every raven tress,
  Or softly lightens o'er her face;
Where thoughts serenely sweet express
  How pure, how dear their dwelling place.

3

And on that cheek, and o'er that brow,
  So soft, so calm, yet eloquent,
The smiles that win, the tints that glow,
  But tell of days in goodness spent,
A mind at peace with all below,
  A heart whose love is innocent!

Stanzas to [Augusta]

1

Though the day of my destiny's over,
  And the star of my fate hath declined,
Thy soft heart refused to discover
  The faults which so many could find;
Though thy soul with my grief was acquainted,
  It shrunk not to share it with me,
And the love which my spirit hath painted
  It never hath found but in *thee*.

2

Then when nature around me is smiling
  The last smile which answers to mine,
I do not believe it beguiling
  Because it reminds me of thine;
And when winds are at war with the ocean,
  As the breasts I believed in with me,
If their billows excite an emotion
  It is that they bear me from *thee*.

3

Though the rock of my last hope is shivered,
  And its fragments are sunk in the wave,
Though I feel that my soul is delivered
  To pain – it shall not be its slave.
There is many a pang to pursue me:
  They may crush, but they shall not contemn –
They may torture, but shall not subdue me –
  'Tis of *thee* that I think – not of them.

4

Though human, thou didst not deceive me,
  Though woman, thou didst not forsake,
Though loved, thou forborest to grieve me,
  Though slandered, thou never could'st shake, –
Though trusted, thou didst not betray me,
  Though parted, it was not to fly,
Though watchful, 'twas not to defame me,
  Nor, mute, that the world might belie.

5

Yet I blame not the world, nor despise it,
   Nor the war of the many with one –
If my soul was not fitted to prize it
   'Twas folly not sooner to shun:
And if dearly that error hath cost me,
   And more than I once could foresee,
I have found that, whatever it lost me,
   It could not deprive me of *thee*.

6

From the wreck of the past, which hath perished,
   Thus much I at least may recall,
It hath taught me that what I most cherished
   Deserved to be dearest of all:
In the desert a fountain is springing,
   In the wide waste there still is a tree,
And a bird in the solitude singing,
   Which speaks to my spirit of *thee*.

Darkness

I had a dream, which was not all a dream.
The bright sun was extinguished, and the stars
Did wander darkling in the eternal space,
Rayless, and pathless, and the icy earth
Swung blind and blackening in the moonless air;
Morn came, and went – and came, and brought no day,
And men forgot their passions in the dread
Of this their desolation; and all hearts
Were chilled into a selfish prayer for light:
And they did live by watchfires – and the thrones,
The palaces of crowned kings – the huts,
The habitations of all things which dwell,
Were burnt for beacons; cities were consumed,
And men were gathered round their blazing homes
To look once more into each other's face;
Happy were those who dwelt within the eye
Of the volcanoes, and their mountain-torch:
A fearful hope was all the world contained;

Forests were set on fire – but hour by hour
They fell and faded – and the crackling trunks
Extinguished with a crash – and all was black.
The brows of men by the despairing light
Wore an unearthly aspect, as by fits
The flashes fell upon them; some lay down
And hid their eyes and wept; and some did rest
Their chins upon their clenched hands, and smiled;
And others hurried to and fro, and fed
Their funeral piles with fuel, and looked up
With mad disquietude on the dull sky,
The pall of a past world; and then again
With curses cast them down upon the dust,
And gnashed their teeth and howled: the wild birds shrieked,
And, terrified, did flutter on the ground,
And flap their useless wings; the wildest brutes
Came tame and tremulous; and vipers crawled
And twined themselves among the multitude,
Hissing, but stingless – they were slain for food:
And War, which for a moment was no more,
Did glut himself again; – a meal was bought
With blood, and each sate sullenly apart
Gorging himself in gloom: no love was left;
All earth was but one thought – and that was death,
Immediate and inglorious; and the pang
Of famine fed upon all entrails – men
Died, and their bones were tombless as their flesh;
The meagre by the meagre were devoured,
Even dogs assailed their masters, all save one,
And he was faithful to a corse, and kept
The birds and beasts and famished men at bay,
Till hunger clung them, or the dropping dead
Lured their lank jaws; himself sought out no food,
But with a piteous and perpetual moan
And a quick desolate cry, licking the hand
Which answered not with a caress – he died.
The crowd was famished by degrees; but two
Of an enormous city did survive,
And they were enemies; they met beside
The dying embers of an altar-place
Where had been heaped a mass of holy things
For an unholy usage; they raked up,

And shivering scraped with their cold skeleton hands
The feeble ashes, and their feeble breath
Blew for a little life, and made a flame
Which was a mockery; then they lifted up
Their eyes as it grew lighter, and beheld
Each other's aspects – saw, and shrieked, and died –
Even of their mutual hideousness they died,
Unknowing who he was upon whose brow
Famine had written Fiend. The world was void,
The populous and the powerful – was a lump,
Seasonless, herbless, treeless, manless, lifeless –
A lump of death – a chaos of hard clay.
The rivers, lakes, and ocean all stood still,
And nothing stirred within their silent depths;
Ships sailorless lay rotting on the sea,
And their masts fell down piecemeal; as they dropped
They slept on the abyss without a surge –
The waves were dead; the tides were in their grave,
The moon their mistress had expired before;
The winds were withered in the stagnant air,
And the clouds perished; Darkness had no need
Of aid from them – She was the universe.

Prometheus

1

Titan! to whose immortal eyes
    The sufferings of mortality,
    Seen in their sad reality,
Were not as things that gods despise;
What was thy pity's recompense?
A silent suffering, and intense;
The rock, the vulture, and the chain,
All that the proud can feel of pain,
The agony they do not show,
The suffocating sense of woe,
    Which speaks but in its loneliness,
And then is jealous lest the sky
Should have a listener, nor will sigh
    Until its voice is echoless.

2

Titan! to thee the strife was given
   Between the suffering and the will,
   Which torture where they cannot kill;
And the inexorable Heaven,
And the deaf tyranny of Fate,
The ruling principle of Hate,
Which for its pleasure doth create
The things it may annihilate,
Refused thee even the boon to die:
The wretched gift eternity
Was thine – and thou hast borne it well.
All that the Thunderer wrung from thee
Was but the menace which flung back
On him the torments of thy rack;
The fate thou didst so well foresee
But would not to appease him tell;
And in thy Silence was his Sentence,
And in his Soul a vain repentance,
And evil dread so ill dissembled
That in his hand the lightnings trembled.

3

Thy Godlike crime was to be kind,
To render with thy precepts less
The sum of human wretchedness,
And strengthen Man with his own mind;
But baffled as thou wert from high,
Still in thy patient energy,
In the endurance, and repulse
Of thine impenetrable Spirit,
Which Earth and Heaven could not convulse,
A mighty lesson we inherit:
Thou art a symbol and a sign
To Mortals of their fate and force;
Like thee, Man is in part divine,
A troubled stream from a pure source;
And Man in portions can foresee
His own funereal destiny;
His wretchedness, and his resistance,
And his sad unallied existence:
To which his Spirit may oppose

Itself – an equal to all woes,
And a firm will, and a deep sense,
Which even in torture can descry
Its own concentrated recompense,
Triumphant where it dares defy,
And making Death a Victory.

Stanzas for Music

There be none of Beauty's daughters
  With a magic like thee;
And like music on the waters
  Is thy sweet voice to me:
When, as if its sound were causing
The charmed ocean's pausing,
The waves lie still and gleaming,
And the lulled winds seem dreaming.

And the midnight moon is weaving
  Her bright chain o'er the deep;
Whose breast is gently heaving,
  As an infant's asleep.
So the spirit bows before thee,
To listen and adore thee;
With a full but soft emotion,
Like the swell of Summer's ocean.

From *Childe Harold's Pilgrimage, A Romaunt, canto III*

109

But let me quit man's works, again to read
His Maker's, spread around me, and suspend
This page, which from my reveries I feed,
Until it seems prolonging without end.
The clouds above me to the white Alps tend,
And I must pierce them, and survey whate'er
May be permitted, as my steps I bend
To their most great and growing region, where
The earth to her embrace compels the powers of air.

110

Italia! too, Italia! looking on thee,
Full flashes on the soul the light of ages,
Since the fierce Carthaginian almost won thee,
To the last halo of the chiefs and sages,
Who glorify thy consecrated pages;
Thou wert the throne and grave of empires; still,
The fount at which the panting mind assuages
Her thirst of knowledge, quaffing there her fill,
Flows from the eternal source of Rome's imperial hill.

111

Thus far I have proceeded in a theme
Renewed with no kind auspices: – to feel
We are not what we have been, and to deem
We are not what we should be, – and to steel
The heart against itself; and to conceal,
With a proud caution, love, or hate, or aught, –
Passion or feeling, purpose, grief or zeal, –
Which is the tyrant spirit of our thought,
Is a stern task of soul: – No matter, – it is taught.

112

And for those words, thus woven into song,
It may be that they are a harmless wile, –
The colouring of the scenes which fleet along,
Which I would seize, in passing, to beguile
My breast, or that of others, for a while.
Fame is the thirst of youth, – but I am not
So young as to regard men's frown or smile,
As loss or guerdon of a glorious lot;
I stood and stand alone, – remembered or forgot.

113

I have not loved the world, nor the world me;
I have not flattered its rank breath, nor bowed
To its idolatries a patient knee, –
Nor coined my cheek to smiles, – nor cried aloud
In worship of an echo; in the crowd
They could not deem me one of such; I stood
Among them, but not of them; in a shroud
Of thoughts which were not their thoughts, and still could,
Had I not filed my mind, which thus itself subdued.

114

I have not loved the world, nor the world me, –
But let us part fair foes; I do believe,
Though I have found them not, that there may be
Words which are things, – hopes which will not deceive,
And virtues which are merciful, nor weave
Snares for the failing: I would also deem
O'er others' griefs that some sincerely grieve;
That two, or one, are almost what they seem, –
That goodness is no name, and happiness no dream.

From *Don Juan, canto I*, stanzas 200–204
and *canto VII*, stanzas 1–7

200

My poem's epic, and is meant to be
  Divided in twelve books; each book containing,
With love, and war, a heavy gale at sea,
  A list of ships, and captains, and kings reigning,
New characters; the episodes are three:
  A panorama view of hell's in training,
After the style of Virgil and of Homer,
So that my name of Epic's no misnomer.

201

All these things will be specified in time,
  With strict regard to Aristotle's rules,
The *vade mecum* of the true sublime,
  Which makes so many poets, and some fools;
Prose poets like blank-verse, I'm fond of rhyme,
  Good workmen never quarrel with their tools;
I've got new mythological machinery,
And very handsome supernatural scenery.

202

There's only one slight difference between
  Me and my epic brethren gone before,
And here the advantage is my own, I ween;
  (Not that I have not several merits more,
But this will more peculiarly be seen)
  They so embellish, that 'tis quite a bore
Their labyrinth of fables to tread through,
Whereas this story's actually true.

203

If any person doubt it, I appeal
  To history, tradition, and to facts,
To newspapers, whose truth all know and feel,
  To plays in five, and operas in three acts;
All these confirm my statement a good deal,
  But that which more completely faith exacts
Is, that myself, and several now in Seville,
Saw Juan's last elopement with the devil.

204

If ever I should condescend to prose,
   I'll write poetical commandments, which
Shall supersede beyond all doubt all those
   That went before; in these I shall enrich
My text with many things that no one knows,
   And carry precept to the highest pitch:
I'll call the work 'Longinus o'er a Bottle,
Or, Every Poet his *own* Aristotle.'

★

1

Oh Love! O Glory! what are ye who fly
   Around us ever, rarely to alight?
There's not a meteor in the Polar sky
   Of such transcendent and more fleeting flight.
Chill, and chained to cold earth, we lift on high
   Our eyes in search of either lovely light;
A thousand and a thousand colours they
Assume, then leave us on our freezing way.

2

And such as they are, such my present tale is,
   A non-descript and ever varying rhyme,
A versified Aurora Borealis,
   Which flashes o'er a waste and icy clime.
When we know what all are, we must bewail us,
   But, ne'ertheless, I hope it is no crime
To laugh at *all* things – for I wish to know
What after *all*, are *all* things – but a *Show*?

3

They accuse me – *Me* – the present writer of
   The present poem – of – I know not what, –
A tendency to under-rate and scoff
   At human power and virtue, and all that;
And this they say in language rather rough.
   Good God! I wonder what they would be at!
I say no more than hath been said in Dante's
Verse, and by Solomon and by Cervantes;

4

By Swift, by Machiavel, by Rochefoucault,
  By Fenelon, by Luther, and by Plato;
By Tillotson, and Wesley, and Rousseau,
  Who knew this life was not worth a potato.
'Tis not their fault, nor mine, if this be so –
  For my part, I pretend not to be Cato,
Nor even Diogenes. – We live and die,
But which is best, you know no more than I.

5

Socrates said, our only knowledge was
  'To know that nothing could be known;' a pleasant
Science enough, which levels to an ass
  Each Man of Wisdom, future, past, or present.
Newton (that Proverb of the Mind) alas!
  Declared, with all his grand discoveries recent,
That he himself felt only 'like a youth
Picking up shells by the great Ocean – Truth.'

6

Ecclesiastes said, that all is Vanity –
  Most modern preachers say the same, or show it
By their examples of true Christianity;
  In short, all know, or very soon may know it;
And in this scene of all-confessed inanity,
  By saint, by sage, by preacher, and by poet,
Must I restrain me, through the fear of strife,
From holding up the Nothingness of life?

7

Dogs, or Men! (for I flatter you in saying
  That ye are dogs – your betters far) ye may
Read, or read not, what I am now essaying
  To show ye what ye are in every way.
As little as the Moon stops for the baying
  Of wolves, will the bright Muse withdraw one ray
From out her skies – then howl your idle wrath!
While she still silvers o'er your gloomy path.

January 22nd 1824.
Messalonghi.
On this day I complete my thirty-sixth year.

1

'T is time this heart should be unmoved
   Since others it hath ceased to move,
Yet though I cannot be beloved
      Still let me love.

2

My days are in the yellow leaf
   The flowers and fruits of love are gone –
The worm, the canker and the grief
      Are mine alone.

3

The fire that on my bosom preys
   Is lone as some Volcanic Isle,
No torch is kindled at its blaze
      A funeral pile!

4

The hope, the fear, the jealous care
   The exalted portion of the pain
And power of Love I cannot share
      But wear the chain.

5

But 't is not *thus* – and 't is not *here*
   Such thoughts should shake my soul, nor *now*
Where glory decks the hero's bier
      Or binds his brow.

6

The Sword – the Banner – and the Field
   Glory and Greece around us see!
The Spartan borne upon his shield
      Was not more free!

7

Awake! (*not* Greece – She *is* awake!)
　　Awake my spirit – think through *whom*
Thy Life blood tracks its parent lake
　　　　And then strike home!

8

Tread those reviving passions down
　　Unworthy Manhood; – unto thee
Indifferent should the smile or frown
　　　　Of Beauty be.

9

If thou regret'st thy youth, why *live*?
　　The Land of honourable Death
Is here – up to the Field! and give
　　　　Away thy Breath.

10

Seek out – less often sought than found,
　　A Soldier's Grave – for thee the best,
Then look around and choose thy ground
　　　　And take thy Rest.

[So, we'll go no more a-roving]

So, we'll go no more a-roving
　　So late into the night,
Though the heart be still as loving,
　　And the moon be still as bright.

For the sword outwears its sheath,
　　And the soul wears out the breast,
And the heart must pause to breathe,
　　And love itself have rest.

Though the night was made for loving,
　　And the day returns too soon,
Yet we'll go no more a-roving
　　By the light of the moon.

THOMAS BABINGTON MACAULAY
1800–59

Macaulay's *Lays of Ancient Rome* (1842) were hugely popular throughout the rest of the nineteenth century and beyond, a staple feature of boys' education as well as a favourite with the general public. W. B. Yeats recalled his father reading the Lays to him when he was eight – 'the first poetry that had moved me after the stable-boy's Orange rhymes', he claimed. At Harrow School Winston Churchill is supposed to have learned by heart all seventy stanzas of the most famous 'lay' (or ballad) of them all, and even more recently, the poet Anne Stevenson has recalled learning the same section by heart 'at a fairly rough school in New Haven, Connecticut.' An excerpt from it is printed here.

Macaulay was born into a strongly evangelical family, and educated accordingly at a school near Cambridge, from which he entered Trinity in 1818. He proved a good classical scholar and a promising writer, winning scholarships and the Chancellor's Medal for English verse. Though graduating without honours (he did not care for mathematics), he was elected to a Fellowship in 1824. He began writing essays for the *Edinburgh Review*, many of which would later be collected in *Essays Critical and Historical* (1843), including one on 'Milton' (1825) which helped to make his name. He was called to the bar and entered politics, being elected a Whig MP for Calne (Wiltshire) and then Leeds. His powers as an orator became evident in the debates preceding the Reform Bill of 1832.

He was elected again as an MP for Edinburgh in 1839 and in 1852, serving as secretary at war (1839–41) and paymaster-general (1846–7). But it was the four years he spent in India from 1834 to 1838 on the new Supreme Council for which his political career is best remembered, not least for the *Minute on Indian Education* (1835) that argued for all instruction in Higher Education to be in English rather than Sanskrit and Arabic. It was in India that he conceived the idea for the *Lays*, influenced by Percy's *Reliques of Ancient English Poetry* and Scott's *Minstrelsy of the Scottish Border*, as well as by his reading of ancient Roman history. He would later declare that the plan occurred to him 'in the jungle at the foot of the Neilgherry hills; and most of the verses were made during a dreary sojourn at Ootacamund and a disagreeable voyage in the Bay of Bengal'.

There was more to their composition than this. On his return to Britain he set out for Rome to see the sites for himself, following in Gibbon's footsteps – and also in a sense Walter Scott's, whose belief in the value of seeing 'real' places he would imitate in work on his *History of England*. The first two volumes of the *History* were published in 1849 to instant acclaim, and the third and fourth in 1855. Like the *Essays* and the *Lays* the *History* was a great success, a best-seller that has never been out of print. The author became wealthy and honoured, as Baron Macaulay of Rothley.

In their first edition, the *Lays* comprised four ballads dramatising episodes from Roman history. 'Horatius' tells the story of a crucial juncture when the Tarquins have been expelled and seek to reinstate themselves with the help of an ally, Lars Porsena of Clusium, and his Etruscan army. Son of the ousted king, 'false Sextus' has raped Lucretia ('the deed of shame') and Rome has been declared a Republic. Horatius leads the resistance to the invading Etruscans by holding the bridge across the Tiber until it can be hacked down, thus saving the city. It was a schoolboy's dream of heroism for at least the next one hundred years.

from *Horatius*

27

Then out spake brave Horatius,
  The Captain of the Gate:
'To every man upon this earth
  Death cometh soon or late.
And how can man die better
  Than facing fearful odds,
For the ashes of his fathers
  And the temples of his gods,

28

'And for the tender mother
  Who dandled him to rest,
And for the wife who nurses
  His baby at her breast,
And for the holy maidens
  Who feed the eternal flame,
To save them from false Sextus
  That wrought the deed of shame?

29

'Hew down the bridge, Sir Consul,
  With all the speed ye may;
I, with two more to help me,
  Will hold the foe in play.
In yon strait path a thousand
  May well be stopped by three.
Now who will stand on either hand,
  And keep the bridge with me?'

★

57

Alone stood brave Horatius,
  But constant still in mind;
Thrice thirty thousand foes before,
  And the broad flood behind.
'Down with him!' cried false Sextus,
  With a smile on his pale face.
'Now yield thee,' cried Lars Porsena,
  'Now yield thee to our grace.'

58

Round turned he, as not deigning
  Those craven ranks to see;
Nought spake he to Lars Porsena,
  To Sextus nought spake he;
But he saw on Palatinus
  The white porch of his home;
And he spake to the noble river
  That rolls by the towers of Rome.

59

'Oh, Tiber! father Tiber!
  To whom the Romans pray,
A Roman's life, a Roman's arms,
  Take thou in charge this day!'
So he spake, and speaking sheathed
  The good sword by his side,
And, with his harness on his back,
  Plunged headlong in the tide.

*

63

'Curse on him!' quoth false Sextus;
  'Will not the villain drown?
But for this stay, ere close of day
  We should have sacked the town!'
'Heaven help him!' quoth Lars Porsena,
  'And bring him safe to shore;
For such a gallant feat of arms
  Was never seen before.'

64

And now he feels the bottom;
  Now on dry earth he stands;
Now round him throng the Fathers;
  To press his gory hands;
And now, with shouts and clapping,
  And noise of weeping loud,
He enters through the River-Gate,
  Borne by the joyous crowd.

65

They gave him of the corn-land,
   That was of public right,
As much as two strong oxen
   Could plough from morn till night;
And they made a molten image,
   And set it up on high,
And there it stands unto this day
   To witness if I lie.

66

It stands in the Comitium,
   Plain for all folk to see;
Horatius in his harness,
   Halting upon one knee:
And underneath is written,
   In letters all of gold,
How valiantly he kept the bridge
   In the brave days of old.

67

And still his name sounds stirring
   Unto the men of Rome,
As the trumpet-blast that cries to them
   To charge the Volscian home;
And wives still pray to Juno
   For boys with hearts as bold
As his who kept the bridge so well
   In the brave days of old.

68

And in the nights of winter,
   When the cold north winds blow,
And the long howling of the wolves
   Is heard amidst the snow;
When round the lonely cottage
   Roars loud the tempest's din,
And the good logs of Algidus
   Roar louder yet within;

69

When the oldest cask is opened,
  And the largest lamp is lit;
When the chestnuts glow in the embers,
  And the kid turns on the spit;
When young and old in circle
  Around the firebrands close;
When the girls are weaving baskets,
  And the lads are shaping bows;

70

When the goodman mends his armour,
  And trims his helmet's plume;
When the goodwife's shuttle merrily
  Goes flashing through the loom;
With weeping and with laughter
  Still is the story told,
How well Horatius kept the bridge
  In the brave days of old.

WINTHROP MACKWORTH PRAED
1802–39

Praed was a brilliant schoolboy at Eton, founding *The Etonian* and writing for it prolifically. Its publisher Charles Knight remembered him as a 'laughing satirist; a pale and slight youth, who had looked upon the aspects of society with the keen perception of a clever manhood'. At Trinity he read classics alongside the slightly older Macaulay, winning medals for Greek odes and epigrams and also for English parody, and a prize for declamation. He was active and witty in debate, and he would in due course deploy these gifts as a Tory MP, as eloquently opposed to Reform as his old friend Macaulay was in support of it. His good looks and confidence attracted admiration at Cambridge. Bulwer Lytton considered that he 'was to the University what Byron was to the world'.

In 1827 Praed was elected to a Trinity Fellowship, but he never took it up. After Cambridge he started writing for the journals and annuals; later he read for the bar, without much enthusiasm, though he continued to practise up to his early death. He was more attracted to politics, leaning heavily now towards the Tories, who were happy to find him a pocket borough in exchange for £1000, and to employ his skill with words both written and spoken. He produced a series of verse satires and argued vigorously against the Reform Bill, returning to Parliament in 1834 and serving as secretary to the Board of Control. Had he lived longer he might have achieved prominence in Sir Robert Peel's Conservative government in the early 1840s, but his health was poor and consumption claimed him shortly after his 37th birthday.

Praed was well enough known in his own time, and he enjoyed for the rest of the century a reputation for skilful 'light verse', for relatively mild satire and light-hearted humour, all turned with a certain grace. His poetry first appeared mainly in periodicals, and was collected after his death: in 1864 his friend Derwent Coleridge (son of the poet) published his *Poems*, prefaced by a memoir, and in 1888 his *Political and Occasional Poems* were published.

Yes or No

I

The Baron de Vaux hath a valiant crest, –
  My Lady is fair and free;
The Baron is full of mirth and jest, –
  My Lady is full of glee;
But their path, we know, is a path of woe,
  And many the reason guess, –
The Baron will ever mutter 'No,'
  When my Lady whispers 'Yes.'

II

The Baron will pass the wine-cup round, –
  My Lady forth will roam;
The Baron will out with horse and hound, –
  My Lady sits at home;
The Baron will go to draw the bow, –
  My Lady will go to chess;
And the Baron will ever mutter 'No,'
  When my Lady whispers 'Yes.'

III

The Baron hath ears for a lovely lay,
  If my Lady sings it not;
The Baron is blind to a beauteous day,
  If it beam in my Lady's grot;
The Baron bows low to a furbelow,
  If it be not my Lady's dress;
And the Baron will ever mutter 'No,'
  When my Lady whispers 'Yes.'

IV

Now saddle my steed, and helm my head,
  Be ready in the porch;
Stout Guy, with a ladder of silken thread,
  And trusty Will, with a torch:
The wind may blow, the torrent flow, –
  No matter, – on we press;
I never can hear the Baron's 'No'
  When my Lady whispers 'Yes.'

Anticipation

'Oh yes! he is in Parliament;
　He's been returning thanks;
You can't conceive the time he's spent
　Already on his franks.
He'll think of nothing, night and day,
　But place, and the gazette': –
No matter what the people say, –
　You won't believe them yet.

'He filled an album, long ago,
　With such delicious rhymes;
Now we shall only see, you know,
　His speeches in the "Times";
And liquid tone and beaming brow,
　Bright eyes and looks of jet,
He'll care for no such nonsense now': –
　Oh! don't believe them yet!

'I vow he's turned a Goth, a Hun,
　By that disgusting Bill;
He'll never make another pun;
　He's danced his last quadrille.
We shall not see him flirt again
　With any fair coquette;
He'll never laugh at Drury Lane.' –
　Psha! – don't believe them yet.

'Last week I heard his uncle boast
　He's sure to have the seals;
I read it in the "Morning Post"
　That he has dined at Peel's;[74]
You'll never see him any more,
　He's in a different set;
He cannot eat at half-past four': –
　No? – don't believe them yet.

'In short, he'll soon be false and cold,
 And infinitely wise;
He'll grow next year extremely old,
 He'll tell enormous lies;
He'll learn to flatter and forsake,
 To feign and to forget': –
O whisper – or my heart will break –
 You won't believe them yet!

FREDERICK TENNYSON
1807–98

Frederick Tennyson grew up in Somersby Rectory, Lincolnshire, son of the Rev. George Clayton Tennyson – a moody, sometimes violent man – and Elizabeth Fytche. He was the oldest of eleven gifted but troubled children, three of whom were poets and three experienced some form of mental breakdown. At Trinity, Frederick was joined by the two other poets in the family: Charles and Alfred (see pp. 162–66 and 180–98). The most rebellious and hot-headed of the children – it was Frederick that George Clayton once threatened to kill, first with a gun, then with a knife, eventually turning him out of the house – he soon came into conflict with the college authorities as well. Refusing to obey the rule that students attend chapel twice a day, he was summoned for an explanation; he was then 'smilingly & satirically impertinent' to the Master, Christopher Wordsworth, and was sent down for three terms – a punishment judged mild at the time. He returned to take his BA in 1832, and after a few more unhappy years at home moved to Florence, where he married and remained for some years before returning to Britain.

In 1827 the three brothers published the confusingly named *Poems by Two Brothers*. Alfred contributed more than half, Charles most of the rest, and Frederick just three or four poems. He was the least gifted of the three, but he did continue to write verse for some years till, disillusioned by the poor reception given to his collection *Days and Hours* (1854) – though we do know that Edward FitzGerald read it – he gave up, and did not publish again till the very end of his life. Music and mysticism began to occupy his time. In 1859 he left Italy and moved to Jersey where he collaborated in mystical researches with a neighbour. In 1872 he visited his old friend FitzGerald in Suffolk and they reminisced together – Frederick explaining the key to the Masonic mysteries, discovered via ancient astrology and soon to be published in a book, *Veritas* (1874). 'All this old Frederic [sic] is as earnest about as a Man – or a Child – can be', FitzGerald commented.

Returning to poetry in his later years, Frederick published *The Isles of Greece* (1890), an epic based on fragments of Sappho and Alcæus, *Daphne* (1891) and *Poems of the Day and Year* (1895). These, however, received little more attention than his earlier works. Though outliving his two younger brothers, his poetic reputation was bound to be, not unjustly, overshadowed by theirs.

To Sorrow

I

O Sorrow, whose inviolable soul
    The God of all things made his dwelling-place,
    Sorrow, whom all must look on face to face
Between their mortal barriers and the goal,
    Whose is the infant's plaint, the funeral knell,
    Thy voice is better than a marriage-bell.

II

Better it is to sit awhile with thee,
    And listen to thy melancholy shell,
    Than sound of festal harpings, and the swell
Of choral triumphs waxing like a sea;
    Better it is to hear thy still small voice
    Than Pæans thundered forth when Kings rejoice!

III

O holy Sorrow, whom the iron Fates
    Alone on earth pass by without a frown,
    When I behold how rebel years discrown
Imperial Youth; how lordly Pleasure waits
    To pass beneath Affliction's dungeon door;
    I'll sit with thee, though thou be old and poor.

IV

How Hope's blue eyes grow dim and blind with tears;
    How Love unplumed, and crazy Mirth forlorn
    Halt after winged Time pursued by Scorn;
How Vanity the last of Youth's frail peers
    Armed with a crooked crutch, and withered wreath
    Goes with Despair to fight the strength of Death;

V

How Glory hears the echoes of his name
    Die down the wind, that wafteth swiftly on
    The thundering sound of victories newly won,
And triumphs louder in the throat of Fame;
    Sorrow, in thy deep bower I'll sit with thee,
    And hear thee sing of Immortality.

CHARLES TENNYSON TURNER
1808–79

Charles Turner (formerly Tennyson) was the second surviving son of
Rev. George Clayton Tennyson and his wife, Elizabeth Fytche. First
educated at Louth Grammar school, Charles, alongside his brother
Alfred, was then taught at home by their father in preparation for
Cambridge. He was admitted to Trinity in 1827, the same year in which
Poems by Two Brothers was published (see pp. 159–60). Charles's first
independent volume, *Sonnets and Fugitive Pieces* (1830), was published
during his time at Cambridge and was much admired by Coleridge.
After graduating in 1832, he was ordained deacon, and then priest in
1833. When a great-uncle, Rev. Samuel Turner, died in 1835, Charles
inherited much of his property, changing his name from Tennyson to
Turner and thereafter publishing as 'Charles Turner', though widely
referred to as 'Charles Tennyson Turner'. A year later Charles married
Louisa Sellwood, whose sister Emily would marry his brother, Alfred,
in 1850. The marriage between Charles and Louisa was severely tested
by his opium addiction, which probably started as early as 1830 and may
have been influenced by his father's similar problem, as well as by her
subsequent periods of mental illness, one of which led to a ten-year sep-
aration. Alfred's horror of opium, no doubt born of a too close, familial
knowledge, emerges in a half-humorous letter written to urge a friend to
avoid the stuff: 'Is there not cakes and ale? is there not toddies? is there
not bacchies? is there not pipes? . . . in the name of all that is near and
dear unto thee I prythee take no opium'. Addictions and depressions,
including Alfred's own 'toddies' and 'bacchies', were all too common in
the Tennyson family.

After their separation Charles and Louisa were reunited in 1849.
He seems to have overcome his addiction, and some five years later he
started to write poetry again, contributing sonnets to the periodicals.
In 1864 he published *Sonnets*, followed by *Small Tableaux* (1868) and
Sonnets, Lyrics, and Translations (1873). In 1866 ill-health forced him to
retire from active ministry, and he died in Cheltenham thirteen years
later. Sadly, Louisa, who also suffered from periodic bouts of religious
mania, had been confined in an asylum near Salisbury some six months
previously, and barely survived him. His death was a severe blow to

Alfred, who declared him 'altogether loveable, a second George Herbert in his utter faith', and commemorated him in the poem 'Frater Ave atque Vale'. He also wrote the prefatory poem to a volume of Charles's *Collected Sonnets* (1880), many of them previously unpublished: 'And thou hast vanished from thine own / To that which looks like rest, / True brother, only to be known / By those who love thee best.' Though his was an often unhappy life, Charles seems to have found in the small compass of the sonnet a form in which to escape the shadow of his much more famous brother.

On the Statue of Lord Byron

by Thorwaldsen,[75] in Trinity College Library, Cambridge

'Tis strange that I, who haply might have met
Thy living self – who sought to hide the flaws
In thy great fame, and, though I ne'er had set
Eyes on thee, heard thee singing without pause,
And longed to see thee, should, alas! detect
The Thyrza-sorrow first on sculptured brows,
And know thee best in marble! Fate allows
But this poor intercourse; high and erect
Thou hold'st thy head, whose forward glance beholds
All forms that throng this learned vestibule;
Women and men, and boys and girls from school,
Who gaze with admiration all unchecked
On thy proud lips, and garment's moveless folds,
So still, so calm, so purely beautiful!

Vienna and In Memoriam

Roused by the war-note, in review I passed
The polities of nations – their intrigues –
Their long-drawn wars and hates – their loves and leagues;
But when I came on sad Vienna, last,
Her scroll of annals, timidly unrolled,
Ran backward from my helpless hands! the woe
Of that one hour that laid our Arthur[76] low,
Made all her chronicle look blank and cold:
Then turned I to that Book of memory,
Which is to grieving hearts like the sweet south
To the parched meadow, or the dying tree;
Which fills with elegy the craving mouth
Of sorrow – slakes with song her piteous drouth,
And leaves her calm, though weeping silently!

Statue of Byron by Bertel Thorvaldsen, Wren Library.

A Brilliant Day

O keen pellucid air! nothing can lurk
Or disavow itself on this bright day;
The small rain-plashes shine from far away,
The tiny emmet glitters at his work;
The bee looks blithe and gay, and as she plies
Her task, and moves and sidles round the cup
Of this spring flower, to drink its honey up,
Her glassy wings, like oars that dip and rise,
Gleam momently. Pure-bosomed, clear of fog,
The long lake glistens, while the glorious beam
Bespangles the wet joints and floating leaves
Of water-plants, whose every point receives
His light; and jellies of the spawning frog,
Unmarked before, like piles of jewels seem!

Gout and Wings

The pigeons fluttered fieldward, one and all,
I saw the swallows wheel, and soar, and dive;
The little bees hung poised before the hive,
Even Partlet hoised herself across the wall:
I felt my earth-bound lot in every limb,
And, in my envious mood, I half-rebelled;
When lo! an insect crossed the page I held,
A little helpless minim, slight and slim;
Ah! sure, there was no room for envy there,
But gracious aid and condescending care;
Alas! my pride and pity were misspent,
The atom knew his strength, and rose in air!
My gout came tingling back, as off he went,
A wing was opened at me everywhere!

Edward FitzGerald was born with the surname Purcell, son of an MP
and his wife Mary Frances, whose father was a wealthy Irish landowner,
John FitzGerald. On the latter's death Mary Frances came into a large
inheritance, and the family changed their name. The FitzGeralds lived
briefly in France, where the young Edward developed an interest in
languages, as well as a knack for dancing and fencing. On returning
to Britain, he attended King Edward VI Grammar School in Bury St
Edmunds – known for its emphasis on literature – and then went up,
aged seventeen, to Trinity. Like many of his contemporaries, FitzGerald
showed little interest in the curriculum of the time, predominantly
natural sciences and mathematics, preferring to read, play music, and
enjoy debates among like-minded friends (including Thackeray), as well
as members of the Cambridge Apostles. He enjoyed his time so much
that, for several years after graduating, he made an annual return and
stayed in his old rooms on King's Parade. Apart from a brief unhappy
marriage he spent most of his life living quietly in Suffolk, a bachelor
and convinced vegetarian (see Tennyson's 'To E. FitzGerald'). His old
friend James Spedding once called him 'the Prince of Quietists', adding:
'His tranquillity is like a pirated copy of the peace of God.'

FitzGerald's first, anonymously published work was 'The Meadows
in Spring', a poem that won the praise of Charles Lamb. But as far
as original poetry went, he believed he lacked 'the strong inward call'
felt by others, including his friends Tennyson and Carlyle. A few of
his minor works are still remembered, such as *Euphranor* (1851), a phil-
osophical dialogue on the topic of education, and *Polonius* (1852), an
anthology of aphorisms. Instead, he was drawn to translation, learning
Spanish and turning six of Calderón's plays into English. When these
were criticised for their infidelity to the originals, FitzGerald retorted
'Better a live Sparrow than a stuffed Eagle'. These were the only
works to which he appended his own name, even if only to distinguish
them from another contemporary translation. In later life he turned
to plays by Aeschylus and Sophocles, and received an award from the
Spanish Royal Academy for his work on Calderón. More importantly,
and of infinite value to scholars of the period, he left behind a large

correspondence with friends and peers which was witty, acerbic, and always readable.

But it is the *Rubáiyát of Omar Khayyám* that made him reluctantly famous. He was approaching fifty when he started translating the *rubáiyát*, or quatrains, attributed to the twelfth-century Persian mathematician and astronomer. In the spring of 1859 a slim brown pamphlet was published privately and anonymously. It would become one of the most popular poems in the English language. Two years later it caught the attention of Dante Gabriel Rossetti and Algernon Charles Swinburne, who helped to spread its fame. John Ruskin later wrote to its anonymous author that he had never 'read anything so glorious'. Glory was the last thing sought by the diffident, reclusive FitzGerald, but growing demand required further editions, enlarged and revised, in 1868, 1872 and 1879. The year after his death in 1883 saw the first of numerous illustrated editions that would give a huge boost to the poem's circulation on both sides of the Atlantic.

The popularity of this work stems from its mix of religious imagery and a profound, aesthetic disengagement, lightly expressed, from all kinds of religious conviction and worldly ambition. FitzGerald had little patience with writers as solemn as Virgil, Dante, Milton, Wordsworth, and George Eliot, who did not, as he said, 'take it easy'. Let them 'dwell apart in the Empyrean', he exclaimed, 'but for Human Delight, Shakespeare, Cervantes, Boccaccio, and Scott!'. As for his friend, Alfred Tennyson, FitzGerald claimed to detest his poetry, but he was loyally generous towards the man. When Tennyson was correcting the proofs of his 1842 volume, tearing the original manuscript into spills for lighting his pipe as he went, it was FitzGerald who retrieved what he could from the fire, and later gave the rescued pieces to Trinity College. He once wrote that he himself was 'an idle fellow, but one whose friendships were more like loves'. He also declared that 'I have not put away childish things, though a man. But, at the same time, this visionary inactivity is better than the mischievous activity of so many I see about me.' FitzGerald's achievement in the *Rubáiyát* was to find an active way of representing such visionary inactivity, with a levity, delicacy and musicality that alleviate what might otherwise be too grim a contemplation of mortality.

from *Rubáiyát of Omar Khayyám*

I

AWAKE! for Morning in the Bowl of Night
Has flung the Stone that puts the Stars to Flight:
 And Lo! the Hunter of the East has caught
The Sultán's Turret in a Noose of Light.

II

Dreaming when Dawn's Left Hand was in the Sky
I heard a Voice within the Tavern cry,
 'Awake, my Little ones, and fill the Cup
Before Life's Liquor in its Cup be dry.'

III

And, as the Cock crew, those who stood before
The Tavern shouted – 'Open then the Door!
 You know how little while we have to stay,
And, once departed, may return no more.'

IV

Now the New Year reviving old Desires,
The thoughtful Soul to Solitude retires,
 Where the WHITE HAND OF MOSES on the Bough
Puts out, and Jesus from the Ground suspires.

V

Irám indeed is gone with all its Rose,
And Jamshýd's Sev'n-ring'd Cup where no one knows;
 But still the Vine her ancient Ruby yields
And still a Garden by the Water blows.

VI

And David's Lips are locked; but in divine
High piping Péhlevi, with 'Wine! Wine! Wine!
 Red Wine!' – the Nightingale cries to the Rose
That yellow Cheek of hers t' incarnadine.

VII

Come, fill the Cup, and in the Fire of Spring
The Winter Garment of Repentance fling:
   The Bird of Time has but a little way
To fly – and Lo! the Bird is on the Wing.

VIII

And look – a thousand Blossoms with the Day
Woke – and a thousand scattered into Clay:
   And this first Summer Month that brings the Rose
Shall take Jamshýd and Kaikobád away.

IX

But come with old Khayyám, and leave the Lot
Of Kaikobád and Kaikhosrú forgot:
   Let Rustum lay about him as he will,
Or Hátim Tai cry Supper – heed them not.

X

With me along some Strip of Herbage strown
That just divides the desert from the sown,
   Where name of Slave and Sultán scarce is known,
And pity Sultán Máhmúd on his Throne.

XI

Here with a Loaf of Bread beneath the Bough,
A Flask of Wine, a Book of Verse – and Thou
   Beside me singing in the Wilderness –
And Wilderness is Paradise enow.

XII

'How sweet is mortal Sovranty!' – think some:
Others – 'How blest the Paradise to come!'
   Ah, take the Cash in hand and waive the Rest;
Oh, the brave Music of a *distant* Drum!

XIII

Look to the Rose that blows about us – 'Lo,
Laughing,' she says, 'into the World I blow:
   At once the silken Tassel of my Purse
Tear, and its Treasure on the Garden throw.'

XIV

The Worldly Hope men set their Hearts upon
Turns Ashes – or it prospers; and anon,
    Like Snow upon the Desert's dusty Face
Lighting a little Hour or two – is gone.

XV

And those who husbanded the Golden Grain,
And those who flung it to the Winds like Rain,
    Alike to no such aureate Earth are turned
As, buried once, Men want dug up again.

XVI

Think, in this battered Caravanserai
Whose Doorways are alternate Night and Day,
    How Sultán after Sultán with his Pomp
Abode his Hour or two, and went his way.

XVII

They say the Lion and the Lizard keep
The Courts where Jamshýd gloried and drank deep:
    And Bahrám, that great Hunter – the Wild Ass
Stamps o'er his Head, and he lies fast asleep.

XVIII

I sometimes think that never blows so red
The Rose as where some buried Caesar bled;
    That every Hyacinth the Garden wears
Dropped in its Lap from some once lovely Head.

XIX

And this delightful Herb whose tender Green
Fledges the River's Lip on which we lean –
    Ah, lean upon it lightly! for who knows
From what once lovely Lip it springs unseen!

XX

Ah, my Belovéd, fill the Cup that clears
To-DAY of past Regrets and future Fears –
    To-morrow? – Why, To-morrow I may be
Myself with Yesterday's Seven Thousand Years.

XXI

Lo! some we loved, the loveliest and best
That Time and Fate of all their Vintage pressed,
    Have drunk their Cup a Round or two before,
And one by one crept silently to Rest.

XXII

And we, that now make merry in the Room
They left, and Summer dresses in new Bloom,
    Ourselves must we beneath the Couch of Earth
Descend, ourselves to make a Couch – for whom?

XXIII

Ah, make the most of what we yet may spend,
Before we too into the Dust descend;
    Dust into Dust, and under Dust, to lie,
Sans Wine, sans Song, sans Singer, and – sans End!

XXIV

Alike for those who for To-DAY prepare,
And those that after a To-MORROW stare,
    A Muezzín from the Tower of Darkness cries
'Fools! your Reward is neither Here nor There!'

XXV

Why, all the Saints and Sages who discussed
Of the Two Worlds so learnedly, are thrust
    Like foolish Prophets forth; their Words to Scorn
Are scattered, and their Mouths are stopped with Dust.

XXVI

Oh, come with old Khayyám, and leave the Wise
To talk; one thing is certain, that Life flies;
    One thing is certain, and the Rest is Lies;
The Flower that once has blown for ever dies.

XXVII

Myself when young did eagerly frequent
Doctor and Saint, and heard great Argument
    About it and about: but evermore
Came out by the same Door as in I went.

XXVIII

With them the Seed of Wisdom did I sow,
And with my own hand laboured it to grow:
    And this was all the Harvest that I reaped –
'I came like Water, and like Wind I go.'

XXIX

Into this Universe, and *why* not knowing,
Nor *whence*, like Water willy-nilly flowing:
    And out of it, as Wind along the Waste,
I know not *whither*, willy-nilly blowing.

XXX

What, without asking, hither hurried *whence?*
And, without asking, *whither* hurried hence!
    Another and another Cup to drown
The Memory of this Impertinence!

XXXI

Up from Earth's Centre through the Seventh Gate
I rose, and on the Throne of Saturn sate,
    And many Knots unravelled by the Road;
But not the Knot of Human Death and Fate.

XXXII

There was a Door to which I found no Key:
There was a Veil past which I could not see:
    Some little Talk awhile of ME and THEE
There seemed – and then no more of THEE and ME.

XXXIII

Then to the rolling Heaven itself I cried,
Asking, 'What Lamp had Destiny to guide
    Her little Children stumbling in the Dark?'
And – 'A blind Understanding!' Heaven replied.

XXXIV

Then to this earthen Bowl did I adjourn
My Lip the secret Well of Life to learn:
    And Lip to Lip it murmured – 'While you live
Drink! – for once dead you never shall return.'

XXXV

I think the Vessel, that with fugitive
Articulation answered, once did live,
    And merry-make; and the cold Lip I kissed
How many Kisses might it take – and give!

XXXVI

For in the Market-place, one Dusk of Day,
I watched the Potter thumping his wet Clay:
    And with its all obliterated Tongue
It murmured – 'Gently, Brother, gently, pray!'

XXXVII

Ah, fill the Cup: – what boots it to repeat
How Time is slipping underneath our Feet:
    Unborn To-MORROW, and dead YESTERDAY,
Why fret about them if To-DAY be sweet!

XXXVIII

One Moment in Annihilation's Waste,
One Moment, of the Well of Life to taste –
    The Stars are setting and the Caravan
Starts for the Dawn of Nothing – Oh, make haste!

XXXIX

How long, how long, in infinite Pursuit
Of This and That endeavour and dispute?
    Better be merry with the fruitful Grape
Than sadden after none, or bitter, Fruit.

XL

You know, my Friends, how long since in my House
For a new Marriage I did make Carouse:
    Divorced old barren Reason from my Bed,
And took the Daughter of the Vine to Spouse.

XLI

For 'Is' and 'Is-NOT' though *with* Rule and Line,
And 'UP-AND-DOWN' *without*, I could define,
    I yet in all I only cared to know,
Was never deep in anything but – Wine.

XLII

And lately, by the Tavern Door agape,
Came stealing through the Dusk an Angel Shape
    Bearing a Vessel on his Shoulder; and
He bid me taste of it; and 'twas – the Grape!

XLIII

The Grape that can with Logic absolute
The Two-and-Seventy jarring Sects confute:
    The subtle Alchemist that in a Trice
Life's leaden Metal into Gold transmute.

XLIV

The mighty Mahmúd, the victorious Lord,
That all the misbelieving and black Horde
    Of Fears and Sorrows that infest the Soul
Scatters and slays with his enchanted Sword.

XLV

But leave the Wise to wrangle, and with me
The Quarrel of the Universe let be:
    And, in some corner of the Hubbub couched,
Make Game of that which makes as much of Thee.

XLVI

For in and out, above, about, below,
'Tis nothing but a Magic Shadow-show,
    Played in a Box whose Candle is the Sun,
Round which we Phantom Figures come and go.

XLVII

And if the Wine you drink, the Lip you press,
End in the Nothing all Things end in – Yes –
    Then fancy while Thou art, Thou art but what
Thou shalt be – Nothing – Thou shalt not be less.

XLVIII

While the Rose blows along the River Brink,
With old Khayyám the Ruby Vintage drink:
    And when the Angel with his darker Draught
Draws up to Thee – take that, and do not shrink.

XLIX

'Tis all a Chequer-board of Nights and Days
Where Destiny with Men for Pieces plays:
    Hither and thither moves, and mates, and slays,
And one by one back in the Closet lays.

L

The Ball no Question makes of Ayes and Noes,
But Right or Left as strikes the Player goes;
    And He that tossed Thee down into the Field,
He knows about it all – HE knows – HE knows!

LI

The Moving Finger writes; and, having writ,
Moves on: nor all thy Piety nor Wit
    Shall lure it back to cancel half a Line,
Nor all thy Tears wash out a Word of it.

LII

And that inverted Bowl we call The Sky,
Whereunder crawling cooped we live and die,
    Lift not thy hands to *It* for help – for It
Rolls impotently on as Thou or I.

LIII

With Earth's first Clay They did the Last Man's knead,
And then of the Last Harvest sowed the Seed:
    Yea, the first Morning of Creation wrote
What the Last Dawn of Reckoning shall read.

LIV

I tell Thee this – When, starting from the Goal,
Over the shoulders of the flaming Foal
    Of Heaven Parwín and Mushtara they flung,
In my predestined Plot of Dust and Soul

LV

The Vine had struck a Fibre; which about
If clings my Being – let the Sufí flout;
    Of my Base Metal may be filed a Key,
That shall unlock the Door he howls without.

LVI

And this I know: whether the one True Light,
Kindle to Love, or Wrath consume me quite,
    One Glimpse of It within the Tavern caught
Better than in the Temple lost outright.

LVII

Oh Thou, who didst with Pitfall and with Gin
Beset the Road I was to wander in,
    Thou wilt not with Predestination round
Enmesh me, and impute my Fall to Sin?

LVIII

Oh, Thou, who Man of baser Earth didst make,
And who with Eden didst devise the Snake;
    For all the Sin wherewith the Face of Man
Is blackened, Man's Forgiveness give – and take!

RICHARD MONCKTON MILNES, LORD HOUGHTON
1809–85

Milnes was an important figure in the world of Victorian letters, not so much for his own writings as for his friendships with Tennyson, Hallam, and Thackeray, all of whom he met at Trinity, and later with Swinburne, the Brownings and Landor. At Cambridge, Milnes was one of the band who set out in November 1829 to debate the respective causes of Shelley and Byron at the Oxford Union – the Cantabrigians defending the Oxford Shelley, and the Oxonians Trinity's Byron. Later, he championed Keats, whose *Life and Letters* he brought out in 1848, and also Blake. His first volume of verse, *Memorials of a Tour in some Parts of Greece, Chiefly Poetical* (1834), was followed by others based on his extensive travels, including *Memorials of a Residence on the Continent, and Historical Poems* (1838) and *Palm Leaves* (1844). His collected *Poetical Works* came out in 1876. Meanwhile he produced tracts, essays, works of biography, history, sociology and Boswelliana. He was also a great bibliophile and collector – of pornography, among other things. His library, including the famous page from a hotel visitor's book where Shelley signed himself *atheist, destined for hell*, was bequeathed to Trinity in 2014.

Elected MP in 1837, Milnes campaigned on behalf of many liberal and progressive causes: for factory education, the Copyright Act, the establishment of Mechanics' Institutes and the repeal of the Contagious Diseases Act. In 1840 he voted for the abolition of capital punishment, and during the American Civil War he supported the North against the Confederacy. In later life, as Baron Houghton, he continued to play a leading role in public affairs. He survives mostly in other people's letters, reminiscences and fiction: as Disraeli's Mr Vavasour in *Tancred* (1847), for example: 'His life was a gyration of energetic curiosity; an insatiable whirl of social celebrity.' In 1879 Henry James described him to a friend as 'a battered and world-wrinkled old mortal, with a restless and fidgety vanity, but with an immense fund of real kindness and humane feeling'.

On Revisiting Cambridge

after a long absence on the continent[77]

I have a debt of my heart's own to Thee,
School of my Soul, old lime and cloister shade,
Which I, strange creditor, should grieve to see
Fully acquitted and exactly paid.
The first ripe taste of manhood's best delights,
Knowledge imbibed, while mind and heart agree,
In sweet belated talk on winter nights,
With friends whom growing time keeps dear to me, –
Such things I owe thee, and not only these:
I owe thee the far beaconing memories
Of the young dead, who, having crossed the tide
Of Life where it was narrow, deep, and clear,
Now cast their brightness from the further side
On the dark-flowing hours I breast in fear.

ALFRED LORD TENNYSON
1809–92

Alfred Tennyson was one of eleven children born to the Rev. George Clayton Tennyson, Rector of Somersby, Lincolnshire, and his wife, Elizabeth. His father was a gifted but moody and violent man, whose rages – he once threatened to kill the oldest boy, Frederick – were sudden and unnerving. His erratic behaviour probably affected all the children. Two of Alfred's brothers would spend periods in a mental asylum, a third was confined for life, while another, Charles, suffered from a lifelong addiction to opium. Alfred would later refer to 'the morbid blood' of the Tennysons. He started writing poetry at an early age, recalling how one of his first compositions, a three-book epic, was composed while walking: 'I never felt so inspired – I used to compose 60 or 70 lines in a breath. I used to shout them about the silent fields, leaping over the hedges in my excitement.' In 1827 he collaborated with two brothers, Frederick and Charles, in a publication titled *Poems by Two Brothers*. That same year he entered Trinity College, joining Frederick and Charles (see pp. 159–66) who had preceded him there.

His 'Lines on Cambridge of 1830', which he later regretted and did not publish, testify to his dislike of the university and its syllabus. However, like many others, he found a way to pursue his own interests. In 1829 he won the Chancellor's Gold Medal for poetry, and at about this time met Arthur Hallam (see pp. 199–202), with whom he formed an intensely close friendship. Both were elected to the secret debating society, 'The Apostles' – a group which included John Kemble and James Spedding, though not Edward FitzGerald or William Makepeace Thackeray, their contemporaries at Trinity. In 1830 Tennyson published his first serious volume, *Poems, Chiefly Lyrical*, which Hallam reviewed intelligently and warmly, comparing it favourably with the work of Shelley and Keats, though warning of an occasional triviality or 'silliness' in subject matter. At this time, he became engaged to Alfred's sister, Emily.

In 1831, at the death of his father, Tennyson left Cambridge without taking a degree. Two years later, while at home with his sisters, he received the news that would change the course of his imaginative life: Hallam had died suddenly while on holiday in Vienna. In the ensuing months of grief he wrote early drafts of some of his greatest poems, including 'Ulysses', 'Break, break, break' and sections of his great elegy for Hallam, *In Memoriam A.H.H.*. This last would occupy him for the next seventeen years, during which time he wandered from place to place, staying with friends or travelling abroad, invested (and lost) his small fortune in a wood-carving scheme, and continually deferred confirmation of his engagement to Emily Sellwood. But these years of mourning and postponement were intensely fruitful. By the time *In Memoriam* was published in 1850, he had also published some of his finest works in *Poems* (1832), *Poems* (1842) and *The Princess* (1847). He once wrote of *In Memoriam*: 'It is rather the cry of the whole human race than mine. In the poem altogether private grief swells out into thought of, and hope for, the whole world. It begins with a funeral and ends with a marriage [...] a sort of Divine Comedy, cheerful at the close. It is a very impersonal poem as well as personal.' *In Memoriam* was published in May; in June, Alfred finally married the long-suffering Emily, and in November, in recognition in particular of this latest work, he was made Poet Laureate on the death of William Wordsworth.

If Tennyson then settled into marriage and renown, the acknowledged grandee of Victorian literature, beloved by the Queen, he nonetheless continued to produce great poems, among them *Maud* (1855) and *Idylls of the King* (1874), as well as many humorous or occasional pieces, like the two poems included here to one-time contemporaries at Trinity: 'To the Rev. W. H. Brookfield' and 'To E. FitzGerald'. Many of his poems were set to music, by Edward Lear for instance, close family friend and frequent visitor. Although Tennyson claimed to be essentially unmusical, it was the sonority of his verse that later poets would remember: 'the finest ear of any English poet since Milton', according to T. S. Eliot, or as Auden put it, a little hedging his bets, 'the finest ear, perhaps, of any English poet'. A poem written towards the very end of Tennyson's life, and included here, recalls a phrase that haunted him as a boy and that runs through his poetry. The lyric, 'Far-Far-Away', subtitled 'For Music', suggests the extent to which this poet's ear was always returning to the sounds of language – to sounds that travel, as if from a great distance, through and beyond the ordinary sense of words.

In 1883 Tennyson reluctantly agreed to a peerage. It was, he declared, only for literature: 'for my own part I shall regret my simple name all my life'. He was buried in Westminster Abbey, the many thousands attending his funeral a witness to his huge and continuing popularity as a poet. He remains one of the major poets of English literature.

Lines on Cambridge of 1830

Therefore your Halls, your ancient Colleges,
Your portals statued with old kings and queens,
Your gardens, myriad-volumed libraries,
Wax-lighted chapels, and rich carven screens,
Your doctors, and your proctors, and your deans,
Shall not avail you, when the Day-beam sports
New-risen o'er awakened Albion. No!
Nor yet your solemn organ-pipes that blow
Melodious thunders through your vacant courts
At noon and eve, because your manner sorts
Not with this age wherefrom ye stand apart.
Because the lips of little children preach
Against you, you that do profess to teach
And teach us nothing, feeding not the heart.

Mariana

Mariana in the moated grange.
MEASURE FOR MEASURE

With blackest moss the flower-plots
  Were thickly crusted, one and all:
The rusted nails fell from the knots
  That held the pear to the gable-wall.
The broken sheds looked sad and strange:
  Unlifted was the clinking latch;
  Weeded and worn the ancient thatch
Upon the lonely moated grange.
    She only said, 'My life is dreary,
      He cometh not,' she said;
    She said, 'I am aweary, aweary,
      I would that I were dead!'

Her tears fell with the dews at even;
  Her tears fell ere the dews were dried;
She could not look on the sweet heaven,
  Either at morn or eventide.
After the flitting of the bats,
  When thickest dark did trance the sky,
  She drew her casement-curtain by,
And glanced athwart the glooming flats.
    She only said, 'The night is dreary,
      He cometh not,' she said;
    She said, 'I am aweary, aweary,
      I would that I were dead!'

Upon the middle of the night,
  Waking she heard the night-fowl crow:
The cock sung out an hour ere light:
  From the dark fen the oxen's low
Came to her: without hope of change,
  In sleep she seemed to walk forlorn,
  Till cold winds woke the gray-eyed morn
About the lonely moated grange.
    She only said, 'The day is dreary,
      He cometh not,' she said;
    She said, 'I am aweary, aweary,
      I would that I were dead!'

About a stone-cast from the wall
  A sluice with blackened waters slept,
And o'er it many, round and small,
  The clustered marish-mosses crept.
Hard by a poplar shook alway,
  All silver-green with gnarled bark:
  For leagues no other tree did mark
The level waste, the rounding gray.
    She only said, 'My life is dreary,
      He cometh not,' she said;
    She said, 'I am aweary, aweary,
      I would that I were dead!'

And ever when the moon was low,
  And the shrill winds were up and away,
In the white curtain, to and fro,
  She saw the gusty shadow sway.
But when the moon was very low,
  And wild winds bound within their cell,
  The shadow of the poplar fell
Upon her bed, across her brow.
     She only said, 'The night is dreary,
      He cometh not,' she said;
     She said, 'I am aweary, aweary,
      I would that I were dead!'

All day within the dreamy house,
  The doors upon their hinges creaked;
The blue fly sung in the pane; the mouse
  Behind the mouldering wainscot shrieked,
Or from the crevice peered about.
  Old faces glimmered thro' the doors,
  Old footsteps trod the upper floors,
Old voices called her from without.
     She only said, 'My life is dreary,
      He cometh not,' she said;
     She said, 'I am aweary, aweary,
      I would that I were dead!'

The sparrow's chirrup on the roof,
  The slow clock ticking, and the sound
Which to the wooing wind aloof
  The poplar made, did all confound
Her sense; but most she loathed the hour
  When the thick-moted sunbeam lay
  Athwart the chambers, and the day
Was sloping toward his western bower.
     Then, said she, 'I am very dreary,
      He will not come,' she said;
     She wept, 'I am aweary, aweary,
      O God, that I were dead!'

The Kraken

Below the thunders of the upper deep;
Far, far beneath in the abysmal sea,
His ancient, dreamless, uninvaded sleep
The Kraken sleepeth: faintest sunlights flee
About his shadowy sides: above him swell
Huge sponges of millennial growth and height;
And far away into the sickly light,
From many a wondrous grot and secret cell
Unnumbered and enormous polypi
Winnow with giant arms the slumbering green.
There hath he lain for ages and will lie
Battening upon huge seaworms in his sleep,
Until the latter fire shall heat the deep;
Then once by man and angels to be seen,
In roaring he shall rise and on the surface die.

Ulysses

It little profits that an idle king,
By this still hearth, among these barren crags,
Matched with an aged wife, I mete and dole
Unequal laws unto a savage race,
That hoard, and sleep, and feed, and know not me.

I cannot rest from travel: I will drink
Life to the lees: all times I have enjoyed
Greatly, have suffered greatly, both with those
That loved me, and alone; on shore, and when
Through scudding drifts the rainy Hyades
Vexed the dim sea: I am become a name;
For always roaming with a hungry heart
Much have I seen and known; cities of men
And manners, climates, councils, governments,
Myself not least, but honoured of them all;
And drunk delight of battle with my peers,
Far on the ringing plains of windy Troy.
I am a part of all that I have met;
Yet all experience is an arch wherethrough

Gleams that untravelled world, whose margin fades
For ever and for ever when I move.
How dull it is to pause, to make an end,
To rust unburnished, not to shine in use!
As though to breathe were life. Life piled on life
Were all too little, and of one to me
Little remains: but every hour is saved
From that eternal silence, something more,
A bringer of new things; and vile it were
For some three suns to store and hoard myself,
And this gray spirit yearning in desire
To follow knowledge, like a sinking star,
Beyond the utmost bound of human thought.

  This is my son, mine own Telemachus,
To whom I leave the sceptre and the isle –
Well-loved of me, discerning to fulfil
This labour, by slow prudence to make mild
A rugged people, and through soft degrees
Subdue them to the useful and the good.
Most blameless is he, centred in the sphere
Of common duties, decent not to fail
In offices of tenderness, and pay
Meet adoration to my household gods,
When I am gone. He works his work, I mine.

  There lies the port; the vessel puffs her sail:
There gloom the dark broad seas. My mariners,
Souls that have toiled, and wrought, and thought with me –
That ever with a frolic welcome took
The thunder and the sunshine, and opposed
Free hearts, free foreheads – you and I are old;
Old age hath yet his honour and his toil;
Death closes all: but something ere the end,
Some work of noble note, may yet be done,
Not unbecoming men that strove with Gods.
The lights begin to twinkle from the rocks:
The long day wanes: the slow moon climbs: the deep
Moans round with many voices. Come, my friends,
'Tis not too late to seek a newer world.
Push off, and sitting well in order smite
The sounding furrows; for my purpose holds

To sail beyond the sunset, and the baths
Of all the western stars, until I die.
It may be that the gulfs will wash us down:
It may be we shall touch the Happy Isles,
And see the great Achilles, whom we knew.
Though much is taken, much abides; and though
We are not now that strength which in old days
Moved earth and heaven; that which we are, we are;
One equal temper of heroic hearts,
Made weak by time and fate, but strong in will
To strive, to seek, to find, and not to yield.

[Break, break, break]

Break, break, break,
    On thy cold gray stones, O Sea!
And I would that my tongue could utter
    The thoughts that arise in me.

O well for the fisherman's boy,
    That he shouts with his sister at play!
O well for the sailor lad,
    That he sings in his boat on the bay!

And the stately ships go on
    To their haven under the hill;
But O for the touch of a vanished hand,
    And the sound of a voice that is still!

Break, break, break
    At the foot of thy crags, O Sea!
But the tender grace of a day that is dead
    Will never come back to me.

The Skipping-Rope

Sure never yet was Antelope
  Could skip so lightly by.
Stand off, or else my skipping-rope
  Will hit you in the eye.
How lightly whirls the skipping-rope!
  How fairy-like you fly!
Go, get you gone, you muse and mope –
  I hate that silly sigh.
Nay, dearest, teach me how to hope,
  Or tell me how to die.
There, take it, take my skipping-rope,
  And hang yourself thereby.

Songs from *The Princess*

'Tears, idle tears, I know not what they mean,
Tears from the depth of some divine despair
Rise in the heart, and gather to the eyes,
In looking on the happy Autumn-fields,
And thinking of the days that are no more.

'Fresh as the first beam glittering on a sail,
That brings our friends up from the underworld,
Sad as the last which reddens over one
That sinks with all we love below the verge;
So sad, so fresh, the days that are no more.

'Ah, sad and strange as in dark summer dawns
The earliest pipe of half-awakened birds
To dying ears, when unto dying eyes
The casement slowly grows a glimmering square;
So sad, so strange, the days that are no more.

'Dear as remembered kisses after death,
And sweet as those by hopeless fancy feigned
On lips that are for others; deep as love,
Deep as first love, and wild with all regret;
O Death in Life, the days that are no more.'

*

Ask me no more: the moon may draw the sea;
  The cloud may stoop from heaven and take the shape
  With fold to fold, of mountain or of cape;
But O too fond, when have I answered thee?
                  Ask me no more.

Ask me no more: what answer should I give?
  I love not hollow cheek or faded eye:
  Yet, O my friend, I will not have thee die!
Ask me no more, lest I should bid thee live;
                  Ask me no more.

Ask me no more: thy fate and mine are sealed:
  I strove against the stream and all in vain:
  Let the great river take me to the main:
No more, dear love, for at a touch I yield;
                  Ask me no more.

*

'Now sleeps the crimson petal, now the white;
Nor waves the cypress in the palace walk;
Nor winks the gold fin in the porphyry font:
The fire-fly wakens: waken thou with me.

Now droops the milkwhite peacock like a ghost,
And like a ghost she glimmers on to me.

Now lies the Earth all Danaë to the stars,
And all thy heart lies open unto me.

Now slides the silent meteor on, and leaves
A shining furrow, as thy thoughts in me.

Now folds the lily all her sweetness up,
And slips into the bosom of the lake:
So fold thyself, my dearest, thou, and slip
Into my bosom and be lost in me.'

from *In Memoriam A. H. H.*

VII

Dark house, by which once more I stand
  Here in the long unlovely street,
  Doors, where my heart was used to beat
So quickly, waiting for a hand,

A hand that can be clasped no more –
  Behold me, for I cannot sleep,
  And like a guilty thing I creep
At earliest morning to the door.

He is not here; but far away
  The noise of life begins again,
  And ghastly though the drizzling rain
On the bald street breaks the blank day.

IX

Fair ship, that from the Italian shore
  Sailest the placid ocean-plains
  With my lost Arthur's loved remains,
Spread thy full wings, and waft him o'er.

So draw him home to those that mourn
  In vain; a favourable speed
  Ruffle thy mirrored mast, and lead
Through prosperous floods his holy urn.

All night no ruder air perplex
  Thy sliding keel, till Phosphor, bright
  As our pure love, through early light
Shall glimmer on the dewy decks.

Sphere all your lights around, above;
  Sleep, gentle heavens, before the prow;
  Sleep, gentle winds, as he sleeps now,
My friend, the brother of my love;

My Arthur, whom I shall not see
  Till all my widowed race be run;
  Dear as the mother to the son,
More than my brothers are to me.

XLIV

How fares it with the happy dead?
  For here the man is more and more;
  But he forgets the days before
God shut the doorways of his head.

The days have vanished, tone and tint,
  And yet perhaps the hoarding sense
  Gives out at times (he knows not whence)
A little flash, a mystic hint;

And in the long harmonious years
  (If Death so taste Lethean springs),
  May some dim touch of earthly things
Surprise thee ranging with thy peers.

If such a dreamy touch should fall,
  O turn thee round, resolve the doubt;
  My guardian angel will speak out
In that high place, and tell thee all.

LXXXVII

I past beside the reverend walls
  In which of old I wore the gown;
  I roved at random through the town,
And saw the tumult of the halls;

And heard once more in college fanes
  The storm their high-built organs make,
  And thunder-music, rolling, shake
The prophet blazoned on the panes;

And caught once more the distant shout,
  The measured pulse of racing oars
  Among the willows; paced the shores
And many a bridge, and all about

The same gray flats again, and felt
  The same, but not the same; and last
  Up that long walk of limes I past
To see the rooms in which he dwelt.

Another name was on the door:
   I lingered; all within was noise
   Of songs, and clapping hands, and boys
That crashed the glass and beat the floor;

Where once we held debate, a band
   Of youthful friends, on mind and art,
   And labour, and the changing mart,
And all the framework of the land;

When one would aim an arrow fair,
   But send it slackly from the string;
   And one would pierce an outer ring,
And one an inner, here and there;

And last the master-bowman, he,
   Would cleave the mark. A willing ear
   We lent him. Who, but hung to hear
The rapt oration flowing free

From point to point, with power and grace
   And music in the bounds of law,
   To those conclusions when we saw
The God within him light his face,

And seem to lift the form, and glow
   In azure orbits heavenly-wise;
   And over those ethereal eyes
The bar of Michael Angelo.

XCIII

I shall not see thee. Dare I say
   No spirit ever brake the band
   That stays him from the native land
Where first he walked when clasped in clay?

No visual shade of some one lost,
   But he, the Spirit himself, may come
   Where all the nerve of sense is numb;
Spirit to Spirit, Ghost to Ghost.

Alfred Tennyson, MS page of *In Memoriam*, XCIII (though numbered 92 by a later hand here), Trinity College MS O.15.13, fol. 38r.

O, therefore from thy sightless range
  With gods in unconjectured bliss,
  O, from the distance of the abyss
Of tenfold-complicated change,

Descend, and touch, and enter; hear
  The wish too strong for words to name;
  That in this blindness of the frame
My Ghost may feel that thine is near.

XCV

By night we lingered on the lawn,
  For underfoot the herb was dry;
  And genial warmth; and o'er the sky
The silvery haze of summer drawn;

And calm that let the tapers burn
  Unwavering: not a cricket chirred:
  The brook alone far-off was heard,
And on the board the fluttering urn:

And bats went round in fragrant skies,
  And wheeled or lit the filmy shapes
  That haunt the dusk, with ermine capes
And woolly breasts and beaded eyes;

While now we sang old songs that pealed
  From knoll to knoll, where, couched at ease,
  The white kine glimmered, and the trees
Laid their dark arms about the field.

But when those others, one by one,
  Withdrew themselves from me and night,
  And in the house light after light
Went out, and I was all alone,

A hunger seized my heart; I read
  Of that glad year which once had been,
  In those fall'n leaves which kept their green,
The noble letters of the dead:

And strangely on the silence broke
   The silent-speaking words, and strange
   Was love's dumb cry defying change
To test his worth; and strangely spoke

The faith, the vigour, bold to dwell
   On doubts that drive the coward back,
   And keen through wordy snares to track
Suggestion to her inmost cell.

So word by word, and line by line,
   The dead man touched me from the past,
   And all at once it seemed at last
His living soul was flashed on mine,

And mine in his was wound, and whirled
   About empyreal heights of thought,
   And came on that which is, and caught
The deep pulsations of the world,

Æonian music measuring out
   The steps of Time – the shocks of Chance –
   The blows of Death. At length my trance
Was cancelled, stricken through with doubt.

Vague words! but ah, how hard to frame
   In matter-moulded forms of speech,
   Or even for intellect to reach
Through memory that which I became:

Till now the doubtful dusk revealed
   The knolls once more where, couched at ease,
   The white kine glimmered, and the trees
Laid their dark arms about the field:

And sucked from out the distant gloom
   A breeze began to tremble o'er
   The large leaves of the sycamore,
And fluctuate all the still perfume,

And gathering freshlier overhead,
  Rocked the full-foliaged elms, and swung
  The heavy-folded rose, and flung
The lilies to and fro, and said

'The dawn, the dawn,' and died away;
  And East and West, without a breath,
  Mixed their dim lights, like life and death,
To broaden into boundless day.

In the Valley of Cauteretz

All along the valley, stream that flashest white,
Deepening thy voice with the deepening of the night,
All along the valley, where thy waters flow,
I walked with one I loved two and thirty years ago.
All along the valley, while I walked to-day,
The two and thirty years were a mist that rolls away;
For all along the valley, down thy rocky bed,
Thy living voice to me was as the voice of the dead,
And all along the valley, by rock and cave and tree,
The voice of the dead was a living voice to me.

To the Rev. W. H. Brookfield

Brooks, for they called you so that knew you best,
Old Brooks, who loved so well to mouth my rhymes,
How oft we two have heard St. Mary's chimes!
How oft the Cantab supper, host and guest,
Would echo helpless laughter to your jest!
How oft with him we paced that walk of limes,
Him, the lost light of those dawn-golden times,
Who loved you well! Now both are gone to rest.
You man of humorous-melancholy mark,
Dead of some inward agony – is it so?
Our kindlier, trustier Jaques, past away!
I cannot laud this life, it looks so dark:
Σκιᾶς ὄναρ[78] – dream of a shadow, go –
God bless you. I shall join you in a day.

To E. FitzGerald

Old Fitz, who from your suburb grange,
　Where once I tarried for a while,
Glance at the wheeling Orb of change,
　And greet it with a kindly smile;
Whom yet I see as there you sit
　Beneath your sheltering garden-tree,
And watch your doves about you flit,
　And plant on shoulder, hand, and knee,
Or on your head their rosy feet,
　As if they knew your diet spares
Whatever moved in that full sheet
　Let down to Peter at his prayers;
Who live on milk and meal and grass;
　And once for ten long weeks I tried
Your table of Pythagoras,
　And seemed at first 'a thing enskied'
(As Shakespeare has it), airy-light
　To float above the ways of men,
Then fell from that half-spiritual height
　Chilled, till I tasted flesh again
One night when earth was winter-black,
　And all the heavens flashed in frost;
And on me, half-asleep, came back
　That wholesome heat the blood had lost,
And set me climbing icy capes
　And glaciers, over which there rolled
To meet me long-armed vines with grapes
　Of Eshcol hugeness – for the cold
Without, and warmth within me, wrought
　To mould the dream; but none can say
That Lenten fare makes Lenten thought,
　Who reads your golden Eastern lay,
Than which I know no version done
　In English more divinely well;
A planet equal to the sun
　Which cast it, that large infidel
Your Omar, and your Omar drew
　Full-handed plaudits from our best
In modern letters, and from two,
　Old friends outvaluing all the rest,
Two voices heard on earth no more;
　But we old friends are still alive,

And I am nearing seventy-four,
    While you have touched at seventy-five,
And so I send a birthday line
    Of greeting; and my son, who dipped
In some forgotten book of mine
    With sallow scraps of manuscript,
And dating many a year ago,
    Has hit on this, which you will take
My Fitz, and welcome, as I know,
    Less for its own than for the sake
Of one recalling gracious times,
    When, in our younger London days,
You found some merit in my rhymes,
    And I more pleasure in your praise.

Far-Far-Away

For Music

What sight so lured him through the fields he knew
As where earth's green stole into heaven's own hue,
        Far-far-away?

What sound was dearest in his native dells?
The mellow lin-lan-lone of evening bells
        Far-far-away.

What vague world-whisper, mystic pain or joy,
Through those three words would haunt him when a boy,
        Far-far-away?

A whisper from his dawn of life? a breath
From some fair dawn beyond the doors of death
        Far-far-away?

Far, far, how far? from o'er the gates of birth,
The faint horizons, all the bounds of earth,
        Far-far-away?

What charm in words, a charm no words could give?
O dying words, can Music make you live
        Far-far-away?

ARTHUR HENRY HALLAM
1811–33

Arthur Hallam was one of eleven children, of whom only four survived into adulthood. His father was the Whig historian Henry Hallam, whose overweening ambition for his clever son was probably intensified by these losses. At Eton Arthur became friends with William Gladstone, the future prime minister, and showed some early promise as a poet. He spent a year in Italy with his family, learning Italian and writing sonnets in the language, before going up to Trinity in 1828. 'There is nothing in this college-studded marsh, which it could give you pleasure to know', he wrote to his sister. Disliking the study of maths and natural sciences, he turned his attention to metaphysics and modern poetry. It was his meeting with Alfred Tennyson in 1829 which marked a turning point. Both had submitted poems for the Chancellor's Gold Medal for poetry (which Tennyson won), and both subsequently joined the secret debating society known as 'The Apostles'. Their meeting, and the friendship which developed from it, was a crucial event in both their lives, as the included poem, 'A Scene in Summer', suggests.

In the vacations Arthur stayed at the Tennysons' family home where he fell in love with Alfred's sister, Emily (see 'Why throbbest thou…') – a relationship matched by Tennyson's own with another Emily (Sellwood) at about the same time. In 1830 the two men travelled to the Pyrenees on a mission to support an insurrection against the King, but Tennyson fell ill and the trip turned into a recuperative holiday at Cauteretz – a time recalled by Tennyson in his poem 'In the Valley of Cauteretz'. The following year Hallam published what is still one of the best reviews of Tennyson's *Poems, Chiefly Lyrical* (1830). Not only a fine account of his friend's 'new species of poetry, a graft of the lyric on the dramatic', it is also an early aestheticist account of modern poetry generally, marked, he claims, by 'melancholy' and a self-conscious 'return of the mind upon itself'. The essay, re-published in his posthumous *Remains in Verse and Prose* (1863), would influence poets and critics of poetry well into the twentieth century.

After leaving Cambridge, and at the instigation of his father, Hallam went to London to train for the bar. Disapproving of his son's engagement, Henry Hallam had forbidden him to visit the Tennysons till he came of age. But in the summer of 1832, while travelling with his father on the continent, Hallam died suddenly in a hotel in Vienna. He was twenty-three. The post-mortem reported that he had died of 'apoplexy' from an inherited malformation of the brain – probably a brain haemorrhage. He left behind some philosophical and literary essays, and a number of well-turned poems. It was left to his grieving friend, Tennyson, to compose in the course of the next seventeen years the poem which would immortalise Hallam's name: *In Memoriam A. H. H.*

A Scene in Summer

Alfred, I would that you behold me now,
Sitting beneath a mossy ivied wall
On a quaint bench, which to that structure old
Winds an accordant curve. Above my head
Dilates immeasurable a wild of leaves
Seeming received into the blue expanse
That vaults this summer noon: before me lies
A lawn of English verdure, smooth and bright,
Mottled with fainter hues of early hay,
Whose fragrance, blended with the rose perfume
From that white flowering bush, invites my sense
To a delicious madness – and faint thoughts
Of childish years are borne into my brain
By unforgotten ardours waking now.
Beyond, a gentle slope leads into shade
Of mighty trees, to bend whose eminent crown
Is the prime labour of the pettish winds,
That now in lighter mood are twirling leaves
Over my feet, or hurrying butterflies,
And the gay humming things that summer loves,
Through the warm air, or altering the bound
Where yon elm-shadows in majestic line
Divide dominion with the abundant light.

[Oh Poetry, oh rarest spirit of all]

Oh Poetry, oh rarest spirit of all
  That dwell within the compass of the mind,
Forsake not him, whom thou of old didst call:
  Still let me seek thy face, and seeking find.
Some years have gone about since I and thou
  Became acquainted first: we met in woe:
Sad was my cry for help as it is now;
  Sad too thy breathed response of music slow;
  But in that sadness was such essence fine,
So keen a sense of Life's mysterious name,
  And high conceit of natures more divine,
That breath and sorrow seemed no more the same.
  Oh let me hear again that sweet reply!
More than by loss of thee I cannot die.

[Why throbbest thou, my heart, why thickly breathest?]

Why throbbest thou, my heart, why thickly breathest?
  I ask no rich and splendid eloquence:
A few words of the warmest and the sweetest
  Sure thou mayst yield without such coy pretence:
Open the chamber where affection's voice,
  For rare occasions is kept close and fine:
  Bid it but say 'sweet Emily, be mine,'
So for one boldness thou shalt aye rejoice.
Fain would I speak when the full music-streams
  Rise from her lips to linger on her face,
Or like a form floating through Raffaelle's dreams,
  Then fixed by him in everliving grace,
  She sits i' the silent worship of mine eyes.
  Courage, my heart: change thou for words thy sighs.

William Makepeace Thackeray was born in Calcutta, in British India; his father Richmond was the Secretary to the Board of Revenue of the East India Company. After the death of his father in 1815, the young Thackeray was sent to school in Britain, first in Chiswick and then at Charterhouse, before he eventually went up to Trinity. He would never return to India; his novels' occasional Anglo-Indian characters and settings were spun out of tales heard among his social connections in Britain. It was in Cambridge that Thackeray began writing, developing a deft touch for light verse, and publishing small, cocksure parodies in magazines like *The Snob* and *The Gownsman*. Though he was always an avid reader, his tastes increasingly turned to travel and self-indulgence, and he left Trinity without a degree after two years, aged nineteen.

After a brief sojourn in Germany, where he had two ill-fated love affairs and made friends with Goethe, Thackeray returned to Britain and for a while studied as a lawyer. This ambition soon passed, as he became engrossed in theatre and the arts. He vacillated over a creative vocation for some time: attempts at publishing and painting came to nothing, and soon, thanks to bank collapses in India, his inheritance was all but lost as well. But on meeting his future wife, Isabella, in 1836, he found new purpose and applied himself properly to an author's life. Over the next few years he pressed on in spite of setbacks – not least the loss of an infant daughter and the onset of his wife's mental illness – writing a large number of magazine pieces under various pseudonyms, and placing some of his poems in *Punch*. His industry and persistence paid off after a decade of hard work, when the serial publication of *Vanity Fair* ran for nineteen months (1847–8). It was Thackeray's first real success, and was picked up by Bradbury and Evans – Charles Dickens's publisher – who went on to publish three of his other major novels, *Pendennis*, *The Newcomes* and *The Virginians*. His reputation was assured, even in the high circles he spent his time mocking; but this would lead to the charge that after *Vanity Fair*, his novels, though still well-received, had lost their satiric bite. Nevertheless, he was recognised as one of the leading

literary figures of the day, becoming in 1860 editor of the influential
Cornhill magazine. When he died suddenly, three years later at the age
of fifty-two, an estimated seven thousand people attended his funeral
in Kensington Gardens.

Ronsard to His Mistress

Quand vous serez bien vieille, le soir à la chandelle
Assise auprès du feu devisant et filant,
Direz, chantant mes vers en vous esmerveillant,
Ronsard m'a célébré du temps que j'étois belle.[79]

Some winter night, shut snugly in
  Beside the fagot in the hall,
I think I see you sit and spin,
  Surrounded by your maidens all.
Old tales are told, old songs are sung,
  Old days come back to memory;
You say, 'When I was fair and young,
  A poet sang of me!'

There's not a maiden in your hall,
  Though tired and sleepy ever so,
But wakes, as you my name recall,
  And longs the history to know.
And, as the piteous tale is said,
  Of lady cold and lover true,
Each, musing, carries it to bed,
  And sighs and envies you!

'Our lady's old and feeble now,'
  They'll say; 'she once was fresh and fair,
And yet she spurned her lover's vow,
  And heartless left him to despair:
The lover lies in silent earth,
  No kindly mate the lady cheers;
She sits beside a lonely hearth,
  With threescore and ten years!'

Ah! dreary thoughts and dreams are those,
  But wherefore yield me to despair,
While yet the poet's bosom glows,
  While yet the dame is peerless fair!
Sweet lady mine! while yet 'tis time
  Requite my passion and my truth,
And gather in their blushing prime
  The roses of your youth!

Commanders of the Faithful

The Pope he is a happy man,
His Palace is the Vatican,
And there he sits and drains his can:
The Pope he is a happy man.
I often say when I'm at home,
I'd like to be the Pope of Rome.

And then there's Sultan Saladin,
That Turkish Soldan full of sin;
He has a hundred wives at least,
By which his pleasure is increased:
I've often wished, I hope no sin,
That I were Sultan Saladin.

But no, the Pope no wife may choose,
And so I would not wear his shoes;
No wine may drink the proud Paynim,
And so I'd rather not be him:
My wife, my wine, I love, I hope,
And would be neither Turk nor Pope.

JAMES CLERK MAXWELL
1831–79

One of the greatest scientists of the nineteenth century, James Clerk Maxwell was born in Edinburgh into a prosperous land-owning family. In his early years he was educated at home on the family estate in Galloway, south-west Scotland, where he would later do much of his writing. In 1841 he started at the Edinburgh Academy, where his eccentric behaviour earned him the nickname 'dafty'. He made close friendships there with two Scots lads who would also go on to distinguished careers: Lewis Campbell, future Professor of Greek at the University of St Andrew's (and Maxwell's future biographer), and Peter Guthrie Tait, mathematical physicist and Maxwell's closest scientific correspondent.

Maxwell was drawn to the beauty of regular geometrical figures, and saw in the study of mathematics the search for harmonious shapes. He found inspiration in the work of the Edinburgh decorative artist David Ramsay Hay, who sought to explain by mathematical principles the harmonious form of geometrical figures and the aesthetics of colour combinations. He developed a particularly keen interest in the study of colour. In 1847 he entered Edinburgh University and three years later arrived in Cambridge, initially at Peterhouse, before moving to Trinity, where he became one of the pupils of William Hopkins, pre-eminent mathematics Fellow. In the winter of 1852–3 Maxwell was invited to be a member of the Apostles Club, where he formed many personal and intellectual friendships. In 1853 he went through an emotional and religious crisis, a 'sort of brain fever' as Campbell described it. He succeeded in winning a Trinity Fellowship at his second attempt in 1855, and set off on the career that took him into many new areas of scientific research, in colour vision and optics, in the study of Saturn's rings, in the kinetic theory of gases and thermodynamics, in field theory and in the electromagnetic theory of light. He was appointed to various distinguished professorships, in Aberdeen, King's College London, and then, in 1871, to the new Chair of Experimental Physics in Cambridge (1871–9).

Maxwell meanwhile had also developed strong literary interests. His biographers record how, upon his election to the Trinity Fellowship, 'he found time for a full course of classical English reading'. He wrote poems himself, often of a jocular nature, with titles such as 'Lines written under the conviction that it is not wise to read Mathematics in November after one's fire is out'; the poem 'Molecular Evolution', re-printed here, belongs in this category. But 'Recollections of Dreamland' is something else. It seems to have been prompted by the death of Maxwell's father two months previously. Mark McCartney writes: 'Released from a day's work from "the midst of facts and figures", he dreams of his idyllic childhood home in Galloway and of hearing and seeing the dead of his past. The poem shows depth of literary skill and psychological insight and given Maxwell's wide reading of literature and poetry, may even be a nod to the genre of medieval dream poems exemplified by Chaucer or Langland.'[80]

Recollections of Dreamland

Cambridge, June 1856

Rouse ye! torpid daylight-dreamers, cast your carking cares away!
As calm air to troubled water, so my night is to your day;
All the dreary day you labour, groping after common sense,
And your eyes ye will not open on the night's magnificence.
Ye would scoff were I to tell you how a guiding radiance gleams
On the outer world of action from my inner world of dreams.

When, with mind released from study, late I lay me down to sleep,
From the midst of facts and figures, into boundless space I leap;
For the inner world grows wider as the outer disappears,
And the soul, retiring inward, finds itself beyond the spheres.
Then, to this unbroken sameness, some fantastic dream succeeds,
Vague emotions rise and ripen into thoughts and words and deeds.
Old impressions, long forgotten, range themselves in Time and Space,
Till I recollect the features of some once familiar place.
Then from valley into valley in my dreaming course I roam,
Till the wanderings of my fancy end, where they began, at home.
Calm it lies in morning twilight, while each streamlet far and wide
Still retains its hazy mantle, borrowed from the mountain's side;
Every knoll is now an island, every wooded bank a shore,
To the lake of quiet vapour that has spread the valley o'er.
Sheep are couched on every hillock, waiting till the morning dawns,
Hares are on their early rambles, limping o'er the dewy lawns.
All within the house is silent, darkened all the chambers seem,
As with noiseless step I enter, gliding onwards in my dream.

What! has Time run out his cycle, do the years return again?
Are there treasure-caves in Dreamland where departed days remain?
I have leapt the bars of distance – left the life that late I led –
I remember years and labours as a tale that I have read;
Yet my heart is hot within me, for I feel the gentle power
Of the spirits that still love me, waiting for this sacred hour.
Yes, – I know the forms that meet me are but phantoms of the brain,
For they walk in mortal bodies, and they have not ceased from pain.
Oh! those signs of human weakness, left behind for ever now,
Dearer far to me than glories round a fancied seraph's brow.
Oh! the old familiar voices! Oh! the patient waiting eyes!
Let me live with them in dreamland, while the world in slumber lies!

For by bonds of sacred honour will they guard my soul in sleep
From the spells of aimless fancies, that around my senses creep.
They will link the past and present into one continuous life,
While I feel their hope, their patience, nerve me for the daily strife.
For it is not all a fancy that our lives and theirs are one,
And we know that all we see is but an endless work begun.
Part is left in Nature's keeping, part is entered into rest,
Part remains to grow and ripen, hidden in some living breast.
What is ours we know not, either when we wake or when we sleep,
But we know that Love and Honour, day and night, are ours to keep.
What though Dreams be wandering fancies, by some lawless force
                                                    entwined,
Empty bubbles, floating upwards through the current of the mind?
There are powers and thoughts within us, that we know not, till they
                                                        rise
Through the stream of conscious action from where Self in secret lies.
But when Will and Sense are silent, by the thoughts that come and go,
We may trace the rocks and eddies in the hidden depths below.

Let me dream my dream till morning; let my mind run slow and clear,
Free from all the world's distraction, feeling that the Dead are near,
Let me wake, and see my duty lie before me straight and plain.
Let me rise refreshed, and ready to begin my work again.

Molecular Evolution

Belfast, 1874

At quite uncertain times and places,
    The atoms left their heavenly path,
And by fortuitous embraces,
    Engendered all that being hath.
And though they seem to cling together,
    And form 'associations' here,
Yet, soon or late, they burst their tether,
    And through the depths of space career.

So we who sat, oppressed with science,
    As British asses, wise and grave,
Are now transformed to wild Red Lions,[81]
    As round our prey we ramp and rave.
Thus, by a swift metamorphosis,
    Wisdom turns wit, and science joke,
Nonsense is incense to our noses,
    For when Red Lions speak, they smoke.

Hail, Nonsense! dry nurse of Red Lions,[82]
    From thee the wise their wisdom learn,
From thee they cull those truths of science,
    Which into thee again they turn.
What combinations of ideas,
    Nonsense alone can wisely form!
What sage has half the power that she has,
    To take the towers of Truth by storm?

Yield, then, ye rules of rigid reason!
    Dissolve, thou too, too solid sense!
Melt into nonsense for a season,
    Then in some nobler form condense.
Soon, all too soon, the chilly morning,
    This flow of soul will crystallize,
Then those who Nonsense now are scorning,
    May learn, too late, where wisdom lies.

The Genius o' Glenlair

*A wee bit doggerel tae mark
the Year o' Maxwell 2006 by Keith Moffatt*[83]

When James Clerk Maxwell was a lad,
His questing mind fair deaved[84] his Dad;
For 'What's the go of it?' he'd speir,[85]
An' hammer on till a' was clear.

They ca'd him 'dafty' at the scule,
An' that, ye'd think, was awfie cruel!
He didna' mind, he was apart
Constructing ovals o' Descartes!

He played wi' colours blue an' green
An' red, enhanced by glorious sheen;
An' took the earliest colour photo,
As good as ony Blake or Giotto.

He analysed the rings o' Saturn,
Resolving their striated pattern,
Predicting weel their composition
By calculus and long division.

Redundant in the granite city
An' spurned by En'bro', mair's the pity,
He ended up awa' doon South,
Nae doot they thocht him gae uncouth!

He liked tae doodle lines o' force,
Wi' charge an' current as the source;
As much at hame wi' rho an' phi,
An' E an' B an' J forbye!

Through these he dreamt up waves o' licht,
An' workit on them day an' nicht;
His mind roamed far whaur ithers durn't,
An' hit upon displacement current.

Syne back tae Galloway he repaired,
He had tae go – he was the laird!
By day conferring wi' the ghillie,
By nicht researching willy-nilly!

At last frae Cambridge cam' the call,
Doon tae thon hallowed Senate Hall,
Where, tho' he held the dons in thrall,
They didna follow him at all!

Blithe son o' Gallovidian hills[86]
O' birk-clad slopes an' tumbling rills,
Wha rose through intellect sublime,
Tae comprehend baith space an' time;

Great Scot! wha's words in prose an' rhyme,
Inspire us yet o'er vales o' time,
In this thine eponymial year[87]
Thy soaring spirit we revere!

EDMUND GOSSE
1849–1928

Edmund Gosse was the only child of Philip Henry Gosse, a zoologist and religious fundamentalist, and Emily Gosse, a painter and evangelical writer, both members of the Plymouth Brethren. With such an unusual mixture of interests at home, it is unsurprising that the young boy's education was fairly haphazard. He read voraciously on his own, then endured a long spell at boarding school following his mother's death. Breaking with his father at the age of seventeen, Gosse worked as a clerk in the library of the British Museum, where he began to make contact with the London literary scene, not only Arthur O'Shaughnessy and Richard Garnett, but later also William Bell Scott and Ford Madox Brown, through whom he was able to distribute copies of his first book, *Madrigals, Songs and Sonnets* (1870), to figures such as Swinburne, Tennyson and Dante Gabriel Rossetti. These poets' responses were generally positive, and Gosse would remain friends with several of them for years to come, though his poetry would never receive general acclaim.

Gosse's most famous book remains *Father and Son: A Study of Two Temperaments* (1907), the memoir of a childhood spent evading his father's fundamentalist shadow. He became well-known as a society figure, George Saintsbury observing that Gosse had 'a genius for knowing people'. Unfortunately, as Henry James would add, he had a complementary 'genius for inaccuracy'. Though his two-volume life of Donne, and his shorter lives of Gray, Raleigh, Congreve and Ibsen, were widely read at the time, they were strewn with errors. One particular scandal surrounded the publication of his grossly inaccurate study *From Shakespeare to Pope*. He was nonetheless a popular lecturer, addressing audiences on both sides of the Atlantic on 'Poetry at the Death of Shakespeare'. This was the first of his Trinity Clark Lectures given in 1884. Despite his lack of formal qualifications he lectured at Trinity for several years, and was formally admitted to membership of the College in 1889.

Towards the end of his life, Gosse relaxed into a position of untroubled high status as a Grand Man of Letters. He moved easily and influentially in high circles, at home and abroad. He was appointed

Librarian to the House of Lords, advised Prime Minister Asquith on matters of arts policy, and served on endless committees. As a good friend to France and French literature – he was a particular champion of André Gide's – he was made Commandeur de la Légion d'honneur and awarded an honorary doctorate from the Sorbonne in 1925. In the same year he was knighted.

1870–71

The year that Henri Regnault[88] died, –
    The sad red blossoming year of war, –
All nations cast the lyre aside,
    And gazed through curved fingers far
        At horror, waste and wide.

Not one new song from overseas
    Came to us; who had ears to hear?
The kings of Europe's minstrelsies
    Walked, bowed, behind the harrowing year,
        Veiled, silent, ill at ease.

For us the very name of man
    Grew hateful in the mist of blood;
We talked of how new life began
    To exiles by the eastern flood,
        Flower-girdled in Japan.

We dreamed of new delight begun
    In palm-encircled Indian shoals,
Where men are coloured by the sun,
    And wear out contemplative souls,
        And vanish one by one.

We found no pleasure any more
    In all the whirl of Western thought;
The dreams that soothed our souls before
    Were burst like bubbles, and we sought
        New hopes on a new shore.

The men who sang that pain was sweet
    Shuddered to see the mask of death
Storm by with myriad thundering feet;
    The sudden truth caught up our breath,
        Our throats like pulses beat.

The songs of pale emaciate hours,
  The fungus-growth of years of peace,
Withered before us like mown flowers;
  We found no pleasure more in these,
    When bullets fell in showers.

For men whose robes are dashed with blood,
  What joy to dream of gorgeous stairs,
Stained with the torturing interlude
  That soothed a Sultan's midday prayers,
    In old days harsh and rude?

For men whose lips are blanched and white,
  With aching wounds and torturing thirst,
What charm in canvas shot with light,
  And pale with faces cleft and curst,
    Past life and life's delight?

And when the war had passed, and song
  Broke out amongst us once again,
As birds sing fresher notes among
  The sunshot woodlands after rain,
    And happier tones prolong, –

So seemed it with the lyric heart
  Of human singers; fresher aims
Sprang in the wilderness of art,
  Serener pathos, nobler claims
    On man for his best part.

The times are changed; not Schumann now,
  But Wagner is our music-man,
Whose flutes and trumpets throb and glow
  With life, as when the world began
    Its genial ebb and flow.

The great god Pan redeified
  Comes, his old kingship to reclaim;
New hopes are spreading far and wide;
  The lands were purged as with a flame,
    The year that Regnault died.

John Henry Newman

August 11, 1890

Peace to the virgin heart, the crystal brain!
   Truce for one hour thro' all the camps of thought!
Our subtlest mind hath rent the veil of pain,
     Hath found the truth he sought.

Who knows what script those opening eyes have read?
   If this set creed, or that, or none be best?
Let no strife jar above this snow-white head!
     Peace for a saint at rest!

R. C. LEHMANN
1856–1929

Rudolph Chambers Lehmann was educated at Highgate School and came to Trinity to read Classics in 1878. After Cambridge he was called to the bar but preferred sport. His enthusiasm for rowing led him to coach both Oxford and Cambridge boat-race crews and to become secretary of the Amateur Rowing Association.

He was also keen on writing and politics. He founded *Granta* while at Cambridge, continuing to edit it for some years afterwards, and for many years contributed to *Punch*. His forays into journalism were less successful. He was active in politics, serving as a Liberal MP from 1906 to 1910, when ill-health and financial worries moved him to give up his seat. Three of his four children went on to make names for themselves: Beatrix as an actress, theatre director and author; John as a poet and man of letters, who followed his father to Trinity and is featured in this volume (pp. 280–3); and Rosamond (who studied at Girton College) as a novelist, of increasingly recognised significance. The occasional poem included here gives a flavour of undergraduate life in the 1870s.

A Ramshackle Room

When the gusts are at play with the trees on the lawn,
    And the lights are put out in the vault of the night;
When within all is snug, for the curtains are drawn,
    And the fire is aglow and the lamps are alight,
Sometimes, as I muse, from the place where I am
My thoughts fly away to a room near the Cam.

'Tis a ramshackle room, where a man might complain
    Of a slope in the ceiling, a rise in the floor;
With a view on a court and a glimpse on a lane,
    And no end of cool wind through the chinks of the door;
With a deep-seated chair that I love to recall,
And some groups of young oarsmen in shorts on the wall.

There's a fat jolly jar of tobacco, some pipes –
    A meerschaum, a briar, a cherry, a clay –
There's a three-handled cup fit for Audit or Swipes
    When the breakfast is done and the plates cleared away.
There's a litter of papers, of books a scratch lot,
Such as *Plato*, and *Dickens*, and *Liddell and Scott*

And a crone in a bonnet that's more like a rag
    From a mist of remembrance steps suddenly out;
And her funny old tongue never ceases to wag
    As she tidies the room where she bustles about;
For a man may be strong and a man may be young,
But he can't put a drag on a Bedmaker's tongue.

And, oh, there's a youngster who sits at his ease
    In the hope, which is vain, that the tongue may run down,
With his feet on the grate and a book on his knees,
    And his cheeks they are smooth and his hair it is brown.
Then I sigh myself back to the place where I am
From that ramshackle room near the banks of the Cam.

Alfred Edward Housman, poet and classical scholar, was the first of seven children born to Edward Housman, a country solicitor, and his wife Sarah, who died when Alfred was twelve. Her dying request to him that he should not lose his Christian faith was perhaps already a lost cause. He recalled how reading *Lemprière's Classical Dictionary*, aged eight, inclined him to paganism, after which 'I became a deist at thirteen and an atheist at twenty-one'. He went up to Oxford in 1877 to study Classics, but after a promising start, stopped going to lectures and generally neglected his studies. Meanwhile, he fell in love with a fellow student, Moses Jackson, who would remain the great love of his life though his feelings were never reciprocated. Alfred failed his Finals and left without a degree.

He then followed Jackson to the Patent Office in London, where he began a ten-year period of service as a higher division clerk. He lodged with Moses and his younger brother Adalbert, of whom he was also fond, but in 1885, for whatever reason (possibly a rejected declaration of love), he dramatically left and did not return. In 1887 Moses moved to India, returning only briefly in 1889 to marry. Alfred was not invited to the wedding and only learned of it later, noting cryptically in his diary: 'I heard he was married'. He kept portraits of the two brothers in his rooms to the end of his life. In London, he also worked at the British Museum Library, and began to publish a series of papers on Greek and Latin authors. By 1892 his reputation for textual scholarship was such that he was offered the Chair of Latin at University College, London. Here he published his first volume of poems, *A Shropshire Lad* (1896). These sparing, formal, reticent verses, often about loved lads and dying soldiers, would be his hallmark.

In 1911 Housman was appointed to the Kennedy Chair of Latin, with a Trinity Fellowship, at Cambridge. He was, by all accounts, a waspish, reclusive presence in college, disinclined to social niceties. As a result stories about him were rife. At one dinner, he and J.M. Barrie exchanged not a word. Barrie then wrote to apologise for his shyness; Housman replied in exactly the same words, but with his name pointedly, correctly spelt. On another occasion he famously refused to allow Wittgenstein, his neighbour in Whewell's Court, to use his newly installed lavatory in a moment of need. He was well known for writing vicious reviews of the work of fellow classicists, but of his poetry writing he said and wrote little. 'Ask me no more, for fear I should reply', the first line of a poem included here, might sum up his reticence in life as well as love. Asked once to explain the nature of poetry, he snapped back: 'I could no more define poetry than a terrier can define a rat.' He was, however, a keen cook and, judging by his many entries in the Kitchen Suggestions Book at Trinity, the food was a trial to him. 'The salmon today was tasteless, and the lamb was both tasteless and tough', he grumbled with metrical force. The story that he introduced *crème brûlée* to High Table may not be far-fetched; he had a sweetness of tooth, if not of manner. In 1922 Housman published *Last Poems*. In spite of the slenderness of his output – only two collections to date – this one sold 21,000 copies in the year of its publication. His was a voice which, in the year of Eliot's *The Waste Land*, still appealed to a wide, general readership. Although he turned down various honours and invitations, he did agree to give the Leslie Stephen lecture at Cambridge in 1933. 'The Name and Nature of Poetry' starts with an excoriation of so called 'literary critics', but then offers a marvellous account of poetry as a form of 'nonsense', having nothing to say beyond its own tune. 'Blake's meaning', he explained, 'is often unimportant or virtually non-existent, so we can listen with all our hearing to his celestial tune.' His own poetry would be set by many composers – Butterworth, Ireland, Barber and Finzi, as well as Vaughan Williams whose *On Wenlock Edge* sets six poems from *A Shropshire Lad*.

Housman died in 1936. He left his large collection of erotica, mostly bought on regular trips to Paris, to the University Library. After his death, two further volumes of poems were published under the editorship of his brother, Laurence: *More Poems* (1936), and *Additional Poems* (1937). These contain verses probably written much earlier but suppressed, like 'Oh who is that young sinner', about the trial and imprisonment of Oscar Wilde. In addition, there were parodies and light verse (see 'Tennyson and the Moated Grange'), hinting at an underlying sense of humour not merely caustic. Trinity probably gave this difficult, divided man a home in which to hide. As Auden once put it: 'No one, not even Cambridge, was to blame / (Blame if you like the human situation): / Heart-injured in North London, he became / The Latin scholar of his generation.' Housman also became, meanwhile, one of the great, if sparingly productive, poets of his time.

from *Tennyson in the Moated Grange* (lines 1–36)

With whittled sticks, the Laureate's plots
   Were thickly covered, one and all;
The Yankee pilgrims lounged in knots
   Expectorating o'er the wall.
Their general air was sad and strange,
   They'd crossed the seas one glimpse to catch
   Of Him; and now they kept their watch
Upon the lonely moated grange.
     They only said, 'This waiting's dreary,
      Calc'late that's *so*,' they said;
     'Reckon that we're aweary, aweary:
      Guess the ole coon's in bed!'

His hair was just as rough as ever;
   His tie was just as much untied;
He never brushed or tied them, never,
   Either at morn or eventide.
After the flitting of the bats
     He drew his casement-curtain by,
     And with his hair-brush took a shy;
It glanced athwart their glooming hats.
     And then they said, 'This ain't so dreary.
      He's riled up *some*,' they said;
     'Let's liquor up! this looks more cheery;
      Wake snakes! was that his head?'

All through the midnight he would sit
   Remarking how the night-fowl crow'd:
A telegram from Downing Street
   Inquiring 'How about the Ode?'
Came to him: and he stamped upon it,
   And set about his weary work: –
   A panegyric on the Turk,
To match the Montenegro sonnet.
     They said, 'He wrote quick slick when Marie
      Alexandrowna wed;
     'Tis *kewrious* how they shift and vary,
      These Britishers,' they said.

from *Oedipus Coloneus* (lines 1211–48)

What man is he that yearneth
    For length unmeasured of days?
Folly mine eye discerneth
    Encompassing all his ways.
For years over-running the measure
    Shall change thee in evil wise:
Grief draweth nigh thee; and pleasure,
    Behold, it is hid from thine eyes.
    This to their wage have they
    Which overlive their day.
And He that looseth from labour
    Doth one with other befriend,
    Whom bride nor bridesmen attend,
Song, nor sound of the tabor,
    Death, that maketh an end.

Thy portion esteem I highest,
    Who wast not ever begot;
Thine next, being born who diest
    And straightway again art not.
With follies light as the feather
    Doth Youth to man befall;
Then evils gather together,
    There wants not one of them all –
    Wrath, envy, discord, strife,
    The sword that seeketh life.
And sealing the sum of trouble
    Doth tottering Age draw nigh,
    Whom friends and kinsfolk fly,
Age, upon whom redouble
    All sorrows under the sky.

This man, as me, even so,
Have the evil days overtaken;
And like as a cape sea-shaken
With tempest at earth's last verges
And shock of all winds that blow,
His head the seas of woe,
The thunders of awful surges
Ruining overflow;

Blown from the fall of even,
  Blown from the dayspring forth,
Blown from the noon in heaven,
  Blown from night and the North.

1887

From Clee to heaven the beacon burns,
  The shires have seen it plain,
From north and south the sign returns
  And beacons burn again.

Look left, look right, the hills are bright,
  The dales are light between,
Because 'tis fifty years to-night
  That God has saved the Queen.

Now, when the flame they watch not towers
  About the soil they trod,
Lads, we'll remember friends of ours
  Who shared the work with God.

To skies that knit their heartstrings right,
  To fields that bred them brave,
The saviours come not home tonight:
  Themselves they could not save.

It dawns in Asia, tombstones show
  And Shropshire names are read;
And the Nile spills his overflow
  Beside the Severn's dead.

[*When I watch the living meet*]

When I watch the living meet,
    And the moving pageant file
Warm and breathing through the street
    Where I lodge a little while,

If the heats of hate and lust
    In the house of flesh are strong,
Let me mind the house of dust
    Where my sojourn shall be long.

In the nation that is not
    Nothing stands that stood before;
There revenges are forgot,
    And the hater hates no more;

Lovers lying two and two
    Ask not whom they sleep beside,
And the bridegroom all night through
    Never turns him to the bride.

[*On Wenlock Edge the wood's in trouble*]

On Wenlock Edge the wood's in trouble;
    His forest fleece the Wrekin heaves;
The gale, it plies the saplings double,
    And thick on Severn snow the leaves.

'Twould blow like this through holt and hanger
    When Uricon the city stood:
'Tis the old wind in the old anger,
    But then it threshed another wood.

Then, 'twas before my time, the Roman
    At yonder heaving hill would stare:
The blood that warms an English yeoman,
    The thoughts that hurt him, they were there.

40

Sav

XXXI

On Wenlock Edge the wood's in trouble;
    His forest fleece the Wrekin heaves;
The wind, it plies the saplings double,
    And thick on Severn snow the leaves.

'Twould blow like this through holt and hanger
    When Uricon the city stood:
'Tis the old wind in the old anger,
    But then it threshed another wood.

Then, 'twas before my time, the Roman
    At yonder heaving hill would stare:
The blood that warms an English yeoman,
    The thoughts that hurt him, they were there.

There, like the wind through woods in riot,
    Through him the gale of life blew high,
The tree of man was never quiet:
    Then 'twas the Roman, now 'tis I.

The wind, it plies the saplings double,
    It blows so hard, 'twill soon be gone:
To-day the Roman and his trouble
    Are ashes under Uricon.

A. E. Housman, 'On Wenlock Edge', Trinity College MS R.I.91, p. 40.

There, like the wind through woods in riot,
　Through him the gale of life blew high;
The tree of man was never quiet:
　Then 'twas the Roman, now 'tis I.

The gale, it plies the saplings double,
　It blows so hard, 'twill soon be gone:
Today the Roman and his trouble
　Are ashes under Uricon.

[Be still, my soul, be still; the arms you bear are brittle]

Be still, my soul, be still; the arms you bear are brittle,
　Earth and high heaven are fixed of old and founded strong.
Think rather, – call to thought, if now you grieve a little,
　The days when we had rest, O soul, for they were long.

Men loved unkindness then, but lightless in the quarry
　I slept and saw not; tears fell down, I did not mourn;
Sweat ran and blood sprang out and I was never sorry:
　Then it was well with me, in days ere I was born.

Now, and I muse for why and never find the reason,
　I pace the earth, and drink the air, and feel the sun.
Be still, be still, my soul; it is but for a season:
　Let us endure an hour and see injustice done.

Ay, look: high heaven and earth ail from the prime foundation;
　All thoughts to rive the heart are here, and all are vain:
Horror and scorn and hate and fear and indignation –
　Oh why did I awake? when shall I sleep again?

[I hoed and trenched and weeded]

I hoed and trenched and weeded,
  And took the flowers to fair:
I brought them home unheeded;
  The hue was not the wear.

So up and down I sow them
  For lads like me to find,
When I shall lie below them,
  A dead man out of mind.

Some seed the birds devour,
  And some the season mars,
But here and there will flower
  The solitary stars,

And fields will yearly bear them
  As light-leaved spring comes on,
And luckless lads will wear them
  When I am dead and gone.

from *Fragment of a Greek Tragedy* (lines 1–28)

Alcmaeon. Chorus.

Cho. O suitably-attired-in-leather-boots
      Head of a traveller, wherefore seeking whom
      Whence by what way how purposed art thou come
      To this well-nightingaled vicinity?
      My object in inquiring is to know.
      But if you happen to be deaf and dumb
      And do not understand a word I say,
      Nod with your hand to signify as much.
Alc. I journeyed hither a Bœotian road.
Cho. Sailing on horseback or with feet for oars?
Alc. Plying with speed my partnership of legs.
Cho. Beneath a shining or a rainy Zeus?
Alc. Mud's sister, not himself, adorns my shoes.
Cho. To learn your name would not displease me much.

Alc.	Not all that men desire do they obtain.
Cho.	Might I then hear at what thy presence shoots?
Alc.	A shepherd's questioned mouth informed me that –
Cho.	What? for I know not yet what you will say.
Alc.	Nor will you ever, if you interrupt.
Cho.	Proceed, and I will hold my speechless tongue.
Alc.	– This house was Eriphyle's, no one's else.
Cho.	Nor did he shame his throat with hateful lies.
Alc.	May I then enter, passing through the door?
Cho.	Go chase into the house a lucky foot.
	And, O my son, be, on the one hand, good,
	And do not, on the other hand, be bad;
	For that is very much the safest plan.
Alc.	I go into the house with heels and speed.

[Oh who is that young sinner with the handcuffs on his wrists?]

Oh who is that young sinner with the handcuffs on his wrists?
And what has he been after that they groan and shake their fists?
And wherefore is he wearing such a conscience-stricken air?
Oh they're taking him to prison for the colour of his hair.

'Tis a shame to human nature, such a head of hair as his;
In the good old time 'twas hanging for the colour that it is;
Though hanging isn't bad enough and flaying would be fair
For the nameless and abominable colour of his hair.

Oh a deal of pains he's taken and a pretty price he's paid
To hide his poll or dye it of a mentionable shade;
But they've pulled the beggar's hat off for the world to see and stare,
And they're haling him to justice for the colour of his hair.

Now 'tis oakum for his fingers and the treadmill for his feet
And the quarry-gang on Portland in the cold and in the heat,
And between his spells of labour in the time he has to spare
He can curse the God that made him for the colour of his hair.

[Ask me no more, for fear I should reply]

Ask me no more, for fear I should reply;
  Others have held their tongues, and so can I,
Hundreds have died, and told no tale before:
  Ask me no more, for fear I should reply –

How one was true and one was clean of stain
  And one was braver than the heavens are high,
And one was fond of me: and all are slain.
  Ask me no more, for fear I should reply.

[He would not stay for me; and who can wonder?]

He would not stay for me; and who can wonder?
  He would not stay for me to stand and gaze.
I shook his hand and tore my heart in sunder
  And went with half my life about my ways.

[When the eye of day is shut]

When the eye of day is shut,
  And the stars deny their beams,
And about the forest hut
  Blows the roaring wood of dreams,

From deep clay, from desert rock,
  From the sunk sands of the main,
Come not at my door to knock,
  Hearts that loved me not again.

Sleep, be still, turn to your rest
  In the lands where you are laid;
In far lodgings east and west
  Lie down on the beds you made.

In gross marl, in blowing dust,
   In the drowned ooze of the sea,
Where you would not, lie you must,
   Lie you must, and not with me.

[Yonder see the morning blink]

Yonder see the morning blink:
   The sun is up, and up must I,
To wash and dress and eat and drink
And look at things and talk and think
   And work, and God knows why.

Oh often have I washed and dressed
   And what's to show for all my pain?
Let me lie abed and rest:
Ten thousand times I've done my best
   And all's to do again.

[From far, from eve and morning]

From far, from eve and morning
   And yon twelve-winded sky,
The stuff of life to knit me
   Blew hither: here am I.

Now – for a breath I tarry
   Nor yet disperse apart –
Take my hand quick and tell me,
   What have you in your heart.

Speak now, and I will answer:
   How shall I help you, say;
Ere to the wind's twelve quarters
   I take my endless way.

[I did not lose my heart in summer's even]

I did not lose my heart in summer's even,
  When roses to the moonrise burst apart:
When plumes were under heel and lead was flying,
  In blood and smoke and flame I lost my heart.

I lost it to a soldier and a foeman,
  A chap that did not kill me, but he tried;
That took the sabre straight and took it striking
  And laughed and kissed his hand to me and died.

MAURICE BARING
1874–1945

Maurice Baring was born at the apex of privilege: his father was Edward
Charles, the first Baron Revelstoke, and his mother was Louisa Emily
Charlotte, grand-daughter of the second Earl Grey. Maurice went to
Eton, and then to Trinity. He never completed his degree, however,
instead moving into the diplomatic service to make use of his undeni-
able talent for languages. Baring began by writing plays, his first, *The
Black Prince*, appearing when he was twenty-eight. Soon he turned his
hand to poetry, producing two collections of learned, elegant, humorous
verse in the 1910s, *Dead Letters* and *Diminutive Dramas*. After resigning
from the Foreign Office in 1904, Baring was sent to Manchuria by
The Morning Post to cover the Russo-Japanese War, after which he
remained in St Petersburg as a foreign correspondent, and developed a
deep feeling for the Russians and their culture. He subsequently pub-
lished his memories of the war: *With the Russians in Manchuria*, as well
as a survey of Russian novels and poetry titled *Landmarks in Russian
Literature*.

Baring became a close friend of G. K. Chesterton's while in St
Petersburg, and he may have been the real-life basis of the character
Horne Fisher in Chesterton's *The Man Who Knew Too Much*. On
leaving Russia, he moved through a string of journalistic postings from
Constantinople to the Balkans, all of which he would describe in *The
Puppet Show of Memory*, an autobiography he penned before he turned
fifty. He describes his reception into the Roman Catholic church there
as 'the only action in my life which I am quite certain I have never
regretted'. During the First World War he was attached to the Royal
Flying Corps, appointed a staff officer of the RAF, and awarded the
OBE. Further honours would come his way later on when he became a
Fellow of the Royal Society of Literature and an Officier de la Légion
d'honneur. These accolades were mostly on account of his elegant
novels of social life, which began to appear in the 1920s and continued
until ill health overtook him in the late 1930s. Those still read today
include *C*, *Cat's Cradle* and *Daphne Adeane*. Versatile and prolific across
many literary genres – his published works number some fifty volumes

– his legacy to poetry lies in the elegies he wrote for friends killed in the Great War, and the *Oxford Book of Russian Verse* that he helped compile towards the end of his life.

August, 1918

In a French Village

I hear the tinkling of the cattle bell,
In the broad stillness of the afternoon;
High in the cloudless haze the harvest moon
Is paler than the phantom of a shell.

A girl is drawing water from a well,
I hear the clatter of her wooden shoon;
Two mothers to their sleeping babies croon,
And the hot village feels the drowsy spell.

Sleep, child, the Angel of Death his wings has spread;
His engines scour the land, the sea, the sky;
And all the weapons of Hell's armoury

Are ready for the blood that is their bread;
And many a thousand men to-night must die,
So many that they will not count the Dead.

Seville

The orange blossoms in the Alcazar,
Where roses and syringas are in flower;
The blinding glory of the morning hour;
The eyes that gleam behind a twisted bar;

The women on the balconies, – a smile;
The barrel-organs, and the blazing heat;
The awning hanging high across the street;
A dark mantilla in a sombre aisle.

A fountain tinkling in a shady court;
The gold arena of the bull-ring's feast;
The coloured crowd acclaiming perilous sport;

The sudden silence when they hold their breath,
While the *torero* gently plays with death,
And flicks the horns of the tremendous beast.

Aleister Crowley was a rum character, whose fascination for magic and the occult started early. He was brought up in a family of devout Plymouth Brethren, but soon found himself attracted to the dark underside of his faith. He would call himself the Great Beast 666, and spent the rest of his life experimenting with varieties of occultism, Satanism, sado-masochism and free love. He came up to Trinity in 1895 to read for the Natural Science Tripos, but quickly persuaded a tutor that his 'business in life was to study English literature'. He read widely, especially the authors he loved, and left without taking his degree. He once wrote: 'I should like the haunted room over the Great Gate of Trinity to be turned into a vault like that of Christian Rosencreutz to receive my sarcophagus' – a desire destined to be unfulfilled. He published his first book of verse while still an undergraduate, *Aceldama* (1898), a sub-Swinburnean fantasy full of poisonous kisses, self-abasing ecstasies and hellish dreams. His second collection, *Songs of the Spirit* (1898), from which 'In Neville's Court' and 'By the Cam' are taken, shows the mix of registers which will characterise future volumes: on the one hand, a stream of orgiastic charnel-house imagery, and on the other a gentler, personal register which will mark his later love poems. Crowley wrote more than sixteen volumes of verse, as well as a novel, *The Diary of a Drug Fiend*, erotic works like *White Stains*, many books about magic (some dictated by angels), including an account of his system, *The Book of the Law* (1904), and a self-styled *Autohagiography* (1929).

After leaving Cambridge, he was able to live on a substantial inheritance from his father, a brewer. He joined the Order of the Golden Dawn, but fell out with its head, MacGregor Mathers, friend of Yeats, and then with Yeats himself whom he accused of pique at his, Crowley's, superior poetic gifts. A keen mountaineer and traveller, his nomadic wanderings took him to Mexico, the Himalayas, North Africa, Russia, Japan, China and India, always driven by his personal creed: 'There is no law beyond Do what thou wilt.' In 1903 he married Rose Edith Skerrett, who would undergo trance-like states on his behalf and helped transmit supernatural dictations. In America, during the First World War, he wrote propaganda for pro-German magazines; in India,

he had to flee the country following an inquiry into the shooting of
two men, and in Sicily, where he had set up a commune of like-minded
spirits who experimented with drugs, nudism and sex, he found himself
banished by the government for indecency. Never short of acolytes
and willing partners in his sexual experiments, he later set up his own
magical Order of the Silver Star.

He ended his life in a boarding-house in Hastings, a chronic heroin
addict. Always inclined to act the guru or magus – he once drove a
scared (or perhaps drunk) Dylan Thomas out of a pub by an act of
clairvoyance – his power of self-belief was prodigious, and his writings
comparably vast. His reputation as a counter-cultural figure was revived
in the 1960s when his portrait appeared on the sleeve of The Beatles'
'Sergeant Pepper' album, and his magical teachings were recalled in The
Rolling Stones' album *Their Satanic Majesties' Request*.

In Neville's Court

Trinity College, Cambridge

I think the souls of many men are here
   Among these cloisters, underneath the spire
   That the moon silvers with magnetic fire;
But not a moon-ray is it, that so clear
Shines on the pavement; for a voice of fear
   It hath, unless it be the breeze that mocks
   My ear, and waves his old majestic locks
About his head. There fell upon my ear:

'O soul contemplative of distant things,
   Who hast a poet's heart, even if thy pen
   Be dry and barren, who dost hold love dear,
Speed forth this message on the fiery wings
Of stinging song to all the race of men:
   That they have hope; for we are happy here.'

By the Cam

Twilight is over, and the noon of night
   Draws to its zenith. Here beyond the stream
   Dance the wild witches that dispel my dream
Of gardens naked in Diana's sight.
Foul censers, altars desecrated, blight
   The corpse-lit river, whose dank vapours teem
   Heavy and horrible, a deadly steam
Of murder's black intolerable might.

The stagnant pools rejoice; the human feast
   Revels at height; the sacrament is come;
God wakes no lightning in the broken East;
   His awful thunders listen and are dumb;
Earth gapes not for that sin; the skies renew
At break of day their vestiture of blue.

MUHAMMAD (ALLAMA) IQBAL
1877–1938

Muhammad Iqbal, widely referred to as 'the spiritual father of Pakistan', was a poet, philosopher, politician and barrister. His father was a tailor, and he was brought up a devout Muslim, undergoing an arranged marriage in his teens. He would later go on to marry two other women, and had several children. In 1895, when he was eighteen, he went to Government College, Lahore to study Arabic, English and philosophy, and two years later took his degree, winning the Gold Medal for outstanding work. In 1905 he came to Trinity on a scholarship to study philosophy, and a year later went on to Munich where he completed his doctorate on metaphysics in Persian thought. There, his German teacher, with whom he formed a close relationship, introduced him to Goethe, Nietzsche and Heine.

Iqbal is recognised as having been a key driver of the movement for the creation of Pakistan. He was a prominent political figure, a lawyer, as well as a philosophical thinker who, after his three years in Europe, developed his own philosophy of 'khudi', from the word 'khud', for self. This defies exact translation, but might be rendered as selfhood, the ego, or even the Nietzschean will to power. Thus, as he writes in one poem, '*Agar khudi ki hifazat karen to ain hayat; / Na karen to sarapa afsoon afsana*'; or, in the translation by Khushwant Singh: 'If we nurture our will, life will have purpose: / If we fail to do so, it will be a tale of frustration.' The singing quality of '*afsoon afsana*' says something about the sound effects of his work, derived from the old Urdu traditions of oral recitative. Iqbal wrote in both Persian and Urdu – his earlier Persian poetry for the educated classes, his later Urdu poetry, often urging political and religious action, for a larger mass readership. His first collection of Persian poetry, *Asrar-e-Khudi* (*The Secrets of the Self*) was published in 1915, though he was already well known from his many public readings. Later works included *Zabur-e-Ajam* (*Persian Psalms*) in 1927, *Bal-e-Jibril* (*The Wings of Gabriel*) in 1935 – reckoned to be his finest volume in Urdu – and *Armaghan-e-Hijaz* (*The Gifts of Hijaz*) in 1938, composed in both Persian and Urdu. Iqbal was knighted in 1922. In 1930, at a session of the All-India Muslim League in London, he delivered his seminal presidential speech (known as the Allahabad Address), in which he argued for the creation of a Muslim state. In a lecture delivered in Cambridge in 1931, he characteristically advised his audience to guard against atheism and materialism – twin evils which, in his view, had been one of the causes of the European War of 1914. Iqbal was named 'National Poet of Pakistan', 'Muhammad Iqbal Day' is a national holiday in Pakistan, and the open university of Pakistan, which has well over a million students, is called the Allama Iqbal University.

At Trinity, Iqbal encountered the Hegelian philosopher John McTaggart, whose work had a lasting influence on his own, particularly on his 1930 work *The Reconstruction of Religious Thought in Islam*. Iqbal was not, however, a systematic thinker, but essentially a poet who often relished contradiction. Singh points out that, while he might exhort the peasantry to rise against oppression, he also wrote eulogies in praise of patrons, kings and princes; he argued that Islam transcended national boundaries while supporting a separate state for Indian Muslims; he was a revolutionary but also a supporter of traditional Muslim values, especially in the home. The poems included here, necessarily in translation, include colloquial conversations with God, witty accounts of the natural world, love poems and politico-religious exhortations, as well as those traditional rhyming rubáiyát, or quatrains, which Edward Fitz-Gerald made popular in England in the previous century.

Beauty's Essence

Beauty asked God one day
This question: 'Why
Didst Thou not make me, in Thy world, undying?'
And God replying –
'A picture-show is this world: all this world
A tale out of the long night of not-being;
And in it, seeing
Its nature works through mutability,
That only is lovely whose essence knows decay.'

The moon stood near and heard this colloquy,
The words took wing about the sky
And reached the morning-star;
Dawn learned them from its star, and told the dew –
It told the heavens' whisper to
Earth's poor familiar;
And at the dew's report the flower's eye filled,
With pain the new bud's tiny heartbeat thrilled;
Springtime fled from the garden, weeping;
Youth, that had come to wander there, went creeping
Sadly away.

Two Planets

Two planets meeting face to face,
One to the other cried, 'How sweet
If endlessly we might embrace,
And here for ever stay! how sweet
If Heaven a little might relent,
And leave our light in one light blent!'

But through that longing to dissolve
In one, the parting summons sounded.
Immutably the stars revolve,
By changeless orbits each is bounded;
Eternal union is a dream,
And severance the world's law supreme.

Six Rubáiyát

1

Thy world the fish's and the winged thing's bower;
My world a crying of the sunrise hour;
In Thy world I am helpless and a slave;
In my world is Thy kingdom and Thy power.

2

Faith is like Abraham at the stake: to be
Self-honouring and God-drunk, is faith. Hear me,
You whom this age's ways so captivate!
To have no faith is worse than slavery.

3

Music of strange lands with Islam's fire blends,
On which the nations' harmony depends;
Empty of concord is the soul of Europe,
Whose civilisation to no Mecca bends.

4

There's breath in you, but no heart's palpitation –
That breath no eager circle's inspiration.
Go beyond Reason's light: hers is the lamp
That shows the road, not marks the destination.

5

Litter- nor camel-faring, I –
Guidepost, no home ensnaring, I –
To burn all dross, my destiny –
Lightning, no harvest-bearing, I!

6

Love's madness has departed: in
The Muslim's veins the blood runs thin;
Ranks broken, hearts perplexed, prayers cold,
No feeling deeper than the skin.

Reproach

Your fate, poor hapless India, there's no telling –
Always the brightest jewel in someone's crown;
Your peasant a carcass spewed up from the grave,
Whose coffin is mouldering still beneath the sod.
Mortgaged to the alien, soul and body too,
Alas – the dweller vanished with the dwelling –,
Enslaved to Britain you have kissed the rod:
It is not Britain I reproach, but you.

Civilisation's Clutches

Iqbal has no doubt of Europe's humaneness; she
Sheds tears for all peoples groaning beneath oppression;
Her reverend churchmen furnish her liberally
With wiring and bulbs for moral illumination.
And yet, my heart burns for Syria and Palestine,
And finds for this knotty puzzle no explanation –
Enlarged from the 'savage grasp' of the Turks, they pine,
Poor things, in the clutches now of 'civilisation'.

God and Man

GOD

I made this world, from one same earth and water,
You made Tartaria, Nubia, and Iran.
I forged from dust the iron's unsullied ore,
You fashioned sword and arrowhead and gun;
You shaped the axe to hew the garden tree,
You wove the cage to hold the singing-bird.

MAN

You made the night and I the lamp,
And You the clay and I the cup;
You – desert, mountain-peak, and vale:
I – flower-bed, park, and orchard; I
Who grind a mirror out of stone,
Who brew from poison honey-drink.

Solitude

I stood beside the ocean
    And asked the restless wave –
To what eternal troubling,
    To what quest are you slave?
With orient pearls by thousands
    Your mantle's edges shine,
But is there in your bosom
    One gem, one heart, like mine?
– It shuddered from the shore and fled,
    It fled, and did not speak.

I stood before the mountain,
    And said – Unpitying thing!
Could sorrow's lamentation
    Your hearing never wring?
If hidden in your granite
    One ruby blood-drop lie,

Do not to my affliction
    One answering word deny!
– Within its cold unbreathing self
    It shrank, and did not speak.

I travelled a long pathway,
    And asked the moon – Shall some
Far day, oh doomed to wander,
    Or no day, end your doom?
Our earth your silver glances
    With lakes of jasmine lace;
Is it a heart within you
    Whose hot glow sears your face?
– It stared with your jealous eyes towards
    The stars, and did not speak.

Past moon and sun I journeyed,
    To where God sits enskied; –
In all Your world no atom
    Is kin of mine, I cried:
Heartless that world, this handful
    Of dust all heart, all pain;
Enchantment fills Your garden,
    But I sing there in vain.
– There gathered on His lips a smile;
    He smiled, and did not speak.

The Night and the Poet

THE NIGHT

Why do you roam about in my moonlight,
So worried,
Silent as a flower, drifting like perfume?
Perhaps you are a jeweller
Dealing in the pearls that are called stars,
Or are a fish that swims in my river of light;
Or a star that has fallen from my brow,
And, having forsaken the heights,
Now resides in the depths below.
The strings of the violin of life are still;
My mirror reflects life as it sleeps.
The eye of the vortex too is sleeping
In the depths of the river;
The restless wave hugs the shore and is still.
The earth, so busy and bustling,
Slumbers as though no one lived on it.
But the poet's heart is never at peace –
How did you elude my spell?

THE POET

I sow pearls in the soil of your moon;
Hiding from men, I weep like dawn.
I am reluctant to come out in the busy day,
And my tears flow in the solitude of night.
The cry pent up inside me,
Whom should I get to hear it,
And to whom can I show my burning desire?
Lying on my chest the lightning of Sinai sobs:
Where is the seeing eye – has it gone to sleep?
My assembly-hall is dead like the candle at a grave.
Alas, night! I have a long way to go!
The winds of the present age are not favourable to it:
It does not feel the loss it has suffered.
The message of love,
When I can no longer keep it to myself,
I come and tell it to your shining stars.

A. A. MILNE
1882–1956

A. A. Milne (Alan Alexander) will always be remembered primarily as the author of the Pooh books, notionally for children but, like all good children's books, also for adults. He was brought up in London, his father being the headmaster of a private school at which H. G. Wells was a science master. An early memory of Alan's was of seeing the coal-man staggering with a sack through a gate. The three-year-old asked: 'Why do they both?' In reply, his father offered a lecture on the economics of co-operation. Milne's own memory, however, was of something more cheerfully unaccountable: 'Nobody knew what I was talking about, and nobody ever did know, and nobody knows now.' The incident hints at that comic mismatch between childish nonsense and adult sense-making which will run through his own children's books. As Pooh puts it, 'nobody knows / (Tiddely pom)…'.

Alan gained a scholarship to Westminster School where he developed a passion for cricket, Jane Austen and light verse, and in 1900 went up to Trinity to read maths. He soon, however, turned his attention to writing instead, submitting comic verses to the student magazine, *Granta*, and later to the satirical magazine, *Punch*, where he would subsequently work as sub-editor. Looking back on this time, he wrote, 'We were very young in those days and young, it still seems to me, in the right sort of way', adding 'let us thank Cambridge and the *Granta* for casting the spell on us.' Any such spell ended decisively with the First World War. In spite of pacifist convictions, Milne volunteered in 1915 and joined the Warwickshire Regiment, spending some months on the Somme (near Mametz Wood where Robert Graves and David Jones also fought), amidst all the horrors of trench warfare. Later, he would recall these experiences in two best-selling books: *Peace with Honour* (1934) and *War with Honour* (1940).

His life as a freelance writer began when he was lucky enough, after four months, to be invalided out of France. He wrote prolifically and in many genres: light verse, short stories, novels, more than thirty screenplays and plays, including a very successful adaptation of Kenneth Grahame's *The Wind in the Willows*: *Toad of Toad Hall* (1929). The rights for the plays alone would come to earn him a substantial £2,000 a year.

Probably his most successful book for adults was a detective novel, *The Red House Mystery* (1922), which was widely translated and reprinted. But instead of following his publisher's wish for more of the same, something changed his direction. His son, Christopher Robin, born in 1920, was given a small teddy bear from Harrods by his parents. Mysteriously called Winnie-the-Pooh by its young owner – nobody knows why – Milne's wife, Daphne, encouraged her husband to write its story. The character first appeared in the verse collection *When We Were Very Young* (1924), then in a short story. *Winnie-the-Pooh* (1926), the novel, soon followed, with illustrations by Ernest Shepard with whom Milne worked closely, often intertwining text and pictures – though it is said that Shepard's bear was more like his own son's teddy than Christopher Robin's. Pooh, Piglet and Eeyore were by this time already toys in the Milne nursery; Owl and Rabbit were inventions, while a mission to Harrods to acquire new characters produced the slightly more exotic (and female!) Kanga, and Roo. The book was a huge success, selling 35,000 copies in its first year in Britain, and 150,000 in the United States. It was translated into many languages, including Latin, *Winnie Ille Pu* (1958) – the only Latin book to reach the New York Times best-seller list. Two more works soon followed: *Now We Are Six* (1927) and *The House at Pooh Corner* (1928). Milne had found his largest, most enduring readership, even if he would sometimes resent the comparative neglect of his other writings. Christopher Robin would also come to resent the public notoriety the books brought him – Milne often used his son in publicity accounts and photographs. Almost immediately after publication there were offers to buy the manuscripts of the two stories, but Milne eventually left them as a gift to Trinity College – perhaps in memory of a time, historical as well as personal, when it was possible to remain 'very young'.

The publication in 1963 of Frederick Crews' parody of a student casebook, *The Pooh Perplex*, containing spoof essays like 'A la recherche du pooh perdu', is only a reminder of the enduring adult fascination of the originals. Commercial products based on the books, whether toys, clothes or films, proliferated, and in 2003 *Winnie-the-Pooh* came seventh in the BBC's poll of the 'best-loved novels' of all time. In his own lifetime, Milne eventually came to accept the success of his works for children. He once wrote some rueful lines on their surprising impact: 'So – the Children's Books: a short / Intermezzo of a sort; / When I wrote them, little thinking / All my years of pen-and-inking / Would be almost lost among / Those four trifles for the young.' As his biographer, Ann Thwaite, concludes, by the time Milne died the 'immortality' of these 'Children's Books', with their delightful verses or 'hums' as Pooh calls them, was assured.

Halfway Down

Halfway down the stairs
Is a stair
Where I sit.
There isn't any
Other stair
Quite like
It.
I'm not at the bottom,
I'm not at the top;
So this is the stair
Where
I always
Stop.

Halfway up the stairs
Isn't up,
And isn't down.
It isn't in the nursery,
It isn't in the town.
And all sorts of funny thoughts
Run round my head:
'It isn't really
Anywhere!
It's somewhere else
Instead!'

The Old Sailor

There was once an old sailor my grandfather knew
Who had so many things which he wanted to do
That, whenever he thought it was time to begin,
He couldn't because of the state he was in.

He was shipwrecked, and lived on an island for weeks,

And he wanted a hat,

and he wanted some breeks;

And he wanted some nets, or a line and some hooks
For the turtles and things which you read of in books.

And, thinking of this, he remembered a thing
Which he wanted (for water) and that was a spring;
And he thought that to talk to he'd look for, and keep
(If he found it) a goat, or some chickens and sheep.

Then, because of the weather, he wanted a hut
With a door (to come in by) which opened and shut
(With a jerk, which was useful if snakes were about),
And a very strong lock to keep savages out.

He began on the fish-hooks, and when he'd begun
He decided he couldn't because of the sun.

So he knew what he ought to begin with, and that
Was to find, or to make, a large sun-stopping hat.

He was making the hat with some leaves from a tree,
When he thought, 'I'm as hot as a body can be,
And I've nothing to take for my terrible thirst;
So I'll look for a spring, and I'll look for it *first.*'

Then he thought as he started, 'Oh, dear and oh, dear!
I'll be lonely to-morrow with nobody here!'
So he made in his note-book a couple of notes:
'*I must first find some chickens*'

and '*No, I mean goats.*'

He had just seen a goat (which he knew by the shape)
When he thought, 'But I must have a boat for escape.

But a boat means a sail, which means needles and thread;
So I'd better sit down and make needles instead.'

He began on a needle, but thought as he worked,
That, if this was an island where savages lurked,
Sitting safe in his hut he'd have nothing to fear,
Whereas now they might suddenly breathe in his ear!

So he thought of his hut… and he thought of his boat,
And his hat and his breeks, and his chickens and goat,
And the hooks (for his food) and the spring (for his thirst)…
But he *never* could think which he ought to do first.

And so in the end he did nothing at all,
But basked on the shingle wrapped up in a shawl.
And I think it was dreadful the way he behaved –
He did nothing but basking until he was saved!

[*The more it* snows]

The more it
snows-tiddely-pom,
The more it
goes-tiddely-pom
The more it
goes-tiddely-pom
On
Snowing.

And nobody
knows-tiddely-pom,
How cold my
toes-tiddely-pom
How cold my
toes-tiddely-pom
Are
Growing.

He sang it like that, which is much the best way of singing it, and when
he had finished, he waited for Piglet to say that, of all the Outdoor
Hums for Snowy Weather he had ever heard, this was the best. And,
after thinking the matter out carefully, Piglet said:

'Pooh,' he said solemnly, 'it isn't the *toes* so much as the *ears*.'

Lines Written by a Bear of Very Little Brain

On Monday, when the sun is hot
I wonder to myself a lot:
'Now is it true, or is it not,
That what is which and which is what?'

On Tuesday, when it hails and snows,
The feeling on me grows and grows
That hardly anybody knows
If those are these or these are those.

On Wednesday, when the sky is blue,
And I have nothing else to do,
I sometimes wonder if it's true
That who is what and what is who.

On Thursday, when it starts to freeze
And hoar-frost twinkles on the trees,
How very readily one sees
That these are whose – but whose are these?

On Friday –

'Yes, it is, isn't it?' said Kanga, not waiting to hear what happened on Friday. 'Just one more jump, Roo, dear, and then we really must be going.'

A. A. Milne – 'Lines Written by a Bear of Very Little Brain', Trinity College Add. MS c.199, fol. 65.

Disobedience

James James
Morrison Morrison
Weatherby George Dupree
Took great
Care of his Mother,
Though he was only three.
James James
Said to his Mother,
'Mother,' he said, said he;
'You must never go down to the end of the town, if you don't go down
with me.'

James James
Morrison's Mother
Put on a golden gown.
James James
Morrison's Mother
Drove to the end of the town.
James James
Morrison's Mother
Said to herself, said she:
'I can get right down to the end of the town and be back in time for tea.'

King John
Put up a notice,
'LOST or STOLEN or STRAYED!
JAMES JAMES
MORRISON'S MOTHER
SEEMS TO HAVE BEEN MISLAID.
LAST SEEN
WANDERING VAGUELY:
QUITE OF HER OWN ACCORD,
SHE TRIED TO GET DOWN TO THE END OF THE TOWN — FORTY
SHILLINGS REWARD!'

James James
Morrison Morrison
(Commonly known as Jim)
Told his
Other relations
Not to go blaming *him*.
James James
Said to his Mother,
'Mother,' he said, said he:
'You must *never* go down to the end of the town without consulting me.'

James James
Morrison's mother
Hasn't been heard of since.
King John
Said he was sorry,
So did the Queen and Prince.
King John
(Somebody told me)
Said to a man he knew:
'If people go down to the end of the town, well, what can *anyone* do?'

(Now then, very softly)
J.J.
M.M.
W.G.Du P.
Took great
C/o his M*****
Though he was only 3.
J.J.
Said to his M*****
'M*****,' he said, said he:
'You-must-never-go-down-to-the-end-of-the-town-if-you-don't-go-
                                        down-with-ME!'

Before he had gone very far he heard a noise. So he stopped and listened.
This was the noise.

Noise, by Pooh

Oh, the butterflies are flying,
Now the winter days are dying,
And the primroses are trying
    To be seen.
And the turtle-doves are cooing,
And the woods are up and doing,
For the violets are blue-ing
    In the green.

Oh, the honey-bees are gumming
On their little wings, and humming
That the summer, which is coming,
    Will be fun,
And the cows are almost cooing,
And the turtle-doves are mooing,
Which is why a Pooh is poohing
    In the sun.

For the spring is really springing;
You can see a skylark singing,
And the blue-bells, which are ringing,
    Can be heard.
And the cuckoo isn't cooing,
But he's cucking and he's ooing,
And a Pooh is simply poohing
    Like a bird.

[Here lies a tree which Owl (a bird)]

'But it isn't Easy,' said Pooh to himself, as he looked at what had once been Owl's House. 'Because Poetry and Hums aren't things which you get, they're things which get *you*. And all you can do is to go where they can find you.'

He waited hopefully...

'Well,' said Pooh after a long wait, 'I shall begin *'Here lies a tree'* because it does, and then I'll see what happens.'

This is what happened:

Here lies a tree which Owl (a bird)
 Was fond of when it stood on end,
 And Owl was talking to a friend
Called Me (in case you hadn't heard)
When something Oo occurred.

For lo! The wind was blusterous
 And flattened out his favourite tree;
 And things looked bad for him and we –
Looked bad, I mean, for he and us –
I've never known them wuss.

Then Piglet (PIGLET) thought a thing:
 'Courage!' he said. 'There's always hope.
 I want a thinnish piece of rope.
Or, if there isn't any, bring
A thickish piece of string.'

So to the letter-box he rose,
 While Pooh and Owl said 'Oh!' and 'Hum!'
 And where the letters always come
(Called 'LETTERS ONLY') Piglet sqoze
His head and then his toes.

Oh gallant Piglet (PIGLET)! Ho!
 Did Piglet tremble? Did he blinch?
 No, no, he struggled inch by inch
Through LETTERS ONLY, as I know
Because I saw him go.

He ran and ran, and then he stood
  And shouted, 'Help for Owl, a bird,
  And Pooh, a bear!' until he heard
The others coming through the wood
As quickly as they could.

'Help-Help and Rescue!' Piglet cried,
  And showed the others where to go.
  [Sing ho! for Piglet (PIGLET) ho!]
And soon the door was opened wide,
And we were both outside!

Sing ho! for Piglet, ho!
Ho!

Poem

Christopher Robin is going.
At least I think he is.
Where?
Nobody knows.
But he is going –
I mean he goes
(To rhyme with 'knows')
Do we care?
(To rhyme with 'where')
We do
Very much.
*(I haven't got a rhyme for that
'is' in the second line yet.
  Bother.)*
*(Now I haven't got a rhyme for
bother. Bother).*
Those two bothers will have
to rhyme with each other
  Buther.
The fact is this is more difficult
than I thought,
I ought –
(Very good indeed)

I ought
To begin again,
But it is easier
To stop.
Christopher Robin, good-bye,
I
(Good)
I
And all your friends
Sends –
I mean all your friend
Send –
*(Very awkward this, it keeps
   going wrong)*
Well, anyhow, we send
Our love
END.

'If anybody wants to clap,' said Eeyore when he had read this, 'now is the time to do it.'

Pooh

EDWARD SHANKS
1892–1953

Edward Richard Butler Shanks was born in London, educated at Merchant Taylor's School, and went to Trinity to read history. During his time there he edited *Granta*, and began to write the neat Georgian verse which would remain indelibly his style for thirty years. He was sent to the war in 1914, but returned the following year as an invalid, and published his first collection, *Songs*. When the war was over, he turned to journalism as a career, writing literary reviews for the *London Mercury* and the *Evening Standard*.

Throughout his life he wrote in a variety of genres, including an early, co-authored study of Hilaire Belloc, collections of essays, a 'tragedy in six scenes' called *Beggar's Ride*, as well as several humorous novels, and a dystopian work, *The People of Ruins*, a transparently anti-Communist tract. He was fairly successful commercially, though he only won critical acclaim for his poetry, in particular *The Queen of China and Other Poems*, which was awarded the first Hawthornden Prize for Imaginative Literature in 1919. Later in life he turned to studies of better-known authors, writing books on Edgar Allan Poe and Rudyard Kipling. He continued to write poetry, but its value is 'largely autobiographical' – as Mark Wormald concludes: 'a fragmentary diary of a poet who uneasily spanned two separate periods and modes of writing, those of Rupert Brooke and of modernism'.

The Rock Pool

To Alice Warrender

This is the sea. In these uneven walls
A wave lies prisoned. Far and far away
Outward to ocean, as the slow tide falls,
Her sisters through the capes that hold the bay
Dancing in lovely liberty recede.
Yet lovely in captivity she lies,
Filled with soft colours, where the waving weed
Moves gently and discloses to our eyes
Blurred shining veins of rock and lucent shells
Under the light-shot water; and here repose
Small quiet fish and dimly glowing bells
Of sleeping sea-anemones that close
Their tender fronds and will not now awake
Till on these rocks the waves returning break.

Armistice Day, 1921

The hush begins. Nothing is heard
Save the arrested taxis throbbing
And here and there an ignorant bird
And here a sentimental woman sobbing.

The statesman bares and bows his head
Before the solemn monument;
His lips, paying duty to the dead
In silence, are more than ever eloquent.

But ere the sacred silence breaks
And taxis hurry on again,
A faint and distant voice awakes,
Speaking the mind of a million absent men:

'Mourn not for us. Our better luck
At least has given us peace and rest.
We struggled when our moment struck
But now we understand that death knew best.

Would we be as our brothers are
Whose barrel-organs charm the town?
Ours was a better dodge by far –
We got *our* pensions in a lump sum down.

We, out of all, have had our pay,
There is no poverty where we lie;
The graveyard has no quarter-day,
The space is narrow but the rent not high.

No empty stomach here is found;
Unless some cheated worm complain
You hear no grumbling underground;
O, never, never wish us back again!

Mourn not for us, but rather we
Will meet upon this solemn day
And in our greater liberty
Keep silent for you, a little while, and pray.'

VLADIMIR NABOKOV
1899–1977

Vladimir Vladimirovich Nabokov was born in 1899 in St Petersburg, into an aristocratic family. His father Vladimir Dmitrievich led the pre-revolutionary Constitutional Democratic Party. After the Revolution, the Nabokovs moved to Berlin, where Nabokov elder would die defending a political rival from an assassination attempt. Even before they moved in 1919, the young Nabokov had published one collection of poetry, *Stikhi* (*Poems*, 1916), and collaborated with Andrei Balashov on a second, *Al'manakh: Dva Puti* (*Two Paths*, 1918). He was accepted into Trinity in 1919 on a scholarship for sons of prominent Russians in exile, and read zoology before switching to French and Russian. He duly received a first class in his second year, but following his father's murder in 1922, he barely managed a second class in his Finals.

Nabokov lived on Trinity Lane, and divided his time in Cambridge between savaging his tutors' Bolshevism, chasing women, and keeping goal for the Trinity football team, which to him involved leaning against the goalpost and 'composing verse in a tongue nobody understood about a remote country nobody knew'. In keeping with this lifestyle, he never visited the University Library, and 'had no interest whatsoever' in the history of Cambridge generally. In the end, the literary fruits of his time at Trinity were poems mostly in Russian, which became two further collections, *Grozd* (*The Cluster*, 1922) and *Gornii Put'* (*The Empyrean Path*, 1923). Both were written under the pseudonym 'V. Sirin', 'sirin' being a bird from the Russian myths of his childhood. He returned to Berlin in 1922, where he met and married Véra Slonim, and began writing novels in Russian.

In 1940 they moved to America, where Nabokov turned to writing in English, a language he had been taught from birth. In *Speak, Memory*, his wry, enchanting autobiography, he recalls how in one childhood summer his father 'ascertained, with patriotic dismay, that my brother and I could read and write English but not Russian (except KAKAO and MAMA)'. He had nine novels to his name by then, all in Russian, but none had made him more than a few hundred dollars. With *Lolita* (1955), and the storm of controversy it whipped up, things finally changed and his reputation was established. Like Joseph Conrad, Nabokov's success came with writing in a new language in middle age, but he differed in having developed an idiom already – a colourful Russian style which would blossom dramatically in the sounds of English. At the same time, he was also an avid lepidopterist, producing eighteen scientific papers on butterflies and moths – 'it is not improbable that had there been no revolution in Russia, I would have devoted myself entirely to lepidopterology and never written any novels at all', he wrote – and an equally devoted compiler of chess problems. Such interactions of the analytic and the playful came to characterise his English poems, which are intensely fine-tuned, and often rhyme and pun like versified riddles – the 'maniac's masterpiece' by Humbert Humbert in *Lolita*, for instance, or John Shade's eponymous 999-line work in *Pale Fire* (1962). But critics found his cerebral games harder to digest outside the world of fiction. The monumental four-volume translation of Pushkin's *Eugene Onegin* (1964) represented Nabokov's combined practice as a translator, critic and poet. Throughout, he kept his version rigorously faithful to the original Russian, while drawing deep from the resources of English. However, its idiosyncratic manner was harshly reviewed, and its poor reception, which the author took badly, ended a long friendship with the disapproving Edmund Wilson.

Despite his focus on the novel, he continued throughout the 1950s and 1960s to write occasional poems in both Russian and English, for émigré reviews and the *New Yorker*, respectively. He translated the Russian ones himself for book publication, and added some of his early work as well – although these, despite being a tiny selection of his younger self's 'steady mass of verse', now provoked in him only 'vague embarrassment'. Instead, he worked principally on new English novels, as well as on the translation of their nine Russian predecessors, rigidly sticking to the principles that made *Eugene Onegin* so unpopular. He was in the process of beginning a ninth English novel, *The Original of Laura*, when he died in Montreux, Switzerland, in 1977.

From *Lolita* (chapter 25)

Wanted, wanted; Dolores Haze.
Hair: brown. Lips: scarlet.
Age: five thousand three hundred days.
Profession: none, or 'starlet'.

Where are you hiding, Dolores Haze?
Why are you hiding, darling?
(I talk in a daze, I walk in a maze,
I cannot get out, said the starling.)

Where are you riding, Dolores Haze?
What make is the magic carpet?
Is a Cream Cougar the present craze?
And where are you parked, my car pet?

Who is your hero, Dolores Haze?
Still one of those blue-caped star-men?
Oh the balmy days and the palmy days,
And the cars, and the bars, my Carmen!

Oh Dolores, that juke-box hurts!
Are you still dancin', darlin'?
(Born in worn levis, both in torn T-shirts,
And I, in my corner, snarlin'.)

Happy, happy is gnarled McFate
Touring the States with a child wife,
Ploughing his Molly in Every State
Among the protected wild life.

My Dolly, my folly! Her eyes were *vair*,
And never closed when I kissed her.
Know an old perfume called *Soleil Vert*?
Are you from Paris, mister?

L'autre soir un air froid d'opéra m'alita:
Son fêlé – bien fol est qui s'y fie!
Il neige, le décor s'écroule, Lolita!
Lolita, qu'ai-je fait de ta vie?

Dying, dying, Lolita Haze,
Of hate and remorse, I'm dying.
And again my hairy fist I raise,
And again I hear you crying.

Officer, officer, there they go
In the rain, where that lighted store is!
And her socks are white, and I love her so,
And her name is Haze, Dolores.

Officer, officer, there they are –
Dolores Haze and her lover!
Whip out your gun and follow that car.
Now tumble out, and take cover.

Wanted, wanted: Dolores Haze.
Her dream-grey gaze never flinches.
Ninety pounds is all she weighs
With a height of sixty inches.

My car is limping, Dolores Haze,
And the last long lap is the hardest,
And I shall be dumped where the weed decays,
And the rest is rust and stardust.

From *Eugene Onegin* (chapter 6)

XXIX

The pistols have already gleamed.
The mallet clanks against the ramrod.
Into the polyhedral barrel go the balls,
and the first time the cock has clicked.
Now powder in a grayish streamlet
is poured into the pan. The jagged,
securely screwed-in flint
is raised anew. Behind a near stump
perturbed Guillot places himself.
The two foes shed their cloaks.
Thirty-two steps Zaretski
with eminent exactness has paced off,
has placed his friends apart at the utmost points,
and each has taken his pistol.

XXX

'Now march toward each other.' Coolly,
not aiming yet, the two foes
with firm tread, slowly, evenly
traversed four paces,
four deadly stairs.
His pistol Eugene then,
not ceasing to advance,
gently the first began to raise.
Now they have stepped five paces more,
and Lenski, closing his left eye,
started to level also – but right then
Onegin fired. ... Struck have
the appointed hours: the poet
in silence drops his pistol.

XXXI

Gently he lays his hand upon his breast
and falls. His misty gaze
expresses death, not anguish.
Thus, slowly, down the slope of hills,
in the sun with sparks shining,
a lump of snow descends.
Deluged with instant cold,

Onegin hastens to the youth,
looks, calls him ... vainly:
he is no more. The youthful bard
has met with an untimely end!
The storm has blown; the beauteous bloom
has withered at sunrise;
the fire upon the altar has gone out! ...

XXXII

Stirless he lay, and strange
was his brow's languid peace.
Under the breast he had been shot clean through;
steaming, the blood flowed from the wound.
One moment earlier
in *this* heart had throbbed inspiration,
enmity, hope, and love,
life effervesced, blood boiled;
now, as in a deserted house,
all in it is both still and dark,
it has become forever silent.
The window boards are shut. The panes with chalk
are whitened over. The chatelaine is gone.
But where, God wot. All trace is lost.

On Translating 'Eugene Onegin'

1

What is translation? On a platter
A poet's pale and glaring head,
A parrot's speech, a monkey's chatter,
And profanation of the dead.
The parasites you were so hard on
Are pardoned if I have your pardon,
O, Pushkin, for my stratagem:
I traveled down your secret stem,
And reached the root, and fed upon it;
Then, in a language newly learned,
I grew another stalk and turned
Your stanza patterned on a sonnet,
Into my honest roadside prose –
All thorn, but cousin to your rose.

2

Reflected words can only shiver
Like elongated lights that twist
In the black mirror of a river
Between the city and the mist.
Elusive Pushkin! Persevering,
I still pick up Tatiana's earring,
Still travel with your sullen rake.
I find another man's mistake,
I analyze alliterations
That grace your feasts and haunt the great
Fourth stanza of your Canto Eight.
This is my task – a poet's patience
And scholiastic passion blent:
Dove-droppings on your monument.

A Literary Dinner

Come here, said my hostess, her face making room
for one of those pink introductory smiles
that link, like a valley of fruit trees in bloom,
the slopes of two names.
I want you, she murmured, to eat Dr James.

I was hungry. The Doctor looked good. He had read
the great book of the week and had liked it, he said,
because it was powerful. So I was brought
a generous helping. His mauve-bosomed wife
kept showing me, very politely, I thought,
the tenderest bits with the point of her knife.
I ate – and in Egypt the sunsets were swell;
The Russians were doing remarkably well;
had I met a Prince Poprinsky, whom he had known
in Caparabella, or was it Mentone?
They had traveled extensively, he and his wife;
her hobby was People, his hobby was Life.
All was good and well cooked, but the tastiest part
was his nut-flavored, crisp cerebellum. The heart
resembled a shiny brown date,
and I stowed all the studs on the edge of my plate.

Ode to a Model

I have followed you, model,
in magazine ads through all seasons,
from dead leaf on the sod
to red leaf on the breeze,

from your lily-white armpit
to the tip of your butterfly eyelash,
charming and pitiful,
silly and stylish.

Or in kneesocks and tartan
standing there like some fabulous symbol,
parted feet pointing outward
– pedal form of akimbo.

On a lawn, in a parody
Of Spring and its cherry tree,
near a vase and a parapet,
virgin practicing archery.

Ballerina, black-masked,
near a parapet of alabaster.
'Can one – somebody asked –
rhyme 'star' and 'disaster'?'

Can one picture a blackbird
as the negative of a small firebird?
Can a record, run backward,
turn 'repaid' into 'diaper'?

Can one marry a model?
Kill your past, make you real, raise a family
by removing you bodily
from back numbers of Sham?

from *The University Poem*

7

And, once again, the crooked alleys,
the gigantic age-old gates –
right in the center of the town,
a barber shop where they shaved Newton,
in ancient mystery enveloped,
the tavern known as the Blue Bull.
There, beyond the stream, the houses,
the century-old turf tramped down
into a dark-green, even carpet
to suit the needs of human games,
the wood-like sound of soccer kicks
in the cold air. Such was the world
where I from Russian clouds was hurled.

8

In the morning, out of bed I'd hop,
and to a lecture rush
with whistling cape; at last a hush
over the chilly amphitheater fell
as the professor of anatomy
mounted the podium, a sage
with vacant, childlike eyes;
with varicolored chalk
a Japanese design he'd trace
of intertwined blood vessels, or
the human skull, and on the way
a naughty joke he might let fly –
stamping of feet was our reply.

9

Supper. The regal dining hall
graced by the likeness of Henry the Eighth –
those tight-sheathed calves, that beard –
all by the sumptuous Holbein limned;
inside that singularly towering hall
that choir lofts made appear so tall,
it was perpetually murky
despite the violet conflagration,
that filtered through the colored panes.

The naked benches stretched along
the naked tables; there we sat,
in the black cowls of brothers' capes,
and ate the over-seasoned soups
made out of pallid vegetables.

10

I lived within an antique chamber,
but, inside its desert silence,
I hardly savored the shades' presence.
Clutching his bear from Muscovy,
esteemed the boxer's fate,
of Italic beauty dreaming
lame Byron passed his student days.
I remembered his distress –
his swim across the Hellespont
to lose some weight.
But I have cooled towards his creations…
so do forgive my unromantic side –
to me the marble roses of a Keats
have more charm than all those stagey storms.

Spring

The engine toward the country flies,
A crowd of tree trunks, shying, nimbly
goes scurrying up the incline:
the smoke, like a white billow, mingles
with birches' motley Apriline.
Velour banquettes inside the carriage
of summer covers are still free.
A yellow trackside dandelion
is visited by its first bee.

Where once there was a snowdrift, only
an oblong, pitted isle is left
beside a ditch that's turning verdant;
of springtime smelling, now grown wet,
the snow is overlaid with soot.

The country house is cold and twilit.
The garden, to the joy of doves,
contains a cloud-reflecting puddle.
The columns and the aged roof,
also the elbow of the drainpipe –
there's need of a fresh coat for all,
a pall of green paint; on the wall
the merry shadow of the painter
and the ladder's shadow fall.

The birches' tops in their cool azure,
the country house, the summer days,
are but the same, recurring image,
yet their perfection grows always.
From exile's lamentations distanced,
lives on my every reminiscence
in an inverted quietude:
What's lost forever is immortal;
and this eternity inverted
is the proud soul's beatitude.

JOHN LEHMANN
1907–87

Rudolph John Frederick Lehmann, son of Rudolph Chambers Lehmann (see pp. 219–20), went to Eton as a King's Scholar, and then to Trinity to study History, and then Modern Languages. At this time he met Julian Bell, nephew of Virginia Woolf, and was introduced to the Bloomsbury circle. On leaving Trinity, he found work with the Woolfs' Hogarth Press – the press that would daringly publish Freud, T. S. Eliot, Rilke, Svevo, Mansfield and Stein, among many others, but also, specifically under Lehmann's influence, poets such as Edmund Blunden, C. Day Lewis, Kenneth Allott and Stephen Spender. He was involved in the publication of the 'Hogarth Letters' in the early 1930s – letters about British imperialism, anti-semitism, and the growing power of Fascism, which, he claimed, caught 'the moods, the pleasures and the preoccupations of the early thirties'. In particular, he discussed with Virginia Woolf her own 'Letter to a Young Poet', at a time when her thoughts were running on the problematic relationship between lyrical privacy and political commitments. In 1931, the press also published his own first collection of poetry, *A Garden Revisited*.

He continued to work for the Woolfs until moving to Vienna in the mid-thirties, to write his precise and sparing verse full-time. Lehmann's major legacy to popular literature was his next project, the left-leaning poetry journal *New Writing*, which he founded in 1935 and developed into the *Penguin New Writing* series when he returned to Britain on the eve of the Second World War. At the height of the war, with pro-British and anti-fascist feelings culturally dominant, this series of new and established leftist poets would publish up to six issues a year, each of which would sell out its 75,000 copies in just a few days. Lehmann returned to the Hogarth Press briefly, then set up his own firm, John Lehmann Ltd, which introduced writers such as Saul Bellow, Gore Vidal and Elizabeth David to British readers. Down the decades he continued to write his elegant, fastidious poetry, accumulating it at a slow rate until a slim *Collected Poems* appeared in 1963. Having received a CBE, a number of international honours and election to the Royal Society of Literature, he taught as a visiting professor at several American universities and wrote reviews for literary magazines, until his death at the age of eighty.

This Excellent Machine

This excellent machine is neatly planned,
A child, a half-wit would not feel perplexed:
No chance to err, you simply press the button –
At once each cog in motion moves the next,
The whole revolves, and anything that lives
Is quickly sucked towards the running band,
Where, shot between the automatic knives,
It's guaranteed to finish dead as mutton.

This excellent machine will illustrate
The modern world divided into nations:
So neatly planned, that if you merely tap it
The armaments will start their devastations,
And though we're for it, though we're all convinced
Some fool will press the button soon or late,
We stand and stare, expecting to be minced, –
And very few are asking *Why not scrap it?*

A Death in Hospital

On the first day, the lifted siege at last
On starving hope: his spirit dropped its load,
And turning once more to the world of friends
   Wept for the love they showed.

Then on the second day, like a black storm
Terror of death burst over him, and pain
Pierced like the jagged lightning, in whose flash
   All he would never gain –

The wine-blue inlets of a home restored,
Peace, and the growth of love in summer's field,
And loaded baskets from a poet's tree –
   Pitiless, stood revealed.

The third night there was battle in the skies:
The tongues of all the guns were hot with steel,
The groaning darkness shuddered, but could add
   No wrench to his ordeal.

The fourth day, when they came with daffodils
And sea-borne fruit, and honey from his home,
They seemed but shadows, where he choked and fought
    There was so little room.

It was the fifth day explanation broke;
There was no fear, nor human longing more,
And all his life in that surprising dawn
    Appeared a dwindling shore

Separate for ever from his tide-kissed boat,
An isle with all its gardens fondly kept
Complete and curious, that belonged to them,
    His friends, who stayed and wept.

After Fever

Yet one day, waking, to emerge at last
From prisons of the brain, more iron than iron,
All mass neurotic dreads, imposed ideas,
    The sick-bed nightmare;

One day, waking, simply to forget
Frontiers, the untrue thought dividing friends,
Only to see the spring's unbroken landscape,
Green plains of corn and darker forest green,
Mottled with farms like fruit in spreading branches,
And south and east the dazzled mountain boulders,
White fells, and streams that quiver down the slopes
Winding through towns to the extreme line of blue;

To be deaf to ghosts that wail in air for blood,
The obscene clamour of the past,
To forget the gathered armies, the machine-guns,
And exchange laughter with Frenchmen in the train
Crossing the Mont Cenis, and bathe in June
With fair-haired brothers happy from the Rhine;

To hear as if new music, men and cranes,
The federated cities of the future rise;

This might be after fever to return
To even pulse and ease of no more dreams,
In a darkened room
Unblind the skylight and be clothed in sun.

Greek Landscape with Figures

Everywhere I walked the olive trees,
Their uncouth, twisted trunks as full of holes
As sculptured torsos, clutched
With plunging roots the peasants' field they shaded.

Some were scooped out by time, it seemed against
Reason of nature that their branches still
Could transmute soil and sun
Into such tender leaves, such fruit for harvest.

Hundreds of years, they said: and all the time
Rough trunks like bulging muscled arms were trying
To screw the roots tighter in,
To resist the pull into space, into nothingness.

I watched the peasants working there, who seemed
Tough like the olive trunks, determined too
To grip the earth with deep
Unflinching will not to be dispossessed.

Quarrelsome, heroic, fruitful in their season
As when the bull roared and the temples rang:
Equally proud against
The rage of history, the whirling globe.

THOM GUNN

1929–2004

William Guinneach Gunn was the child of a tempestuous marriage
between two very different journalists: Bert, a brash, hard-drinking
reporter and editor, and Annie, a literary, independent-minded woman
who inspired a love of reading in her son. It ended disastrously with
their divorce in 1940. Four years later, when William was fifteen, Annie
committed suicide. It was William and his brother, Ander, who found
her body on the floor beside the gas poker from which she had inhaled.
As late as 1979, the fifty-year-old poet was still wondering if he would
ever be able to write about the mother whom he had adored. Eventu-
ally, in 2000, he published the movingly simple poem, 'The Gas-Poker'
(included here), about the object which he describes as a 'sort of back-
wards flute' – as if that instrument of death also lay behind much of
his own poetic music. William was reclusive and awkward in his teens,
not only from the shock of his mother's death, but also from a growing
awareness of his homosexual feelings. Literature became his refuge.
After two years' National Service and six months working in Paris, he
went up to Trinity to read English in 1950. During this time he changed
his name to Thomson William Gunn – 'Thom' for short – Thomson
being his mother's maiden name.

At Trinity his writing blossomed, partly inspired by the lectures of
F. R. Leavis – 'better than any creative-writing class', he declared. He
read widely, discovering Donne and the Elizabethans who gave him
his lasting sense of form and metre, as well as the whole range of liter-
ature from Chaucer to Auden. He edited poetry magazines, organised
readings – one by a surprisingly 'sober and punctual' Dylan Thomas
– encountered the newly arrived Ted Hughes who would later become
a friend, and fell in love with the man who would be his lifelong com-
panion, Mike Kitay. In his autobiographical essay 'Cambridge in the
Fifties', Gunn recalls a night in Trinity gardens, acting in a Shakespeare
play: 'It was Cambridge at its sweetest – Shakespeare, the moonlit
summer night, the park-like private gardens of wealthy colleges, friends
I hoped would be friends for life – different kinds of happiness rolled
into one.' The poems in his first volume, *Fighting Terms* (1954), were all
written during these undergraduate years, including 'The Secret Sharer'

(included here), about looking up at his own lighted room in Whewell's Court, and seeing another self moving behind the curtain.

After Cambridge Gunn went to Stanford on a creative writing fellowship – a reminder of new openings for poets in the mid-twentieth century – where he studied under the influential poet and critic, Yvor Winters. Gunn's strictly formal style led to his inclusion in Robert Conquest's anthology *New Lines*, alongside Donald Davie and Philip Larkin. Being classed as one of the 'Movement' poets, formal, anti-modernist and plain-speaking, was not comfortable however. The predominant fashion was changing, and by the time he came to publish *Touch* (1967) Gunn was also experimenting with syllabics and free verse. But he always refused to be tied to any one school. Of the two opposing strains in poetry, 'the New Formalism and the Language Poets', he once declared: 'Neither interests me. I'm interested in individual poets, not in poetics.' He took various teaching posts in Texas, Berkeley and San Francisco, while continuing to publish new collections, including *Moly* (1971), *Jack Straw's Castle* (1976) and *The Passages of Joy* (1982).

Once settled for good with Mike in San Francisco, Thom experimented with the counter-cultural movements of the sixties: LSD, free love, and commune life. He came out as gay in *Jack Straw's Castle*, and in the following decades also wrote criticism and reviews. Then, as AIDS started to ravage the gay community in the 1980s, his subject matter changed. A close friend who was dying asked Thom to nurse him – a difficult vigil which resulted in the powerful long poem 'Lament', included here. With the deaths of more friends, his register became predominantly elegiac, and in 1992 he published the collection for which he is perhaps best known: *The Man with Night Sweats*. Of it he once commented: 'Everybody noticed the gay poetry, but there are many poems about friendship in that book and a great many more in a new one that have to do with friendship, or imply it as a value, as indeed it is for me.' His last book, *Boss Cupid* (2000), continued the themes of death and friendship.

Gunn retired from teaching in 2000. Though he had always taken drugs recreationally, he now lost the discipline of self-restraint. In the last few years he wrote little, and eventually, his system overloaded with a concoction of substances, he died of heart failure. His will remain, as his editor Clive Wilmer puts it, 'a body of work more consistently well written than that of any of his contemporaries'.

The Secret Sharer

Over the ankles in snow and numb past pain
I stared up at my window three stories high:
From a white street unconcerned as a dead eye,
I patiently called my name again and again.

The curtains were lit, through glass were lit by doubt.
And there was I, within the room alone.
In the empty wind I stood and shouted on:
But O, what if the strange head should peer out?

Suspended taut between two equal fears
I was like to be torn apart by their strong pull:
What, I asked, if I never hear my call?
And what if it reaches my insensitive ears?

Fixed in my socket of thought I saw them move
Aside, I saw that some uncertain hand
Had touched the curtains. Mine? I wondered. And,
At this instant, the wind turned in its groove.

The wind turns in its groove and I am here
Lying in bed, the snow and street outside;
Fire-glow still reassuring; dark defied.
The wind turns in its groove: I am still there.

Tamer and Hawk

I thought I was so tough,
But gentled at your hands,
Cannot be quick enough
To fly for you and show
That when I go I go
At your commands.

Even in flight above
I am no longer free:
You seeled me with your love,
I am blind to other birds –
The habit of your words
Has hooded me.

As formerly, I wheel
I hover and I twist,
But only want the feel,
In my possessive thought,
Of catcher and of caught
Upon your wrist.

You but half civilize,
Taming me in this way.
Through having only eyes
For you I fear to lose,
I lose to keep, and choose
Tamer as prey.

The Outdoor Concert

At the edge
of the understanding:
    it's the secret.

You recognize not
the content of it but
the fact that it is
there to be recognized.

Dust raised
by vendors and dancers
shimmers on the windless air
where it hovers
as if it will never settle.

The secret
is still the secret

is not a proposition:
it's in finding
what connects the man
with the music, with
the listeners, with the fog
in the top of the eucalyptus,
with dust discovered on the lip

and then in living a while
at that luminous intersection,
spread at the centre
like a white garden spider
so still
that you think it
has become its web,

a god existing
only in its creation.

The Missed Beat

Above the harsh clods blanked-white in the sun
                    Where hour by hour
                Ants labor one by one:
A petal-face of pinkish-red so sheer
            That flux itself misses a beat,
                    I hold my breath. Bent here,
Absorbed in wonder, shaken by my power,
I try to stop the moment, this, complete:
                    Down of the flower
                Seemed like the down that might invest
Both look and looked-at, being inseparable.
                    Can it be repossessed?
I feel my pulse's climb, and the long fall.

Ms of Thom Gunn's poem 'The Missed Beat'. Reproduced from
a personal copy of Clive Wilmer's. In his bibliography of *The
Gruffyground Press: The First Four Decades* (Chestnut Editions, 2012),
Mark Askam explains how Gunn wrote out the poem by hand in five
defective copies of the chapbook to which it gave the title, and sent
these to friends.

His Rooms in College

All through the damp morning he works, he reads.
The papers of his students are interrupted
Still by the raw fury, the awkward sadness
His marriage has become. The young serious voices
Are drowned by her remembered piteous wail
'Discovering' the one unfaithfulness
He never did commit.
                              Be more specific.
What do they have ahead of them, poor dears,
This kind of thing?
                              Today no supervisions;
But though he meant these hours for his research
He takes a book, not even in his 'field',
And some note touches him, he goes on reading
Hours long into the afternoon from which
The same low river fog has never lifted.
If every now and then he raises his eyes
And stares at winter lawns below, each time
He sees their hard blurred slopes the less. He reads,
He reads, until the chapel clock strikes five,
And suddenly discovers that the book,
Unevenly, gradually, and with difficulty,
Has all along been showing him its mind
(Like no one ever met at a dinner party),
And his attention has become prolonged
To the quiet passion with which he in return
Has given himself completely to the book.
He looks out at the darkened lawns, surprised
Less by the loss of grief than by the trust.

The Hug

It was your birthday, we had drunk and dined
    Half of the night with our old friend
        Who'd showed us in the end
    To a bed I reached in one drunk stride.
      Already I lay snug,
And drowsy with the wine dozed on one side.

I dozed, I slept. My sleep broke on a hug,
      Suddenly, from behind,
In which the full lengths of our bodies pressed:
      Your instep to my heel,
    My shoulder-blades against your chest.
    It was not sex, but I could feel
    The whole strength of your body set,
        Or braced, to mine,
      And locking me to you
    As if we were still twenty-two
    When our grand passion had not yet
      Become familial.
    My quick sleep had deleted all
    Of intervening time and place.
      I only knew
The stay of your secure firm dry embrace.

The Man with Night Sweats

I wake up cold, I who
Prospered through dreams of heat
Wake to their residue,
Sweat, and a clinging sheet.

My flesh was its own shield:
Where it was gashed, it healed.

I grew as I explored
The body I could trust
Even while I adored
The risk that made robust,

A world of wonders in
Each challenge to the skin.

I cannot but be sorry
The given shield was cracked
My mind reduced to hurry,
My flesh reduced and wrecked.

I have to change the bed,
But catch myself instead

Stopped upright where I am
Hugging my body to me
As if to shield it from
The pains that will go through me,

As if hands were enough
To hold an avalanche off.

Lament

Your dying was a difficult enterprise.
First, petty things took up your energies,
The small but clustering duties of the sick,
Irritant as the cough's dry rhetoric.
Those hours of waiting for pills, shot, x-ray
Or test (while you read novels two a day)
Already with a kind of clumsy stealth
Distanced you from the habits of your health.
    In hope still, courteous still, but tired and thin,
You tried to stay the man that you had been,
Treating each symptom as a mere mishap
Without import. But then the spinal tap.
It brought a hard headache, and when night came
I heard you wake up from the same bad dream
Every half-hour with the same short cry
Of mild outrage, before immediately
Slipping into the nightmare once again
Empty of content but the drip of pain.
No respite followed: though the nightmare ceased,
Your cough grew thick and rich, its strength increased.
Four nights, and on the fifth we drove you down
To the Emergency Room. That frown, that frown:
I'd never seen such rage in you before
As when they wheeled you through the swinging door.
For you knew, rightly, they conveyed you from
Those normal pleasures of the sun's kingdom
The hedonistic body basks within
And takes for granted – summer on the skin,
Sleep without break, the moderate taste of tea
In a dry mouth. You had gone on from me
As if your body sought out martyrdom
In the far Canada of a hospital room.
Once there, you entered fully the distress
And long pale rigours of the wilderness.
A gust of morphine hid you. Back in sight
You breathed through a segmented tube, fat, white,
Jammed down your throat so that you could not speak.
    How thin the distance made you. In your cheek
One day, appeared the true shape of your bone
No longer padded. Still your mind, alone,

Explored this emptying intermediate
State for what holds and rests were hidden in it.
   You wrote us messages on a pad, amused
At one time that you had your nurse confused
Who, seeing you reconciled after four years
With your grey father, both of you in tears,
Asked if this was at last your 'special friend'
(The one you waited for until the end).
'She sings,' you wrote, 'a Philippine folk song
To wake me in the morning... It is long
And very pretty.' Grabbing at detail
To furnish this bare ledge toured by the gale,
On which you lay, bed restful as a knife,
You tried, tried hard, to make of it a life
Thick with the complicating circumstance
Your thoughts might fasten on. It had been chance
Always till now that had filled up the moment
With live specifics your hilarious comment
Discovered as it went along; and fed,
Laconic, quick, wherever it was led.
You improvised upon your own delight.
I think back to the scented summer night
We talked between our sleeping bags, below
A molten field of stars five years ago:
I was so tickled by your mind's light touch
I couldn't sleep, you made me laugh too much,
Though I was tired and begged you to leave off.

Now you were tired, and yet not tired enough
– Still hungry for the great world you were losing
Steadily in no season of your choosing –
And when at last the whole death was assured,
Drugs having failed, and when you had endured
Two weeks of an abominable constraint,
You faced it equably, without complaint,
Unwhimpering, but not at peace with it.
You'd lived as if your time was infinite:
You were not ready and not reconciled,
Feeling as uncompleted as a child
Till you had shown the world what you could do
In some ambitious role to be worked through,
A role your need for it had half-defined,

But never wholly, even in your mind.
You lacked the necessary ruthlessness,
The soaring meanness that pinpoints success.
We loved that lack of self-love, and your smile,
Rueful, at your own silliness.
                              Meanwhile,
Your lungs collapsed, and the machine, unstrained,
Did all your breathing now. Nothing remained
But death by drowning on an inland sea
Of your own fluids, which it seemed could be
Kindly forestalled by drugs. Both could and would:
Nothing was said, everything understood,
At least by us. Your own concerns were not
Long-term, precisely, when they gave the shot
– You made local arrangements to the bed
And pulled a pillow round beside your head.
    And so you slept, and died, your skin gone grey,
Achieving your completeness, in a way.

Outdoors next day, I was dizzy from a sense
Of being ejected with some violence
From vigil in a white and distant spot
Where I was numb, into this garden plot
Too warm, too close, and not enough like pain.
I was delivered into time again
– The variations that I live among
Where your long body too used to belong
And where the still bush is minutely active.
You never thought your body was attractive,
Though others did, and yet you trusted it
And must have loved its fickleness a bit
Since it was yours and gave you what it could,
Till near the end it let you down for good,
Its blood hospitable to those guests who
Took over by betraying it into
The greatest of its inconsistencies
This difficult, tedious, painful enterprise.

The Gas-Poker

Forty-eight years ago
– Can it be forty-eight
Since then? – they forced the door
Which she had barricaded
With a full bureau's weight
Lest anyone find, as they did,
What she had blocked it for.

She had blocked the doorway so,
To keep the children out.
In her red dressing-gown
She wrote notes, all night busy
Pushing the things about,
Thinking till she was dizzy,
Before she had lain down.

The children went to and fro
On the harsh winter lawn
Repeating their lament,
A burden, to each other
In the December dawn,
Elder and younger brother,
Till they knew what it meant.

Knew all there was to know.
Coming back off the grass
To the room of her release,
They who had been her treasures
Knew to turn off the gas,
Take the appropriate measures,
Telephone the police.

One image from the flow
Sticks in the stubborn mind:
A sort of backwards flute.
The poker that she held up
Breathed from the holes aligned
Into her mouth till, filled up
By its music, she was mute.

KIT WRIGHT
1944–

Kit Wright has published more than twenty-five books for children and adults, among them *The Bear Looked Over the Mountain* (1978), which won the Geoffrey Faber Memorial Prize, *Hot Dog and Other Poems* (1982), *Bump-Starting the Hearse* (1983), *Short Afternoons* (1989), which won both the Heinemann Award and the Hawthornden Prize, *Hoping It Might Be So: Poems 1974–2000* (2001) and, most recently, *Ode to Didcot Power Station* (2014). After working for a time as a university lecturer in Canada, he returned to Britain and became a freelance writer. He came to Trinity as a Fellow Commoner in Creative Arts in 1977.

Kit describes how he 'continued to pursue [his] secondary role as itinerant bard to schoolchildren' during his time at Trinity, to supplement what was then the rather modest stipend attached to his post. Of that time he recalls a 'rollicking birthday poem' he wrote for Ralph Leigh, Professor of French and Rousseau specialist, which he declaimed at the party Ralph hosted:

Seventy summers have gone by
Since R. A. Leigh first saw the sky
 And shortly came to cable
Massive messages from Rousseau.
Others were not skilled to do so:
 Ralph alone was able…

'It's fair to say that when I began to recite', Kit writes, 'I was more pleased with the enterprise than he was; but by the end he seemed genuinely touched by the tribute.' The two seem to have formed a great friendship, Ralph having a keen interest in poetry and a readiness to disseminate his 'refreshing opinions'. In particular, Kit remembers his suggestion that W. H. Auden's 'Musée des Beaux Arts' would be improved by omitting all the adjectives.

Kit recalls having friends at Trinity among the Fellows, the students and the staff, and seeing poems by people in all three categories. Indeed, despite the fact that his own work was 'not in line with the then predominant school of Cambridge poetry', he remembers there being 'plenty of poets in Cambridge, younger and older, whose work I admired and whose company I enjoyed, including Elaine Feinstein, Clive Wilmer, Richard Burns, Steven Romer and Abigail Mozley'. The immediate product of this time, reading and company – apart, no doubt, from the impact Kit had on contemporary Trinity members – was the collection, *Bump-Starting the Hearse*; and then, much later, a play, *Bowling in the Dark*, set in that same Fellows' Bowling Green which was the site of many of his poetic conversations. Kit sums up his experience at Trinity by writing, 'it was a great time for me and I thank the College and its members for their generosity and hospitality'.

The Roller in the Woods

Who would imagine a cricket ground
Had ever existed here,
Folded into a farm on the downland pasture,
Lapping the edge of the oakwood
And the buttercup-quilted rides?

For the Toll is returned to plough
After a century of combat,
Sown to a sea of blue-green waves
Beneath which it lies drowned.
And now,
Stick nor stone of the old pavilion,
Hook nor slat of the scoreboard left:
Never an echo of tumbling children,
Tattle of Edwardians,
Knocking their pipes out on the rough deal benches.

Foaming hawthorn and rhododendron
Have colonised the field-edge, spreading
Through copper beech and flowering chestnut
And adventitious saplings.
                              Where
Is the *camaraderie*
Of the side I played for so often here:

Their thunderous blows and heroical overs,
The days that flowed with sun and wind:
Stalemates in dismal drizzle,
And the finger of death uplifted in the dusk?

Where,
I might ask,
Are Nobby and Dave and the Colonel and Phil,
The two Pauls and the one and only
Moggy Worsfold and Arthur Spark?
I have failed to raise them
By staring out at the level meadow
As if I were Cadmus who had sown
The dragon's teeth and awaited
His armed men springing from the earth.

But I did untangle my way
Through the canopied darkness of what had been
The boundary. Among the laurel bushes
And snagging goose-grass and rabbit holes,
I found what I'd forgotten, hidden
Under a wide oak. For this

Was what they could not lightly move
In the rhythm of abandonment:
Here was the deep ground-bass and the solemn
Measure of constancy, foundry-born,
That had lasted so long.
                          And I laid
My arms across the surface, feeling
Under the rust and dust and pollen,
The summers that never seemed to move
And all the years gone by to the creak of iron.

Stabat Mater[89]

Consider the young girl, who for homework or recreation,
Was drawing a tree that rose in soaring flight from the gardens
Behind the ground-floor flat. And these
Were dark with buildings in the daytime;
Pressed by walls of lichened brick and a grove of ash and plane.

But this was an evening of lemon September sunlight.
Her mother was taking the washing down from the line.
And the girl from her bedroom window, a sketchpad on her knees,
Looked and looked at the ash tree, saw

It move. It shouldn't have done that.
For this was no shivering of the leaves, or a branch dipping, it stepped
Forward on its own authority,
Made the decision. She screamed.

Her mother, with a clothes-peg in her mouth,
Looked up and saw the great tree like an animal
Considering her and manoeuvring. She hurled
Her body that dragged in dreamtime over the lawn,

Made the back door as it came down like the sky.
It had seemed to rise a shade and swivel,
Then crack like thunder in two along
Three garden walls of shattered masonry
And rubble. From its grave,
Lain where the woman had been standing,
Only the seething of the leaves.

Disbelieving in retribution or providence,
We recoup the moral: proof
That God has a sense of theatre? Salvation through Art?
But the woman and the child,
Crying and shaking in each other's arms,
Come back to me, and what broke cover there
Still feels like the wind of an energy not then blind.

Cold Harbor

On the night before the Battle of Cold Harbor in 1864, many of the doomed Federal soldiers wrote their names on slips of paper which they pinned to their backs, so that their families could be told of their deaths. One made a last diary entry, a line reproduced here.

The hour my blood is to be spilled
I know. I therefore write it in:
June 3. Cold Harbor. I was killed.

Upon our backs our lives are billed,
Our names and numbers on a pin,
The hour my blood is to be spilled.

As though toward this ending willed,
I carve my tombstone for my kin:
June 3. Cold Harbor. I was killed.

For this dawn dying we were drilled,
A battle no known God can win
Nor stop the hour our blood is spilled,

Which cannot ever be distilled
As balm, but only re-begin:
June 3. Cold Harbor. I was killed.

So all our dreams flow unfulfilled
To death by this blind creek. Within
The hour my blood is to be spilled.
June 3. Cold Harbor. I was killed.

George Herbert's Other Self in Africa

Thinking another way
    To tilt the prism.
I vowed to turn to light
    My tenebrism
    And serve not night
        But day.

Surely, I cried, the sieves
    Of love shake slow
But even. Love subsists
    Though pressed most low:
    As it exists,
        Forgives.

But my stern godlessness
    Rose through the sun,
Admonished me: Fat heart,
    So starving's fun?
    Whom have they art
        To bless?

Thereat my false thought froze,
    Seeing how plain
The field was where they died,
    How sealed their pain,
    And I replied
        God knows.

That Was The Summer

That was the summer as I recall,
the man next door and I began
to call each other Sir,
in a kind of roguish formality or
mock-combative collusion. Why,
I cannot say, but keep it up
we somehow did for some little time;
for as long, you might almost say, as it took.
'Are you all right, sir?' 'Quite all right, sir.
You all right, sir?' 'Sir, I'm well.'
Nor did we fail to operate
attendant quasi-theatrical business:
the stiff half-turn; the ritual bow;
the planted stare of profound regard,
as we met on our doorsteps, housekeys poised...
or bellowed across the howling High Road
'ARE YOU ALL RIGHT, SIR?' 'QUITE ALL RIGHT, SIR!'
as though in loyal defence of a principle
both were prepared to die for, soon.
But the ending seemed as inexplicable
as the beginning: the disappearance,
ambulance sirens, police, old pressmen
hogging the bar at the Horse and Artichoke,
cats gone skinny, the haunted dog.
And of course I know no more than anyone
else as I walk these streets at midnight,
hoping to coax from neon or starlight
a final reflexive *Sir, I'm well.*

PETER ROBINSON
1953–

Peter Robinson has published several works of literary criticism, among them *Poetry, Poets, Readers: Making Things Happen* (2002), *Twentieth-Century Poetry: Selves and Situations* (2005) and *Poetry and Translation: The Art of the Impossible* (2010). He has also published at least four works of fictional prose, including *Foreigners, Drunks and Babies: Eleven Stories* (2013) and, most recently, *September in the Rain* (2016). In addition to translations of the Italian poets Ungaretti, Sereni and Erba, he has produced more than twenty volumes of his own poetry, among them *The Benefit Forms* (1978), *This Other Life* (1988), which won the Cheltenham Prize, *Entertaining Fates* (1992), *Selected Poems: 1976–2001* (2003), *The Returning Sky* (2012) and *Buried Music* (2015). He has taught in Cambridge and at the University of Tohoku in Japan, but returned to Britain in 2007 to take up the post of Professor of English and American literature at the University of Reading. He first came to Trinity in 1975 to do a PhD on modern poetry.

Peter describes himself at that time as 'not in good spiritual shape', 'emotionally involved with two women and having just witnessed at gunpoint the sexual violation of one of them'. This event has been important to his writing, and has featured in several of his works. In these circumstances he found the routine of college life difficult to adopt, and moved to a rented room outside college. 'Nevertheless,' he recounts, 'Trinity was my base for the following five years, the place I would meet some inspiring people – such as the painter Fellow Commoner, David Inshaw.'

Of Trinity's literary culture, Peter writes: 'I have no doubt that it had a profound and permanent influence on my poetry. It was a place where intensely urgent close reading was sustained and promoted, where, if it were to be taken seriously, such attention to individual words, phrases and cadences had to be backed by remorseless literary and philosophical knowledge – especially as derived from Wittgenstein.' Wittgenstein himself attended Trinity, arriving in 1911, and Peter recalls 'as touchstone' for his poetry one of many characteristic ripostes the philosopher is said to have made: 'To the philosopher's asking whether some recently purchased classical music 78s were good, the college's future director of studies in English, Theo Redpath, hedged: "It depends what you mean by 'good'?"; "I mean what you mean", Wittgenstein replied.' 'The same', Peter hopes, 'may be said of the poems here.'

Autobiography

Morning, in the small hotel
on the edge of the industrial

quarter of town, the light
settles on the breakfast table's white

which becomes the notebook page.
You read me like a book. You're telling me,

'When they write the biography
this will be called *A Brief Affair*.'

Over butter, vermicelli, bread
and jams the phrases carry.

Outside, they trouble the air,
smoky across the tramlines. The days,

now a life intact and separate,
are glazed with association. Flats

that rise at the edge of the street
would tell a convenient story

could they speak of the crossroads set
for the so difficult goodbyes.

Our expressions in the photograph
taken with a time device

will bear the double illusion.
Looking like we think we look,

other than what we look like,
it is the false perspective

carries us away. The cars
merely drive as we go off

beneath a skyline captioned:
It is not enough just to live.

1976

A Woman a Poem a Picture

for David Inshaw

The flattened cumulus darker than slate allows bright sunshine to
break across the gap between cloud-banks and the tumuli as, elsewhere,
topiary hedges. Would it be a woman reaches up to readjust her –
what's it called? – a parasol. Or, no, she waves goodbye.

Dilapidated circumstances: lacking its flimsy white covering, Thomas
Hardy ('greatest of the moderns') imagined the one he had come
across a skeleton. Well, he would, wouldn't he.

The deepening presence of … what if she leaves him? Clouds are
heaped. A mackerel sky has evening written all over it. Not very
much gets finished. Now you count two women, together, playing
shuttlecock. Best to keep it under your hat was William Blake's advice,
for love that's told can never be.

And she has turned face into the sun. The yellow verso of her breasts
diminishing, this shadow may well be extended – and to whatsoever
distance. Embed small dabs of darker tone in the field behind her.

It's difficult to draw with the woman in his light. The painter's set up
his easel in that green, but his model refuses, point-blank, to stand still.

At the Invitation View, it remains unclear who has returned and
from what oblique, unwished-for angle. The colour match depends
on whatever she is wearing: no, hardly the original air-blue gown. It's
the unexpected appearance of another person's wife, who stops herself
from smiling and goes on up the stairs.

Cleaning

Seeing as she submerges
disturbances of the foamy water,
unnoticed here, I look at her

skin suffused with warmth, the margins
of her self and I acknowledge
urges he pressed home, my fears.

Lathering reaches of her front
to punish in herself another's want
and be clean, she is fierce:

roughly imagined by him;
taken as though insubstantial;
dispossessed, possessed – my victim.

Unannounced, I lightly touch
her streaming upper arm to speak.
Only it startles her so much

an over-faint quiet is thickening.
My mistake, never reckoning
how still you are afraid of me

or my imagination. Being
not specially alone, alive I'm
far from the person who endured him.

My love, this is the dirty thing.

Convalescent Days

for the Friends

I wake as a cock crows into the haze
of Lacrilube eye-gel. My convalescence
has blurred slow, changeable summer.
Arranged rose petals imperceptibly age
on a window sill. The sloping lawn
is speckled with daisies and dark birds.

Leisurely debates about what birds
have dared to feed bring back a haze
of handbook illustrations to the lawn.
Lunching with friends helps convalescence.
Chaffinch, thrush, a starling? At my age
I ought to know. It's already late summer.

You've made a present of this summer,
its lost hamster, hurt ginger tom, the birds
taking dust-baths. Bad news in our age
of domestic wars homes through a haze
brought by too much sun. Convalescence
is no trouble. Someone mows the lawn.

In avenues and parks beyond edged lawn
life expands across distances all summer,
then shrinks to headaches of convalescence.
On a video, forgotten hits by the Byrds
start into a fiercely yearning haze
that means remorse. So this is middle age,

and we have begun to feel our age.
The shadowy figures around your lawn
are husbands and wives lost in the haze
or manoeuvrings of a different summer.
What went wrong? We're not free birds,
and life itself's become a convalescence.

Keeping going is what convalescence
mainly entails. One daughter's of an age
(or thinks so) to act like the little birds
and bees; she sunbathes, sulking on cut lawn,
plays social tennis or piano through summer.
Carol, she's your own Dolores Haze.

Most of these birds will abandon your lawn,
and convalescence is another way to age;
just so the summers must become autumnal haze.

Unheimlich Leben [90]

Seeing that far-fetched look of yours,
again I have you coming home
from Valparaíso, as it might be,
to the Isle of Ely.

Maltings, greens, a sunken lane
seen then on a daily basis
turn aside, as if withdrawn,
at your coming home –
home to hear how the natives complain
and with so little reason,
to find its quiet brick streets and walks
grating on you all the more.

I see them as though through your eyes,
those drowned lands with their roundabouts,
industrial parks, estates
now high and dry
when a local bus fails to materialize …
but what would these glimpses be for
if not to make peace with our places and times?
Leafage is thick like the summers before,
your guess, as good as mine.

Like a Railway Station

somewhere, on the edge of landscape
abstracted by deep autumn mist,
a grey-ness in the troubled woods'
threatened ash and remnant elm
as from a local train or platform,
its blur's this slow reminder –
'depending on your nearness,
forgive me, to the grave,' he says.

But I have had that thought already
with the various aches and pains;
and carrying my own inside me,
look out across deserted tracks
past people waiting on connections
to where fields fade in distance.
A voice announces some delays
and the distance takes no notice,

not having that much time for time.

ANGELA LEIGHTON
1954–

Angela Leighton has published various works of criticism on nineteenth- and twentieth-century poetry, including *Victorian Women Poets: Writing Against the Heart* (1992), *On Form: Poetry, Aestheticism, and the Legacy of a Word* (2007) and *Voyages over Voices: Critical Essays on Anne Stevenson* (2011). In addition she has published four volumes of poetry: *A Cold Spell* (2000), *Sea Level* (2007), *The Messages* (2012) and, most recently, *Spills* (2016) – a collection of memoirs, stories, translations and poems. She was elected Senior Research Fellow at Trinity in 2006.

She begins some recollections of her time at Trinity thus: 'I've been addressed as all sorts in my time, but only in Boulder, Colorado, and at Trinity, Cambridge have I been addressed as "Ma'm". It has a lovely old-world ring, apparently unconnected with any title or status. "Ma'm!", one of the Trinity porters called after me one day, soon after my arrival, as I walked to the Wren Library through Nevile's Court. "Fellows are *allowed* to walk on the lawn!" Walking on the lawn doesn't come naturally – it seems bad for the grass and bad for my shoes – but I was tickled to remember a less hospitable reaction to Virginia Woolf, who was unceremoniously shooed off a college lawn back in the 1920s. Since then women, and women Fellows, have come to Trinity – and have had to learn rules often as ancient as the college, and sometimes as unpredictably strange.'

Of her early days at Trinity, she recalls, first, 'the magic-carpet spread of crocuses on the Backs in February-March – a sight the late Anne Barton used to ask about every spring, when unable to go out to see them for herself'. Her elegy for Anne, 'Crocus', celebrates these particular elysian fields. Secondly, 'the flowering of the lime trees down the avenue, when on warm spring days you hear that soft machinery of bees over your head – Tennyson's "innumerable bees" still "murmuring"'. Thirdly, 'the sound of the chapel choir singing at evensong – George Herbert, gazing down from the stained glass windows at the congregation below, and outside, in winter, the mist drawing veils over Great Court and the fountain hanging in icicles, like points of stopped time'. Several poems in this collection, including her own sonnet on a sculpture by Maggi Hambling, '"Aftermath: Parasite"', echo Herbert's poem

'Prayer'. Fourthly, more darkly, there is her memory of 'a very clever postdoctoral student, for whom life seemed too hard to bear, and whose death during my first months at Trinity is recalled in my elegiac poem 'Crack-Willow' (about the fallen, split, re-rooting willows on Lammas Land), with its epigraph from Dante's wood of the suicides'. And fifthly, she recalls, 'always, beyond all these local sights and sounds, the flats of land and depths of sky that make up the Fens of East Anglia, and give Cambridge that feel of always going out, beyond its own privileged halls and quirky traditions, to a world beyond'.

Crack-Willow

Non fronda verde, ma di color fosco;
non rami schietti, ma nodosi e involti...   DANTE

[No green frond, but dusky coloured;
no clear cut branches, but knotty and involved...]

It is the look of muteness that cries out –
bare trunks with all their willow-pattern gone,
anatomies of trees, stripped to the bone.

So Dante asked, skirting the suicides,
how souls get cramped into these knotty types?
On Lammas Land crack-willow splits its sides.

These broken shapes have lost the power to speak.
Their summer eloquence, that whispery blur,
is all club-fists and withered musculature,

stranded, beached, in light too clean to hide,
a wickerwork long ditched and pared and dry.
Is this the last imagination of a cry?

On Lammas Land crack-willow stops my tongue.
These botched hulks rot, a warning sign,
grounded stumps nuzzling the fen's damp groin

as if they'd suck the land again for life,
rooting in ancient cuts and leams and lodes
for sap to rise into their arms once more.

I'm cold as hell and lost for words to say.
I'd snap a twig to hear his voice retort.
The winter sky has nothing to report.

Crack-willow, break your back and crack your case,
knuckle into the fen, dig in, die down.
You'll fetch again in whispers. He'll not respond.

Library

and the innocent wood lifts line-long with its leaves and libraries.   LES MURRAY

Bone-set, head-strong, I wonder at trees
(a thought spreads out, branching from seed),

how year after year they stand to hear
nothing but air and necessary weather,

sturdy patients of the passing sky,
pilots, taking the wind for a ride.

They're lynch-pins, joins between ether and grit,
fastenings locked to the edge of things,

forks of attention, each to itself
a mirror-image irreversibly set

wherever the earth settles its level,
and skies open, forever vertical.

My small bones knock on tables, shelves –
soft tymps, sly hints, like hearing self's

shut spirit rap on this and that,
cold calls within. Soon I'm tracked

to the library's hall, lifting a book,
looking to know (thin slices of wood)

how the folded time of a mind unfolds
word by word, tone by tone.

So I, in my bones, wonder at trees
that inch invisibly along new lines

and stand their ground and seem at ease,
shadowed in their own shadowing,

yet rooting deeper than the mind might dig,
probing how near, how dark earth is.

And I, in my bones, articulately free,
(touching wood, imagining leaves)

stay to read – while far and wide,
largo assai, the weather of the sky

nourishes tap-roots, leaf-shoots, tree-rings,
growing like thoughts, heard like listenings.

Sluice

It's pitch and sudden in a brick siding.
Toadflax and stonecrop shiver in a draught –
precarious frills whiskering the brickwork,
tickling a shaft that dives to the dark

where an old cellar-smell wells up from a drain,
where walls contain the whisk and tarry
of blacker water, and a gate regulates
its Stygian takings, drop by drop.

We stop to watch a swallow draw
wish-lists of hills on the fossed flats,
where stacked mops of reed-mace make
populous outcrops, heads above us.

Below, a sluice-grid monitors the flow.
Water queues in straight dug channels,
where all its leafy detritus scums
in unmoved pools, in pausing stills –

till quick and under, a black coil of wet
sucks through the fipple of a blade.
We watch the runaway water swell
in undercurrents to the shining levels.

Crocus

i.m. Anne Barton, Trinity College

l'animo nostro informe... come un croco...   MONTALE

[our formless spirit... like a crocus...]

From Hebrew, *Karkom*, Arabic, *Kurkum* –
once, she asked me: are the crocuses out?
Come spring, who'll walk that terrestrial ground?

Night after night her high lit windows
signed the passing weather of the sky.
Now they're dark, heights clarify.

The scholar's gain and loss contend
beyond the Court's palaestra of lawn,
through windy arches where the river bends.

Christopher Wren or Christopher Robin –
will some bird carry us over the Cam
to the crocus fields, to see them again?

It's late. I plant six bulbs in a ring.
My soil's small-holding holds them in
and makes a handsel, though it weighs deadweights.

Sicilian Road

An open runway tacks and plays for time.
Its cursive outline coasts, then loops and veers
across the valley bottom, changing its mind,
turning aside from ease – there are heights to climb.

The hills above are black and secretive.
The road unravels a spoor, dangles a trail,
then takes the ground in its stride and picks, at last,
a path that starts to climb, barely at first,

rising on each stepped foot, aloof and clear
above this shaky land that cracks and gapes –
like something traced, freehand, above the facts,
a phrase spun out of air, and fixed in place.

Imagine a river on stilts, bird-flight on steps,
a flow expressed in the poised footwork of a dance,
a flourish made by a fool who bows to a king,
mocking the grandeur there, yet gracing him.

It runs far up into dark primitive hills –
from here, a skater's turn, a rope to the winds.
Imagine a wavelength braced, pinned on its way,
as if you dreamed a tune, and could make it stay.

Even-Song

that roar which lies on the other side of silence.   GEORGE ELIOT

Something wants in.
Who'll mourn by halves
the vacuum quiet
of a slew of stars
and the moon's thin
shifting anchor
crux and mover
fascinator.

Out in the woods
is owlscope's scare
(you don't look there).
How would stars sound
if you could hear?
From old provençale
(call it a prayer)
le gai saber.[91]

We belong in the calends
of accountable days.
Our currency's air.
Its obstacle carries
breakthrough soundwaves.
(My love in the desert
of a fatal regret
turns blind and deaf.)

Yet something wants in.
A moth, is it?
flutter-tonguing the pane
the dead still beckoning.
We're bound to this
perpetual audition
this second-hearing
of a silent thing.

Now mourn by halves.
A slow coronach
through darkened glass
sings the after-
silence that must start.
Like roaring starlight
(unimaginable din)…
something wants in.

'Aftermath: Parasite'⁹²

for Maggi Hambling

What's this? War work? So call it 'Aftermath'.
All flesh is grass. The second mowing's art.

A broken torso strung to its carrying cross,
wood-nymph or totem, curious nubby boss,

stickler, unsightly gobbet, raw impress,
a newborn fledgling set to fly the nest,

a touching kiss in two-step, *pas de deux*,
meat-hook or metastasis, *faute de mieux*,

the stuff of life, parasite or specimen case,
the heart itself coupled to heights and base,

an instrument fine-strung from root-stock wood,
accord and touch, a sound not understood:

this human foreign body flush on its log,
a stranger metaphored, the finger of God.

JAMES HARPUR
1956–

James Harpur has published five volumes of poetry: *A Vision of Comets* (1993), *The Monk's Dream* (1996), *Oracle Bones* (2001), *The Dark Age* (2007), which won the Michael Hartnett Award and, most recently, *Angels and Harvesters* (2012). He has worked as an editor, adjudicator, translator, teacher of English and workshop facilitator. He has also enjoyed writing residencies in Monaco, Cork and Exeter Cathedral.

James came to Trinity in 1976 to read classics, his 'brain', he says, 'pickled with Jebb and Jowett and my body encased with a tweed jacket'. He soon changed to English literature – 'indecently soon' – and recounts, 'my head now buzzed with Hughes and Larkin, and my body sported a fine pair of trendy dungarees'. He picks out 'the world of Gawain, Yeats's *Vision*, and Eliot's *Four Quartets*' as a great influence in his first year. He also wrote a dissertation on Ted Hughes's *Crow* that delved 'into shamanism and Jung'. 'Ted was an early model of what a poet might be', he writes: 'I still remember the frisson of seeing him read in a small Cambridge art gallery: it was wintry, the audience was anxious because Ted was late (he had already postponed the reading from the previous week because of snow drifts in Devon)... then Old Crow appeared with a bevy of fur-clad females, and seemed to fill the room.'

In his time at Trinity – which he remembers as having 'the atmosphere of a place of infinite possibilities and inducements to experiment with ideas and words' – he wrote two plays for the Dryden Society: the first, a one-act play about computer dating and fate, the second about an adulterous classics don (containing 'a bravura performance by a young Stephen Fry'). For a while he saw himself becoming a dramatist; but once he submitted an entry for the Powell Prize for poetry – and won first equal – he didn't look back. 'There may have been only two entries', he jokes humbly, 'but it was enough to make me fantasise about life after Trinity and living in a remote place and scribbling away'. It was a fellow student who set this 'pipe-dream' on the path to fruition, suggesting he put James in touch with his father, who was in the business of teaching English as a foreign language. 'Within four weeks', he recalls, 'I was stepping off the plane at Herakleion, Crete, and spent a glorious year of teaching, thinking, and writing poetry. It set me on the course I have followed ever since'.

Cranborne Woods (17 May, 1994)

for my mother

We stopped the car, ducked below the fence
Felt time unravelling in a revelation
The seconds fall and scatter into thousands

Of tiny saints, a reborn multitude
Flowing past the trees, through pools of sun,
Each earthly form a spirit flame, pure blue.

They watched us drift among them, large as gods,
As if we'd come as part of their parousia
To stay with them forever in these woods.

As time grew darker we slipped away like ghosts
And slowly drove... towards your death next May
When once again I saw the risen host

Could watch you walking weightlessly among
The welcomers, the gently swaying throng.

The White Silhouette

for John F. Deane

There went a whisper round the decks one morning, 'We have a mysterious passenger on board'... Often I thought of that rumour after we reached Jerusalem... When I saw the man all in white by the Golden Gate carrying in all weathers his lighted lamp, I always thought, 'There is a mysterious pilgrim in Jerusalem.'
STEPHEN GRAHAM, from *With the Russian Pilgrims to Jerusalem* (1913)

I thought we would meet in a holy place
Like the church in the hamlet of Bishopstone
Empty on a Wiltshire summer's day
The trees full of rooks and hung in green
And the stream in the meadows a rush
Of darkling silver beneath the bridge
Where I saw my first kingfisher flash
Its needle, leaving its turquoise stitch
In my memory; and I would sit
In the church and close my eyes
And wait in vain for something to ignite
And wonder whether this was my life
Wasting away in my mother's home.
Sometimes I'd bring Herbert's Temple
And read the quiet order of his poems
And picture him, as once he was glimpsed,
Hugging the floor in his church at Bemerton
Asking love to bid him welcome.
I sat with an upright praying disposition
Preoccupied in self-combing
Too callow and spiritually impatient
To notice if you had slipped in
As a tourist to inspect the choir or font
And buy a picture postcard and sign
The book with 'lovely atmosphere';
Or as a walker taking refuge from rain
Or a woman primping flowers by the altar.

Or somewhere like the island of Patmos
Out of season and the tourist flow,
The sea leeching blue from the skies.
In the cave of St John, pointillist gold

On tips of candles and highlights of icons,
You might have visited that day in September
When I was there, absorbing the coolness,
Imagining John on the Day of the Lord
Prostrate on the ground as if before a throne
And you not dressed in a 'robe and gold sash'
Nor with hair 'as white as wool or snow'
But as a pilgrim with camera and rucksack
Respectful, curious, guide-book in hand
Appreciating the grain of raw stone
Catching my eye and pausing for a second
As if I were a schoolfriend from years ago.
I never saw you, if you were there,
For I was too blinded by the new Jerusalem
Flashing out jasper, topaz, sapphire
Descending from heaven like a huge regal crown.

Or somewhere like Holycross in Tipperary,
The abbey at the meeting of road and river,
You might have stopped to break a journey
As I often do, and seen me there in the nave
Ambling down the sloping floor
Towards the relic-splinter of the Cross
Or sitting outside on the banks of the Suir
On a bench on a swathe of tended grass
Perhaps that day when, heading north,
I paused by the car park to watch
A bride, fragile, and frozen by the door
Her bridesmaids huddled in the cold of March
Waiting and waiting to make her entrance
Into the sudden shine of turning faces
Like a swan gliding in its snowdress
From an arch of the bridge in a state of grace.
I was too mesmerised by her destiny
To see you start your car, drive off,
And raise your hand as you passed me by
On the way to Cashel, Fermoy and the south.

But there was that time I was so certain
That I had finally found you;
Sick at home, I turned to meditation
And prayer to overcome self-pity

For weeks accumulating quietude
Till that morning when seconds were emptied out
My thoughts cleansed, my self destroyed
Within an uncanny infusing light
That seemed to deepen and unfold
More layers of radiance and lay me wide open
So you could cross the threshold
Or I could cross, at any moment.
But I closed the door of my heart, afraid,
Who knows, that I might have met you
Afraid I would pass to the other side
And never return to all that I knew;
I thought I could always re-open myself
And greet you properly, well prepared.
I never did. I feared that sudden shift
Into the zone of timelessness; too scared
I looked for you in public, for safety,
I kneeled in churches, gave the sign
Of peace in St James's Piccadilly,
I recited prayers, took bread and wine
And I concentrated so hard, but failed
To believe they were your blood and body;
I heard staccato prayers, like nails
Banged in, as if to board up windows.

Sometimes I'd sense you as a glimmer
As in that dream I once had out of the blue
When you stood at night on a Greek island shore;
Your face was hidden, but it was you;
The stars pinned in place the layers of darkness
Then came the comets, perhaps a dozen,
Their tails fanned out with diminishing sparks;
Slowly they twisted and turned – your hands
Moving in concert, as if you were guiding them,
As if they were on strings, like Chinese kites.
The comets slowed and stopped, and changed
Into letters of Hebrew, emblazoning the night.
And I knew if I could grasp those words,
Your silent message across the stars,
I'd know my destiny on earth.
Instead I woke, as puzzled as Belshazzar.

I do not search for you any more
I don't know whom to seek, or where;
Too weary, disillusioned, I'm not sure
What I think or if I really care
That much; my last hope – that my resignation
Might be a sign of the Via Negativa,
A stage of my self-abnegation –
That hope prevents the thing it hopes for.

And yet

I still write to you, poem after poem,
Trying to shape the perfect pattern
Of words and the mystery of their rhythm,
An earthly music audible in heaven –
Each poem is a coloured flare
A distress signal, an outflowing
Of myself, a camouflaged prayer
Dispatched towards the Cloud of Unknowing
And all I have to do is stay
Where I am, ready to be rescued
Not move, speak or think but wait
For the brightening of the Cloud
For your white silhouette to break
Free from it and come nearer, nearer,
Till I see your essence and I can ask
Where in the world you were
Throughout my days – and only then
Will I grasp why I never found you
Because you were too close to home
Because I thought I'd have to die
To see you there, right there, removing
The lineaments of your disguise –
My careworn wrinkled skin
My jaded incarnation of your eyes –
My face becoming your face
My eyes your eyes
I   you   us   I you us
Iesus.

BEN OKRI

1959–

Ben Okri has published more than ten novels, including *Flowers and Shadows* (1980), *Infinite Riches* (1998) and *The Famished Road* (1991), this last being awarded the Booker Prize, as well as three volumes of short stories and three of essays. In addition he has published three volumes of poetry: *An African Elegy* (1992), *Mental Fight* (1999) and *Wild* (2012). He has been the recipient of the Commonwealth Writers Prize, the Aga Khan Prize for Fiction, the Premio Palmi, the Guardian Fiction Prize, and has received honorary doctorates from the Universities of Westminster, Essex, Exeter, SOAS and Bedfordshire. In 2001 he was awarded an OBE. He came to Trinity as a Fellow Commoner in Creative Arts in 1991.

'It felt like a second youth being at Trinity', Ben remembers; 'an unimaginable amount of energy and exploration had gone into the writing of *The Famished Road*, and I felt drained and empty… In the midst of these pressures, the Trinity Fellowship was a godsend. In a way the years at Trinity were among the happiest of my life.' He especially loved High Table, 'with its intellectual conversation and excellent food and wines', and the post-dinner haunt of the upstairs Combination Room 'where we retired for further intellectual badinage'. At one particular dinner-time conversation he remembers speaking at length about Homer: 'I was listened to politely, and then it was quietly suggested to me that I have another look at Virgil. I did, and this began a new Virgilian phase that lasted many years. That is what I loved about Trinity: the casual illumination.'

In addition to writing short stories, essays and poems, including 'half poems on the back of High Table menus', he gave workshops and readings, wrote a secular sermon for the chapel, and composed a poem about Isaac Newton 'which was set to music by the late Richard Marlow as part of a splendid commemoration feast'. But there was also time for quiet: 'I went to the gardens every evening after the Combination Room. At night I had it all to myself. To sit on a bench, invaded by the night fragrance of flowers, was to be borne into Arcadia.'

But he also recalls less pleasant aspects of his time. 'There were things I saw which still shock… Sometimes I glimpsed frozen arrogance, other times a coldness in the heart, and occasionally it occurred to me that a few of the Fellows could do with a pungent dose of ordinary life. It was an unreal world there, and it needs to be. I understand that now. But it also needs to change. The two years of semi-sequestration were just what I needed. But the years went by very quickly. Before I knew it they were seeking for my successor. Before I knew it I was in a van, with all my Cambridge belongings, departing from that spiked paradise in the middle of the night.'

An Undeserved Sweetness

After the wind lifts the beggar
From his bed of trash
And blows him to the empty pubs
At the road's end
There exists only the silence
Of the world before dawn
And the solitude of trees.

Handel on the set mysteriously
Recalls to me the long
Hot nights of childhood spent
In malarial slums
In the midst of potent shrines
At the edge of great seas.
Dreams of the past sing
With voices of the future.

And now the world is assaulted
With a sweetness it doesn't deserve
Flowers sing with the voices of absent bees
The air swells with the vibrant
Solitude of trees who nightly
Whisper of re-invading the world.

But the night bends the trees
Into my dreams
And the stars fall with their fruits
Into my lonely world burnt hands.

Migrations

The world is a cauldron
In which we are mixed.
Time is an illusion.
No condition is fixed.

And so in our millions
We walk or swim or break
Across boundaries, fleeing
Wars, evils and hunger to make

A new home in what seems
A void, an empty space,
Without our histories,
Or tales of our race.

But about us scream the inhabitants
Who've never known barren
Lands, or tyranny, or such pain
That pushes us from the warren

Of cruel histories into lands
Whose earth may not receive
Us. But we're like pollen.
We're fertile, and we grieve.

Heraclitus' Golden River

1

'Change is good, but no change
Is better.' The words rang
Through the great hall
As they have resounded
Silently through bygone ages.

The air is dryer where no change
Is better. Old ways kept
Old, protected from the devils
At the gate, stiffen
The mind's luminous dance.
Change is a god that Heraclitus saw
In the ancient river.

And as we keep
Things the same, the river
Works beneath us,
The god works ironies
On our lives. The river runs;
Fields unfurl strange
New mushrooms; libraries yield
New books in the charged
Margins of the old.
And reason, trapped in iron philosophies,
Turns on itself, and prowls
The diminished boundaries
Of a shrinking world,
Shrinking because of the horror
Of the devils at the gates.

Poets pray to the goddess of surprise:
Love is seduced by change,
Itself unchanging. Time,
Serene, remains indifferent
To our iron will, our willed philosophies.
The world grows or shrinks of its own
Necessity, its own vision.
The river makes all things
Dance to a music they
Never understood at the time.

2

The giants who built walls
Meant to be proof against
Time and the desert ravages
Found in their sleep
That the walls had become
Change, had moved, had dissolved;
Or worse, that the feared things
Had seeped in underfoot,
Or through the air;
Or changed the frontiers
Of their rigid dialogue.

Walls invite invasion.
Walls end up trapping within the demons
Meant to be kept out; for
The demons merely turn into
The giants, grow in them,
Like a silent cancer.

Oases attract the eyes of the hungry.
Protected places, illuminated
By fame, attract the rage
Of the unlucky, the unfortunate,
The dispossessed, and all those
Shut out in the outer
Darknesses of our age.

All around, leonids, planets,
Stars are whirling.
The cosmos shrinks and grows,
It dreams and flows
Beneath the immutable spell of change.
All around lives collapse, empires
Quietly fall and cave in from
Natural exhaustion; dynasties
Give up the ghost of ambition,
Continents drift apart,
And wars eat up fathers and frail sisters,
And roads break out
Into unhallowed speech.

It is natural to want calm places
Where stillness grows,
It's natural to want
Virgil's spreading beeches.

But the river flows, and so must we.
Change is the happy god Heraclitus
Glimpsed in the golden river.
Spread illumination through this darkening world,
Spread illumination through this darkening world.
No change is good; dancing
Gracefully with change is better.

[Angled willows of the river]

Angled willows of the river
Dripping their leaves
Into the shallow water.

Frosted evergreens
Round the monumental library
Blunting its power,
Its proud disdain.

Nostalgia of bridges
Over glittering brown waters.

The clear places
Winter creates
Between windowpane spaces
Of the trees.

Shimmering distances
Weaving a fraternity
Among spires.
A royalty of crests.

Remoulding the ruins
Of antiquity
To a receding dream
And river.

High Table
November 1992

SOPHIE HANNAH
1971–

Sophie Hannah is an internationally best-selling crime writer and poet. Her first psychological thriller, *Little Face*, was published in 2006, and her thirteenth, *The Narrow Bed*, in 2016. In 2013, her novel *The Carrier* won Crime Thriller of the Year at the Specsavers National Book Awards UK. With the approval of Agatha Christie's estate, she has written two novels featuring the detective Hercule Poirot: *The Monogram Murders* (2014) and *Closed Casket* (2016). In addition to verse translations of Tove Janssen, she has published several volumes of poetry, including *The Hero and the Girl Next Door* (1995), *Hotels like Houses* (1996), *Leaving and Leaving You* (1999), *First of the Last Chances* (2003), *Pessimism for Beginners* (2007) and, most recently, *Marrying the Ugly Millionaire* (2015). She has also published three other novels and three collections of short stories, *The Fantastic Book of Everybody's Secrets* (2008), *Something Untoward: Six Tales of Domestic Terror* (2012) and *The Visitors Book* (2015). She was Fellow Commoner in Creative Arts at Trinity between 1997 and 1999.

She describes her time at the College as 'utter bliss', 'one of the best experiences of my entire life'. She continues: 'It gave me the confidence to pursue my writing and think of myself as a proper writer (rather than as a secretary who skived off work to write poems, which was my official job title before Trinity rescued me!)'. Her praise for Trinity is effusive: 'I am still waiting to be invited onto Radio Four's *Desert Island Discs*, so that I can name Trinity College, Cambridge as the one luxury I would take with me to the desert island.'

After her Fellowship ended, Sophie moved to Yorkshire, but 'always hoped to move back to Cambridge, which, after my Trinity experience, was my favourite place in the world and the place where I had been happiest'. In 2010 she bought a house in Cambridge city centre, not before someone had made a comment to her, 'in an attempt to put me off Cambridge, about how it was not ideal because everyone was too clever; but I love being surrounded by very clever people!' Her poem, 'Unbalanced', takes this comment as its starting point.

Long For This World

I settle for less than snow,
try to go gracefully like seasons go

which will regain their ground –
ditch, hill and field – when a new year comes round.

Now I know everything:
how winter leaves without resenting spring,

lives in a safe time frame,
gives up so much but knows he can reclaim

all titles that are his,
fall out for months and still be what he is.

I settle for less than snow:
high only once, then no way up from low,

then to be swept from drives.
Ten words I throw into your changing lives

fly like ten snowballs hurled:
I hope to be, and will, long for this world.

The Cancellation

On the day of the cancellation
The librarian phoned at two.
My reading at Swillingcote Youth Club
Had regrettably fallen through.

The members of Swillingcote Youth Club
Had just done their GCSES
And demanded a rave, not poems,
Before they began their degrees.

Since this happened at such short notice
They would still have to pay my fee.
I parked in the nearest lay-by
And let out a loud yippee.

The librarian put the phone down
And muttered, 'Oh, thank the Lord!'
She was fed up of chaperoning
While the touring poet toured.

The girl from the local bookshop
Who'd been told to provide a stall
But who knew that the youth club members
Would buy no books at all

Expressed with a wild gyration
Her joy at a late reprieve,
And Andy, the youth club leader,
And the youth arts worker, Steve,

Both cheered as one does when granted
The gift of eternal life.
Each felt like God's chosen person
As he skipped back home to his wife.

It occurred to me some time later
That such bliss, such immense content
Needn't always be left to fortune,
Could in fact be a planned event.

What ballet or play or reading,
What movie creates a buzz
Or boosts the morale of the nation
As a cancellation does?

No play, is the simple answer.
No film that was ever shown.
I submit that the cancellation
Is an art form all of its own.
To give back to a frantic public
Some hours they were sure they'd lose
Might well be my new vocation.
I anticipate great reviews.

From now on, with verve and gusto,
I'll agree to a month-long tour.
Call now if you'd like to book me
For three hundred pounds or more.

Unbalanced

Cambridge has a very unbalanced demographic – there's an unnaturally high concentration of intelligent people.

There is a lot that's wrong with Cambridge, yes:
Houses are too expensive and too thin,
The Clifton Leisure Park is nothing less
than standing proof that a grave mortal sin
can be committed by a multiscreen
cinema allied with a Travelodge.
A Cambridge street is no idyllic scene –
often, on King's Parade, I have to dodge
tourists who seek to bash me in the face
with their huge cameras. I contain my rage,
remind myself that I don't own the place –
I must play nice and share my Chronophage,[93]
and thank my stars. Hemmed in by Hills Road traffic,
I savour the unbalanced demographic.

The Storming

There are differences, one assumes,
between us and the people we know who storm out of rooms,

sometimes crying, but not every time;
sometimes muttering, sometimes an angry marching mime

is their exit mode. Where do they go,
all those people who storm out of rooms? Will we ever know?

Are there sandwiches there, and a flask
of hot tea? We won't find out if we never ask.

Once they've fled the provoking scene,
do they all get together somewhere? Do they reconvene

in a basement, an attic, a flat?
Do they also reserve the right to storm out of that,

and if so, do they take turns to storm
or link arms and desert *en masse* in a furious swarm,

leaving nobody in their wake?
Would there be any point in the storming, for nobody's sake?

There are differences, one fears,
between us and the people who storm out of rooms in tears,

as if, having ruined it all,
in the snug, they imagine they'll be better off in the hall,

and that anyone left in a chair
automatically gets to be wrong and to blame and unfair,

unaware of how bad stormers feel,
and quite lacking in feelings themselves. That is part of the deal.

Notice how I don't leap to my feet,
how I nestle in cushions and curl myself into my seat.

Leave at once for the moral high ground.
I'll stay here by the fire, mocking storms and just lounging around.

Did You Put on a Shirt?

Author's Note: In November 2014, scientist Matt Taylor, part of a team of scientists that
successfully landed a probe on a comet, was publicly shamed online for wearing a shirt with a
comic strip-style design of scantily-clad women. In June 2015, Nobel-prize-winner
Sir Tim Hunt received a similarly severe public shaming after he was reported to have made
a sexist joke at a conference. It was later established that Sir Tim had been comprehensively
misunderstood and misrepresented. His joke was very much pro-women and at
his own expense.

I blogged about Tim Hunt again.
I argued hard and long,
but other women, other men,
might also need a strong
defence, and so I'm asking folks
in Harlem, Hull, Hong Kong –
have you told any harmless jokes?
Have you done nothing wrong?

Then let me leap to your defence!
Did you put on a shirt
you liked (which would make perfect sense)?
Did nobody get hurt?
Did you walk past an antelope
and grin in mild surprise,
not smack it with a stethoscope
nor rub salt in its eyes?

And was your grin then misconstrued
as cause for great alarm,
and did the most enormous feud
spring from the lack of harm
you did? Have you been made to feel
that now you don't belong?
I'm not surprised. The danger's real
if you do nothing wrong.

Have you neglected, all these years,
to learn to play Mahjong?
I warn you – that will end in tears.
Did you once sing the song
Come on Eileen? Or eat pea soup?
Or watch the film *King Kong*?
Then welcome to that hated group:
those who did nothing wrong.

Smugly, you think, 'I won't be next.
I steal and cheat and lie.'
Just wait, though, till you send a text
saying, 'No milk – please buy'.
That's when the haters will descend.
Trust me, it won't be long.
I urge you: save yourself, my friend:
NEVER do nothing wrong.

SEAN BORODALE
1973–

Sean Borodale has published three volumes of poetry: *Notes for an Atlas* (2007), *Bee Journal* (2012), later issued as a Vintage Classic, and *Human Work* (2015). He has also written a radio poem, *Mighty Beast*, which won a Radio Academy Gold Award. He studied and then taught for a time at the Slade School of Fine Arts, and has had residencies at the Miró Foundation in Mallorca, the Rijksakademie van Beeldende Kunsten in Amsterdam, the Wordsworth Trust in Grasmere, Bluecoat in Liverpool, and Trinity College, Dublin. He was appointed Fellow in Creative Arts at Trinity (Cambridge) in 2013.

Sean reflects on the 'extraordinary qualities of freedom' that Trinity offered him, 'to read expansively, to write without limits, to ask questions, to spend protracted, undisturbed time articulating ideas or developing manifestos around creative work'. It was a productive period in which he amassed a great body of notes and thoughts to go on with. He was struck by the college bells and their peculiar rhythms that 'gave days a time-pattern that at first seemed alien. What at first felt like imposition on pure, unsaturated air turned slowly into almost astrological configurations of the intervals of day'. Further vivid impressions include the darkness of winter, of breakfast 'in the gloom and clatter of the hall', of dinner 'among others reduced to darkness beyond the halo of a guttering candle', of 'black gowns flapping around figures hurrying across a snow-covered Great Court', of 'white swans gliding on black water beyond the Wren library', and of 'the red and bloody shape of an eclipsed moon above the court in which Newton measured the speed of sound'. Other poets were never far to find. A porter from Northern Ireland in Great Court read to him a poem by Paul Muldoon about the Belfast ship-yards. He haunted places in Cambridge where other writers had lived and passed through: Ted Hughes, Sylvia Plath, Virginia Woolf, Tennyson, Wordsworth, Coleridge, Wittgenstein. After much searching he at last found Wittgenstein's grave 'in a tangled weed-strewn churchyard – a place not unlike his handwriting'. He remembers the 'brilliant students' who ventured into his poetry workshop and finally, 'the chaos across my desk, maybe a hundred books out on loan from the college library at once'.

2nd May

The North Wind leans against your house
containing a mind of its own again;
its song, its bursts of breath are wilful cold reminders
of the dangerous airs.

Slowly you are tuning yourselves
into the small misheard scales, into a purpose.

A bee, a tine being struck was out:
sound like a rooting of thin flash
in liquid form poured from a bucket the size of an adult
tooth.
Magnet of listening, I to hear it
turned the pole of my head.

The hive door is there,
the landing board's grey slope of bleached wood.

One worker there,
banded as piano wire, freakish hands strumming.

Those *are* wings.
I was out, all my apertures very unfrightened.
Calm holes in my head heard the exact creak
of breaking nettles across the buzz.

23rd July: Noise & Waste

Today the hive
is trying out *its* harmonics,

a weepy low fugue I think to burning sun.
The loss of flowers is overwhelming:

dry sheaths and packets
stapled onto brown skulls.

The nagging air swings gibbets of drought.
Some clumps of the world are barred.
The dump stinks in flowerbeds, weedbeds,
and the river's clogged two miles of hemlock rots.

Mangled carapaces fall out of air
skinny in their little traps of make-up.

A chimera of scrap parts.
Grass-blade emerald twisted.
Glitter paste of bumps & grazes.
The air's ears are traumatised,

and on the flames of the hour
just a whiff of decline,
just a whiff more.

The white dry heat jangles;
it's like a kiln is shaking at the corners.

Tomorrow,
must search the dawn's damp ash
for broken mirrors.

7th August: Property

A frame of honeycomb is in the kitchen:
just a candle, vigil, out of respect.
It's like a body I visit
laid on the table's midnight.

The smell is first; under its pinewood resin
the smell of light is in a miracle:
I – criminal – touch

its tear-easy skin of skeletal reef.
(Best use of space for minimal effort.)
No waste for them, just work,
and days of nectar flow are nearing end.

Flowers are here, springs of them,
wells and weightless drops of briefest sex;
a wax shroud turned down at its corners;
a dead skin most beautifully scented,
drawn out of dark.

When touched,
observe the way
that light swells in the crack
and golden-eyes.

But it is cold,
I paid for it with hooks across my flesh.

Apple Jelly (On-going)

I was asking, *is a body ever at peace?*

Like, how does it look to be stewed
until a skin develops an absence of flesh?
Pressed through the gauze of a wire mesh,
stripped of seed, boiled old with sugar
[*granulated, refined: do not burn*];

like, how does it look
whose creepy lack of minerals sets it searching:
gel-coloured torchlight, *grandmother sweets.*
Whatever fruit is, pressing its fidget to set-point;
ingredient of pectin working.

(Grim tales of utterly deformed woods
derange on the scum.)

Only the exosphere of a garden,
bubbling up time: the alembic miracle of the kitchen.

Test on a cold spoon the hot, sly, wild juice
snared in the syrup.

I have only this medium of result:
stickier on my hands, weirdly comforting.

It boils on, it lifts up and down on the puckering distress,
signals what kind of interrogation this is.

Washing-Up

I was washing up, when
an owl flew to the window
(this kitchen window)

and grew the splay of its fan;
a pale halo of wingspan,
white and eerie; the traveller

or a similar apparition, caught partially;
I remember it all.

The hour grave; I lurked in the form
of what a human is, stooped over cleaning
utensils, disorder;

pressed to a mouse-fear at the back of me,
a tenure in doom; astonished at the pull
of this predator: every feather and claw,

the detailed grease-print
on the glass and my own, living, tensed light.

It has shaken off its own anatomy
into outer minutiae.

I thought, to get glass clean: vinegar.

I remember it all:
    it squeaked like shrews
being killed
as I polished the owl away.

And against my own reflection on the black, dark night,
I continued to scour
the film off crockery –
rinsing the suds,
perfecting the gleam.

Soil at Cockle's Field

What did I dig for, which are not the dreams I will get?
I am so cold I have to dig the sodden staining of a century,
and the black felt of twenty dialects
which are dead only in upper spaces. Here they still thrive;
small, congesting bodies in organic silt
many would have dredged for a second coming.
But this is England. I cannot adhere to the surface-country.
I ask for a way through the blacker cooling reaches of areas.
I will go dark with it, go in attempting illuminations
of another order, without geography; only the sticky-weight of oblivion,
or the tunnels of voles, streams, trickles, the blood-soak
I will drink when I am cold, without myself.
Will not feel the frost freezing my hair stiff
but be below
the frost's liturgy of scrap metal, its water-shrapnel.

I will loiter, nameless, waiting for the hole to absorb me. *Bury me* I say,
with my fish skeleton eyes, my wasting jaws, my cold patience
losing the battle. By the black pond beyond the pond edge,
where it is black, below the porous swarming
of matter, the frog's gelatinous clotting of eggs;
which is all an eye and another eye staring in. Where there is no light,
                                                                    lifeless,
into the hole I am about to enter; I said, *Here is a weight to keep*,
under dead leaf and root-shake and creature pausing,
like the mole, antisocial
inside the sinew of its machinery;
digging to depths under fur.
All is shallow, all is deep too.
Impossible to register what worms do under the footprint,
without digging up the long voices of them
casting dead miles into potent food;
the lines of them in the dark, tubular and single-minded.
All of them together, one writhing single mind of twisting multiplicity,
touching sides to mate.
A single worm-parent rope frayed to millions,
totally sensed, but blind;
blindly feeling along tunnels below horizons;
bleeding through patches of the soil's skull.

JACOB POLLEY
1975–

Jacob Polley has published four volumes of poetry, *The Brink* (2003), a Poetry Book Society Choice, *Little Gods* (2006), *The Havocs* (2012), which won the Geoffrey Faber Memorial Prize, and most recently, *Jackself* (2016), which won the T. S. Eliot Prize. He has also published a novel, *Talk of the Town* (2009), which won the Somerset Maugham Award, as well as film scripts, installation and musical pieces. He came to Trinity in 2005 as a Fellow Commoner in Creative Arts, from where he went on to become a lecturer at the Universities of St Andrews and then Newcastle.

Jacob recalls living on Green Street with his then partner, 'spending a lot of time looking down at the street from what I seem to remember was a third-floor window, watching people coming in and out of Heffers and the Slug and Lettuce'. He was also writing his novel, *Talk of the Town*, though he remembers that 'this involved a lot of not writing, and walking from Cambridge to Grantchester, thinking about writing. There were probably a lot of people doing the same as I was, I used to think, and there was succour in that'. 'For a lot of the time', he writes – in language that echoes the title of one of Ben Okri's poems selected here – 'I felt like an imposter, which seems only right and proper, as to feel anything otherwise – like I *deserved* these two years, gazing out of various windows, thinking about writing – would have made me a stranger to myself.'

He recalls meeting some 'extraordinary people' during his spell at Trinity, 'not least the members of the writing group I gathered about me, semi-informally, which was made up of some Trinity students, some students from other colleges, and some people from outside the University'. It is a group which, as several of the poets here testify, has continued to fuel aspiring poets in and around the College in recent years. Jacob ends his recollections by writing, 'I can't believe it's now over a decade since we parked up at the College and I wondered what on earth I was supposed to do as the Fellow Commoner. No one ever told me, of course, and I think I pretty much did whatever it was anyway…'

A Jar of Honey

You hold it like a lit bulb,
a pound of light,
and swivel the stunned glow
around the fat glass sides:

it's the sun, all flesh
and no bones
but for the floating
knuckle of honeycomb.

The Owls

I hear the owls in the dark yews
behind the house – children out late
or lost, their voices worn away.
They've forgotten their names and wait

to be called again by mothers
who miss them, so they might return
with fingers and human faces.
But their sadness, too, is long gone.

Their voices are as empty
and unlovable as glass
and no one calls into the trees.

Little gods, they've forsaken us
as we have them. They sit and cry,
glorified, and couldn't care less.

You

under the dripping trees, listening to the crows'
knackered songs while the estuary glints
in the winter light. You holding your mother's purse,
the woods bare, the fields dark, and on the hill
that shocked white house where you're no longer welcome.
You setting off, the collar of your brother's coat

pulled up to your chin and the back of your neck dripped down,
wondering about London, the Thames, Dover and boats.
The hedgerows are snagged with the rain that woke you
where you lay last night in a hayloft, dreaming of rats.
You walking wet-trousered, wet-socked towards town.
You scranning Rich Teas from your rucksack.

You avoiding main roads. You warming your hands on a cow.
You on the outskirts, an industrial estate
where the kerbs are high and the corrugated sheds
hum and grind as their arc-lit interiors swing.
You in a lorry, learning Spanish with the driver
from a Teach Yourself tape. Grey miles, grey thoughts:

the rockslides caught in metal nets,
the pine forests' green domes; bare earth and bridges:
the lumpy, guileless country.
You with your fingers in the payphones' coin-trays,
palming dust from under the fruit machines.
You eating piecrusts from the plates left out

in Little Chef, watching ravens tugging bin-bags.
You in the afternoon, in the South,
in a city made of billboards and roundabouts,
looking for somewhere to ask to be dropped.
You asleep in a church porch, asleep in a graveyard,
asleep in a garden, a greenhouse, a warehouse, a wardrobe.

You washing in the yellow-tiled bogs with liquid soap,
waiting round the back of Tesco's for them to throw out the loaves.
You robbed, you running, your long fingernails.
You in the library, reading *Which?*
You on the Underground, riding all the way round,
finding the shopping list tucked in her purse:

milk potatoes broccoli cheese cheese-spread peas margarine

Langley Lane

Stand up straight, my son. Don't slouch.
Mother, I'm not slouching.
There's nothing you need hide from me.
You know I don't like touching.

A mother must – it's in my hands
to touch what's mine so briefly,
to touch my son for one small proof
that he's still strong and loves me.

Mother, I wish you weren't at home
and I could sit in peace.
I'd hoped to meet the dark alone
and not to cause a fuss.

My son, I'm bound to love no less
the child who brings me pain.
My son, what spreads across your shirt?
You need not hide a stain.

What I hide won't be undone
and I'd not see your face
to spare myself the sight of one
whose grief is my disgrace.

Take a chair, my son, you're tired.
Drink a glass of milk.
You're up, you're down. Your brain's still soft.
Your adulthood half built.

You're pale, my son – you'll fade away:
    you need a bite to eat.
Once I was young and like you swayed
    unsteady on my feet –

Mother, soon I'll get my rest
    so while I can I'll stand.
My son, what's loose at your left wrist?
    What's spilling from your hand?

Mother, my hand is full of shame.
    It's pouring from my heart.
I've walked it in from Langley Lane
    where trouble's known to start.

If trouble starts, you've said to me
    just turn and walk away.
But Langley Lane's blind corner led
    to five who blocked my way.

You're on our turf, one said, and spat.
    The youngest-looking shoved
me first; I shoved him harder back.
    He punched me in the chest.

The leaves were still. The sun came out
    to scatter coins of light
and I saw gripped in his right fist
    a little silver spike.

A spike at which I stared, surprised –
    a bloody silver spike
at which he also stared, surprised,
    our two boys' looks alike.

The sun went in. A siren moaned.
    Clouds crawled across the blue.
They grabbed my phone. I started home –
    what else was there to do?

My son, you walked from Langley Lane?
I walked from Langley Lane.
I took small steps and often stopped
to breathe around the pain.

My son, you walked from Langley Lane.
I walked from Langley Lane.
I held myself to slow the stain
and walked from Langley Lane.

Peewit

a little one
    drab   barely skyborne, with nothing
of the gut-unravelling acumen
of the scavenger   this is Jackself
limping across marshland, making a decoy
of himself, piping up when the day goes dim
so close to the ground he's almost it

    small wonder Peewit
is the name the other boys have given him
    not Jackdaw, not Rook

        the gods of bracken and fly-tipped
black plastic sacks will expose themselves to the pilgrim
who has faith in the star
at the centre of the crab apple, in the ditchful
of frogspawn and the shed door
hinged with spiders' webs

    so it comes to pass
for Peewit, whippy stick in his right hand
    as he tramps the far-out lanes with those
who had diminished him,
a breeze
starts to ratch in the dust   the foxglove
jangles   his legs
buckle and he goes down, his eyes a white
flutter in his head

the boys circle him
where he fits,
grinding his teeth so hard they sing
     and when they heft him,
heavier than he should be,
his bird-soul batters
into him   they process so slowly the light's
all gone by halfway home
     when

Peewit's no longer between them   has flown
     and blank with terror
the boys go round and round
in the dark and cold and are not ever found

EMMA JONES
1977–

Emma Jones's first volume of poems, *The Striped World*, was published in 2009 and won the Forward Prize for Best First Collection as well as the Queensland Premier Literary Award. She has held residencies in Rome, Riga and at the Wordsworth Trust in Grasmere, and has been tutor in creative writing at Oxford. In 2011 she returned to Trinity to take up the post of Gould Lector in Writing, during which time she completed a libretto, *City Songs*, for music by the then Creative Arts Fellow in Composition, Ēriks Ešenvalds. She is now Lecturer at the University of St Andrew's.

Emma recalls her two years at the college: 'Trinity has always struck me as having a geometrical kind of beauty: Great Court's near-square, the precise lines of the mown lawns and the massive tended hedge in the Bowling Green. If the beauty of a mathematical proof lies in its elegant compressions, its sense of inevitability – a tendency it shares, the idea goes, with music and with poetry – then this seems a suitable beauty for what is, famously, a mathematicians' college, and also a college of poets.'

Her rooms were under the clock-tower, and she got to know its habits. 'There's the famous double chime, of course. But there are subtler, associated sounds: a kind of chirring on the stairs, machine-like and bird-like, and the cries and flights of the actual birds who congregate around and about the clock, pigeons mainly, but ravens too. One of the Fellows had figured out what it cost the clock in terms of annual time to have pigeons land on its enormous hands – several minutes a year, if it isn't corrected. So measures are taken against the birds: strategic wire, dummy ravens and, from time to time, the hawk man.'

A poem excerpted here tells of this hawk man. Emma recalls her first encounter with him, 'on a June afternoon when many of the students had gone and the buildings seemed sunk in their own rumi-nations. The air was stunned and summery. Crossing the court, I became aware of the sound of a sort of small, toy-like, infrequent and almost rustling bell. This, it turned out, was attached to the leg of a small brown-gold hawk sitting on the chapel roof. It looked dignified, even with its jester's get-up. From time to time the hawk would be summoned with a gesture or a whistle by a man in the court below, and would fly, activating that dreamy bell again, to a crenellated wall or to the top of the fountain, where again it would sit, impassive, occasionally shifting its wings. The man told me he and his hawk were a form of pest control: they kept away clock-bothering birds. He said he and his hawk were employed by hospitals, chicken runs, public parks. But it seemed to me so fitting to Trinity, this mix of grandeur and efficiency – this housekeeping-cum-falconry.'

Farming

The pearls were empire animals.
They'd been shucked from the heart of their grey mothers
which is why, so often, you'll find them
nestled at the neck and breast.
It stood to reason.
The sea was one long necklace,
and they often thought of that country.

Its customs waylaid them,
and it occupied their minds.
Nobody missed them.
The oysters felt nothing,
neither here nor there,
down on the farm and miles out to sea,
those swaying crops.

Rolled to create circumference.
Opened to accommodate
the small strange foreign irritant
that hones itself to a moon.
The oysters say
'it's a lulling stone, that outside heart
turned in, and beating.'

They knit their fields of nacre, and are quiet.
The clouds converge.
It's a sad constabulary,
the sky and the sea, and the boats.
Because piracy is common
the farmers carry guns. Does the sea
object, marshalling its edges?

Do the fish know
their glint, those inward birds
in the fields of the Pacific?
It's a singing bone,
the indivisible pearl.
It's a bright barred thing. And pearls
are empire animals. And poems are pearls.

Conversation

'Oh this and that. But for various reasons' –
(the season, and the change in season, the season of grief

and retrospection, the rooftop pulled from the childhood
house, and the internal doll in its stuck seat,

that is, the fictive soul in its brute cathedral, and because of memory,
maybe, and organs in niches, and the beat to things,

and the knowledge that the body is the soul and vice versa,
but that false distinctions are sometimes meaningful,

and that difference, all difference, is just distance, not a state,
not a nation, and because nothing *matters*, not really,

or everything does, I don't mind being an animal, at all,
because a sentient thing is nothing else, and because toward matter

I feel neither love nor hate but the kind of shuttered
Swiss neutrality a watch might feel for time

if it had an animal's sentiments, knowing itself a symbol
and function, knowing itself a tool, and because I feel

the dull culmination of various phenomena informing me
and am that culmination, I feel ill in some small way,

though not ill really, just idle, and I prefer, you see,
to keep an impassive inviolable pact with things that tick,

with solitary, shifted things, and because my life's approximate act
is the sister to some other life, with different tints, I carry

and nurse, my diffident twin, I'm often morose, and think
of those statues that lean above themselves in water,

those fountains, stone, with commemorative light,
with disfiguring winds, and because reflection is an end in itself

and because there's an end even to reflection, and an end to the eye,
that heated room, I prefer to keep my artifice and my arsenal

suspended, close; like an angled man; like the stationed sun;
and because matter ends, or I should say, matter turns to matter,

and my small inalienable witness to this is real, I can't pretend
to wish to be a rooted thing, full-grown, concerned

with practical matters, in a rooted world, and careful of borders,
when an ineradicable small portion glints, my mind, that alma mater,

and says, make your work your vicarage) – 'I put off going back'.

from *The Hawk Man*

I

The hawk man is in the court;
the hawk is on the chapel.
Around, the sourceless yellow light.

At first the hawk seems hobbled
by its bell. It doesn't fly
but sits and shifts its wings and legs.

Bird on the house of the son
and the father, inhabit
your wings the way the painting stands

in the house of the father.
As both an image and thing.
You needn't contradict yourself.

The hawk man's not your father.
But now, when he lifts his arm
and calls, that relative

sound is a thing and a kinship.
You come, and demonstrate
with open wings the wind's own shape.

II The Closeup

Here's the thing. The hawk and hawk
man courting. The staining saints.
The returned, reducible scene.

The hawk man is a local
hire from a nearby village,
a specialist in various

forms of what he likes to call
'pest control' but which retain
archaic names of: poisoning,

entrapment, etcetera,
just as he's a falconer
of sorts. His soft Hawaiian shirt

is a soughing doublet. Noon
and the sourceless light have made
him particular; his shadow

is a constant man come close;
it pools now at his feet. It comes
back to him the way the tutored hawk

comes back, the shadow, the bird;
noon too, and the palindromic
ease with which it dips and follows

back again, against itself,
ante and post, a double queen
wavering, on a playing card.

The garrisons of learning
reeled them in. Hawk and hawk
man, one tutored, one tutoring.

Viridian holiday
shirt, hawk man! deliver us
from ravens and profligate

doves, and the wasteful civic birds.

III   The Urban Field

is fleet and grained
and above the field three flotsam hawks
impel their bit of wind.

And alternate. In reticular
drifts, they till those gusts
that are their flock and their pasture.

They're triplicate: not of one mind.
Below them, the farmer,
or the farmer's man, flusters

the tractor. It's a green steed
in the standing sun. He wields it,
that laboured man, with a drubbing love.

Consider the field. The crimped
heft of the breached wheat
in the wake of the diligent cropper.

Consider the cropper. No,
consider its mechanical
sidekick, the man. The hawks do

consider him. They consider the man.
Birds, man, the shepherd wind,
rooted to the common grain.

The earth is particular,
in the solstice noon. Now and then
the vigilant, bored hawks stutter

and stop; staunch their drifts; suspend
and so compel themselves to
shutter the white wind, and beat,

and beat nowhere. It's a real point!
They're seeing things! The matter
below them, in the moving grain.

The hawks say: compel yourself.
Consider the wind, that harvest,
and the ape in its natural machine.

IV   The Scarecrow

And did the field mouse have a god?
And did the mouse intone
'the face of God! in the moving grain!'

Listen. The mammalian grist
in the subtle crop, when the shadow hangs,
the wing, machine and the man, that

afflatus in thrown clothes.

V   Hawk

The hawk man is in the court,
the court is in the chapel.
The field is in the court
and the hawk man's a hawk.
And the hawk is a shadow
and the shadow's fleet.
Every bird a paraclete.

REBECCA WATTS
1983–

Rebecca Watts' first collection, *The Met Office Advises Caution*, was published in 2016. She was an undergraduate at Trinity from 2001 to 2004, and explains: 'It had been my academic ambition to return to Trinity for a PhD on twentieth-century poetry, but as soon as I started I knew it wasn't right for me just then – I was too restless – and I left in 2008 to see what else I could do.' She moved to London and started an evening course at City University, where she began writing her own poems. It was an enthusiasm which led her to Grasmere, 'to work for the Wordsworth Trust as a museum intern in a thriving literary community'. There she attended workshops led by the then resident poet Emma Jones, and began writing regularly. She now works as a librarian at St John's College, Cambridge.

It is Jacob Polley that Rebecca credits with first introducing her to contemporary poetry. Of his collection *The Brink* she writes, 'its images and unpretentious language blew me away; it is still my go-to book when I want to be reminded what brilliant poems are like.' On returning to work at St John's College library, she jokes: 'I have not escaped Wordsworth.' She recalls of that time: 'By a stroke of luck, when my university email account was reactivated I was still on the Trinity Literary Society mailing list, from which I learned that Emma had also moved to Cambridge and was starting a workshop group there.' She attended these fortnightly sessions for two years under Emma, and then another two under her successor, Sean Borodale. 'My writing improved immeasurably thanks to the generous attention and encouragement I received', she recalls, estimating that about half the poems in her debut collection went through the Trinity Poetry Workshop.

She notes that her time at Trinity gave her direct material for poems on more than one occasion. 'Though I didn't care to know it at the time, the bat that flew in through the window of my room in 2003 would return seven years later, a memory triggered when another of its kind disturbed the peace of a holiday in the Yorkshire Moors. As an undergraduate I also competed in college and university athletics, and spent many an afternoon attempting to improve my technique ('Long

Jump'). While I can no longer get away with referring to myself as an athlete, I'm still a keen runner, and the beginnings of poems often occur to me as I run, not realising I'm thinking about anything at all.'

Two Bats

The first I met was a baby,
an accidental landing on the pillow.
Four floors up, the night was hot
and the window wide and receptive as an eye.
Though it hadn't meant to come, its two short flights
cast suspicion on the room, before it joined us, trembling.
In the lamplight it was little more than fur and wing,
no bigger than a thumb; a pulse. Humbled,
it held still as we slid the pint glass under
then raised it slowly to the moon.

The second was sent. Full-grown,
it knew its way around the landscape better than I
who'd thrown the sash down early to inhale the moors –
so it slipped in at dusk unnoticed.
When I hit the switch for the big light
it flung itself back and forth above our heads,
a glove, issuing a challenge over and over.
No instincts rose. Perhaps we were too familiar;
perhaps we already knew that if it settled
we'd be repulsed by black eyes, membranous skin,
bared teeth like a little man's. Instead,
we waited sheepishly on the landing
not looking at much, while someone else
nobler with a tea towel dealt with it.
Afterwards, though we were left to sleep,
something hung on in the dark between us.

Insomniac

Midnight.
Sky hung like ink in a jar of water.
Moon smooth as a glacier mint on its way to dissolution.

Walking the towpath
cheeks pale
I am dissolving

but not in the way I seek;
not as the mind's fingers reach out
and fuse with the fingers of sleep

to cradle eight hours of dreams; more
as the line between solid and liquid
might be rubbed out,

as path tree grass bench bin everything
blurs. Amid the vagaries
of unsleep

the spirit of the old city is rising like damp,
feeling its blind way back to the fens,
groping at my face and lungs. Here

river has taken to air,
let go of silt,
shrugged off houseboats and swans

to hover over its essence:
to kiss me. When
all I want

is everything to slot into
its proper place:
flat sky, round moon, straight path, dark river.

To lie down still as a woman between new sheets:
eyes closing effortlessly, mind empty
as a jar of water.

Long Jump

I don't have to take a run-up any more.
I haven't measured out my approach in advance
in pigeon steps. I didn't spend Tuesday afternoon
tiptoeing on imaginary eggshells
or Thursday slouching backwards down the lane
loosening each muscle's hold on its bone.

To start up from zero and gather speed
and feel myself opening out like a hairpin,
crescendo right up to the bam of the board,
toes pushing, arch lifting, knee driving, and fly –
and hang before the silent drop,
moving through stillness, arms outstretched,

is rare now. I don't need to brush myself off
and walk away as though I don't care for the result.
But I sometimes jog down Wilberforce Road to the track,
over which a grey sky's spread; where crows
saunter by stray hockey balls, and the wind
sweeps across unimpeded from Siberia.

After Rain

here's mist
slung like a belt on the evening's waist

here's nettle and thistle's
uprisings, suppressed

there's the herd,
huddled, waiting for blindness to lift

here's a cloudmass
stretching to the far-off edge

there's the city,
a mirage crowned with red

here's a fisherman
in silhouette

the flicker of a pipistrelle
overhead

plink
of surface tension punctured by a fish

German Tinder Box, c. 1800

Here's day awaiting itself without realising,
holed up on the mantelpiece in a souvenir tin.
It smells of old conspiring coins:
the morning's tender. Inside it's restless,
flinching in snug dark, dreaming of fire.

Waking is never easy: it happens gradually
with metal, oil, rag, splint; from the patient
clock, clock, clock of flint on steel
a spark is drawn and flown on a paraffin flag
till dawn's incensed, and left to burn.

A box worth more than its weight in gold
to anyone knelt at the cold grate:
to see their own sun born and lifted
out of the heart of a black forest.

The Molecatcher's Warning

Nobody asked or answered questions out there.
Ten miles from the nearest anywhere
the landscape was a disbanded library.

Only the moles remained,
strung on a barbed wire fence,
a dozen antiquated books forced open.

It must've been the north-east wind
or a bandit crow
that picked them over so –

not a scrap hanging on
inside the stretched skins,
their spines disintegrating.

Read in me
they wanted to declare
how it all ends.

But the threads that once
had a hold on their hearts
dangled, loose and crisp.

And their kin
can't read anything
but earth.

Deep Six[94]

now you've gone down
and retrieval isn't possible

now there's no chance of you
washing up on any shore

I find I can cast off
at night

in a boat I do not own
and row

straight into the middle of the lake
(too deep for police divers to check)

and there when everything is still
take from my pocket a stone

and hold it over the side
and let it go

how easy it is

opening my hand above the water
seeing your white face goggle

(and the cold)
(and the pressure)

as the glow of your outstretched fingers recedes
I pull my head through the noose

of my sweater
and breathe

NOTES

1   *Byron's Letters and Journals*, ed. Leslie A. Marchand, 12 vols (London: John Murray, 1973–82), VII: 170.

2   Tom Clayton, 'Suckling, Sir John', *Oxford Dictionary of National Biography* (hereafter ODNB).

3   His monument in Westminster Abbey proclaims him 'The Pindar, Horace, and Virgil of the English, the glory and favourite of his age' (Alexander Lindsay, 'Cowley, Abraham', ODNB).

4   He was formally admitted to membership of the College in 1889.

5   The first holder of the post was the composer Nicholas Maw (1967–71), and the list since then has included other composers including Judith Weir (1983–5), Thomas Adès (1995–7) and Ēriks Ešenvalds (2011–13), visual artists including David Inshaw (1975–7) and Ulyana Gumeniuk (2009–11), the writer Deborah Levy (1989–91) and the film-maker Eugenio Polgovsky Ezcurra (2015–17).

6   Robert Creighton, quoted by Paul Hammond, 'Dryden, John', ODNB.

7   Quoted by John Drury, *Music at Midnight: The Life and Poetry of George Herbert* (London: Penguin Books, 2014), p. 84.

8   *Byron's Letters and Journals*, 1: 79, 136.

9   *The Letters of Alfred Lord Tennyson*, eds. Cecil Y. Lang and Edgar F. Shannon, Jr., 3 vols (Oxford: Clarendon Press, 1982–90), 1: 23.

10 Drury, *Music at Midnight*, p. 100.

11 Hammond, 'Dryden', ODNB.

12 quadrangle: an Oxford term. At Cambridge they are called 'courts'.

13 Ch. 1. Woolf was invited to give the Clark Lectures in 1932 but declined.

14 Properly, 'Nevile's Court'.

15 Woolf's father, Leslie Stephen, would write a study of George Eliot (London: Macmillan, 1902).

16 From 'George Eliot', in the *Century Magazine* (November 1881).

17 *The Letters of Edward FitzGerald*, ed. Alfred McKinley Terhune and Annabelle Burdick Terhune, 4 vols (Princeton: Princeton University Press, 1980), 1: 133.

18 Ann Thwaite, 'Milne, Alan Alexander', ODNB.

19 kine: cows

20 wray: reveal

21 in raffe and ruffe: coarsely, in a disorderly manner; referring to alliterative verse

22 griff: graft

23 quite: requite

24   gite: type of gown
25   Si fortunatus infoelix: 'If [a man is] fortunate, [he is bound to be] unhappy'
26   Littleton: author of legal textbook
27   Fitzherbert: Sir Anthony Fitzherbert, barrister
28   Tully: Cicero
29   fleereth: grimaces, sneers
30   Peter pence: money, coins
31   Flushing frays: wars in Holland
32   Old Parkins, Rastell, and Dan Bracton's books: authors of standard legal works
33   many maistries mo: many more masteries
34   Haud ictus sapio: 'Having been struck, I am not wise'
35   Bacon's poem is a kind of riff on this Greek epigram, which is printed immediately before the poem in Thomas Farnaby's 1629 *Florilegium Epigrammatum Graecorum*. Chris Scott's translation:
   What kind of path through life might a man wish to cut? Strife and harsh business are in the heart of the city; worries in our homes; troubles aplenty in the country; in the sea, terror; and from across it comes fear for what you have, and, as distressing, fear on account of what you already lack. Will you wed? You will not be free from care. Will you not wed? Then you will whittle yourself away, in solitude. Children are hard work; a childless life disables. Youth is foolish; old age, on the contrary, grey and impotent. Your course of action is one of two things: never to have been born, or born, at once to die.
36   Ego Sum Vitis: 'I am the vine' (see John 15:5)
37   transelement: transform the elements of
38   Incarnationis Profundum Mysterium: The Profound Mystery of the Incarnation
39   Ocyroe: a stock mythological name for a nymph. In Ovid's *Metamorphoses*, a nymph named Ocyroe is transformed into a horse.
40   sudding: foaming
41   Itys: son of Procne by Tereus
42   furt: theft (from Latin 'furtum')
43   chymick: alchemist
44   Ad Amicum Litigantem: To a litigant friend
45   Parians: people from Paros, famous ancient source of marble
46   Socinus: Fausto Sozzino, controversial theologian who denied the truth of the Trinity
47   Jack Bond: a friend of Suckling's
48   Dr Harvey: William Harvey, English physician (1578–1657)
49   Pellaean Prince: Alexander the Great
50   corslet: piece of armour
51   Hampton: Hampton Court
52   Caresbrook's: Caresbrook Castle on the Isle of Wight, to which Charles 1 fled
53   clymacteric: epochal

54   the marvel of Peru: a foreign flower, *Mirabilis Jalapa*

55   Ormus: Hormuz, strait in the Persian Gulf, famous for its gem trade

56   the town bays: the London Laureate (John Dryden)

57   drugget: heavy cloth of wool

58   her: the Roman Catholic church

59   the Host: the consecrated wafer in the mass, understood in Catholic doctrine as bread turned into the body of Christ

60   Etherege, Southerne, Wycherley: all English and Irish dramatists

61   Thomas Rymer became Historiographer Royal on Thomas Shadwell's death in 1692.

62   *This whole line is taken from Sir* John Denham. [Dryden's note]

63   salvage: savage

64   Brunswick: George I

65   The chapel was begun in 1554–5 by Mary I and completed in 1567 by Elizabeth I.

66   'I say that you alone are wise and know how to live well, whose wealth is conspicuous from your elegant villas.' Horace *Letters* 1.15.

67   [Author's note] Alain-René Le Sage (1668–1747), *Le Diable Boiteux* (1707), chap. 3. [Byron refers to Le Sage's novel, in which the demon Asmodeus perches Don Leandro Cleofas on the steeple of San Salvador in Madrid and magically lifts the roofs off all the houses so that Cleofas can see into them.]

68   Henry Petty-Fitzmaurice, Third Marquess of Lansdowne (Trinity), defeated Henry John Temple, Third Viscount Palmerston (St John's) for the University of Cambridge parliamentary seat in February 1806.

69   Lord Hawke: Edward Harvey Hawke, Third Baron Hawke

70   [Author's note] Sele's publication on Greek metres, displays considerable talent and ingenuity, but, as might be expected in so difficult a work, is not remarkable for accuracy. [Byron refers to John Barlow Seale's *Analysis of the Greek Metres* (Cambridge, 1785).]

71   [Author's note] The Latin of the schools is of the CANINE SPECIES and not very intelligible.

72   [Author's note] The discovery of Pythagoras, that the square of the hypotenuse, is equal to the squares of the other two sides of a right-angled triangle.

73   [Author's note] On a Saint Day, the Students wear Surplices, in Chapel.

74   Peel's: Sir Robert Peel (1788–1850), conservative politician, Home Secretary at the time this poem was written, subsequently Prime Minister, 1834–5 and 1841–6.

75   Thorwaldsen: Bertel Thorvaldsen or Thorwaldsen (*c.*1770–1844), Danish sculptor. Refused for Poets' Corner in Westminster Abbey and rejected for the College Chapel, this statue of Byron was introduced into the Wren Library in 1845.

76   Arthur: Arthur Hallam (1811–33), whose death in Vienna prompted Alfred Tennyson's *In Memoriam A.H.H.*

77   The second of two sonnets with this title, headed 'The Same'.

78 Σκιᾶς ὄναρ: 'Skias onar': 'man is a dream of a shadow'. From Pindar's *Pythian 8*.

79 'When you are truly old, sitting at eve near the fire by candlelight, spinning and winding thread, you will say, marvelling as you recite my verses, "Ronsard sang my praise in the days when I was fair".' (Editors' translation)

80 *James Clerk Maxwell: Perspectives on His Life and Work*, eds. Raymond Flood, Mark McCartney, Andrew Whitaker (2014).

81 'The "Red Lions" are a club formed by Members of the British Association, to meet for relaxation after the graver labours of the day.' [Note in original]

82 '"Leonum arida nutrix." – *Horace.*' [Note in original]

83 Keith Moffatt, FRS, born and bred in Edinburgh, a Fellow of Trinity College from 1961 to 1977 and again, on his return to the Chair of Mathematical Physics, from 1980 to the present, Director of the Isaac Newton Institute for Mathematical Sciences (1996–2001). His research interests lie within the broad field of fluid dynamics, particularly in magnetohydrodynamics and the theory of turbulence.

84 deave: stun

85 speir: ask

86 Gallovidian hills: hills of Galloway

87 eponymial year: the year to which Maxwell gave his name (2006 being the 175th anniversary of his birth)

88 Henri Regnault: French painter (1843–71), killed in the siege of Paris at the battle of Buzenval.

89 Stabat Mater: the opening words of a famous mediaeval hymn to Mary, 'Stabat mater dolorosa' (literally, 'the grieving mother stood'), depicting Christ's mother at the crucifixion.

90 *Unheimlich Leben*: literally, 'to live in an un-homely way': as an adjective the German 'unheimlich' also carries the sense of 'eerie', 'uncanny', 'terrible'

91 *le gai saber*: 'gay knowledge' or 'gay science' – the art of composing love poetry among the troubadours

92 Title of a flesh-coloured sculpture on pointed wooden base by Maggi Hambling. 'Aftermath' is the second mowing of grass.

93 Chronophage: literally, 'time-eater', the Corpus clock represents a monstrous grasshopper-like insect on top of a clock, apparently devouring the minutes as they pass. It was designed by Dr John C. Taylor and has been much photographed by tourists since its installation on Trumpington Street in 2008, at the north-west corner of Corpus Christi College.

94 [Author's note]: 'Deep six' is a nautical expression indicating a water depth of six fathoms (thirty-six ft), traditionally thought to be the minimum depth required for a sea burial.

SOURCES

Texts based on first publication in volume form except where otherwise specified by an asterisk.

GEORGE GASCOIGNE

'The Green Knight's Farewell to Fancy'. *A Hundreth Sundrie Flowres...* (1573).

'A Sonnet Written in Praise of the Brown Beauty', 'Gascoigne's Woodmanship'. *The Poesies of George Gascoigne Esquire* (1575).

FRANCIS BACON

The Poems of Francis Bacon, for the first time collected and edited after the original texts, with introduction by Alexander B. Grosart (1870).

WILLIAM ALABASTER

'Upon the Crucifix (III)'. J. H. Pollen, 'William Alabaster, a newly discovered Catholic Poet of the Elizabethan Age', *The Month* (April 1904).*

'Incarnationis Profundum Mysterium'. Louise Imogen Guiney, *Recusant Poets: with a selection from their work* (1938).

All other sonnets first published in *The Sonnets of William Alabaster*, eds. Helen Gardner and G. M. Storey (1959).

GILES FLETCHER

Sorrowe's Joy, or a Lamentation for our Deceased Soveraigne Elizabeth, with a Triumph for the Prosperous succession of our Gratious King James (1603).

GEORGE HERBERT

The Temple: Sacred Poems and Private Ejaculations (1633).

THOMAS RANDOLPH

'In Praise of Women in General'. *Poems with The muses looking-glass, and Amyntas; whereunto is added The jealous lovers* (1668; 5th ed.).

All other poems first published in *Poems with the Muses looking-glasse: and Amyntas: By Thomas Randolph Master of Arts, and late fellow of Trinity Colledge in Cambridge* (1638).

SIR JOHN SUCKLING

'Out upon it! I have loved'. *Selections from the Works of Sir John Suckling*, ed. Alfred Inigo Suckling (1836).

All other poems first published in *Fragmenta Aurea* (1646).

ABRAHAM COWLEY

'Upon Dr Harvey'. *The Works of Mr Abraham Cowley* (1668).

'The Grasshopper'. *Poems Written by A. Cowley* (1656).

'Against Fruition'. *The Mistress; or, Several Copies of Love Verses* (1647).

ANDREW MARVELL

'On Mr Milton's Paradise Lost'. John Milton, *Paradise Lost. A Poem in Twelve Books* (1674; 2nd ed.).

All other poems first published in *Miscellaneous Poems* (1681).

JOHN DRYDEN

'Prologue to the University of Oxford', 'Mac Flecknoe'.* *Miscellany Poems* (1684).

'To the Memory of Mr Oldham'. *Remains of Mr John Oldham in Verse and Prose* (1684).

The Hind and the Panther (1687).

A Song for St CECILIA's Day (1697).

'To My Dear Friend Mr Congreve'. *The Double-Dealer, A Comedy* (1694).

The works of Virgil containing his Pastorals, Georgics and Aeneis. Translated into English Verse (1697).

'Palamon and Arcite'. *Fables Ancient and Modern* (1700).

CHARLES MONTAGU, EARL OF HALIFAX

An Epistle to the Right Honourable Charles, Earl of Dorset and Middlesex (1690).

LEONARD WELSTED

Epistles, Odes &c. Written on Several Subjects (1724).

LAURENCE EUSDEN

Poetical Miscellanies, the sixth part (1709).

JOHN BYROM

Miscellaneous Poems (1773).

ROBERT LLOYD

'The Cit's Country Box, 1757'. *Poems* (1762).

'A Familiar Epistle, to J.B. Esq'. *St James's Magazine* (October, 1762).*

GEORGE GORDON, LORD BYRON

'Granta, a Medley'. *Hours of Idleness. A Series of Poems Original and Translated* (1807).

'She walks in beauty, like the night'. *Hebrew Melodies* (1815).

'Stanzas to [Augusta]'. *The Prisoner of Chillon and Other Poems* (1816).

'Darkness'. *The Prisoner of Chillon and Other Poems* (1816).

'Prometheus'. *The Prisoner of Chillon and Other Poems* (1816).

'Stanzas for Music'. *Poems* (1816).

Childe Harold's Pilgrimage. A Romaunt. Canto III (1816).
Don Juan. Cantos I–II (1816); *Don Juan.* Cantos VI–VIII (1823).
'January 22nd 1824'. *Morning Chronicle* (29 October 1824).*
'So, we'll go no more a-roving'. *The Works of Lord Byron, in Six Volumes* (1831).

THOMAS BABINGTON MACAULAY

Lays of Ancient Rome (1842).

WINTHROP MACKWORTH PRAED

The Poems of Winthrop Mackworth Praed, 2 vols (1864).

FREDERICK TENNYSON

Days and Hours (1854).

CHARLES TENNYSON TURNER

'On the Statue of Lord Byron'. *Sonnets* (1864).
'Vienna and In Memoriam', 'A Brilliant Day'. *Small Tableaux* (1868).
'Gout and Wings'. *Sonnets, Lyrics, and Translations* (1873).

EDWARD FITZGERALD

Rubáiyát of Omar Khayyám: The Astronomer-Poet of Persia. Translated into English Verse (1859).

RICHARD MONCKTON MILNES

The Poems of Richard Monckton Milnes, 2 vols (1837), vol. 1.

ALFRED LORD TENNYSON

'Lines on Cambridge of 1830'. Hallam Tennyson, *Alfred Lord Tennyson: A Memoir,* 2 vols (1897), vol. 1.

All others from *The Works of Tennyson* (Eversley Edition), 9 vols., ed. Hallam, Lord Tennyson, 1908.*

ARTHUR HENRY HALLAM

Remains in Verse and Prose of Arthur Henry Hallam (1863).

WILLIAM MAKEPEACE THACKERAY

The Works of William Makepeace Thackeray, 12 vols (1872), vol. XI.

JAMES CLERK MAXWELL

Lewis Campbell and William Garnett, *The Life of James Clerk Maxwell* (1882).

'The Genius o' Glenlair', by Keith Moffatt. By permission of the author.

EDMUND GOSSE

The Collected Poems of Edmund Gosse (1911).

R. C. LEHMANN

The Vagabond and Other Poems from Punch (1918).

A. E. HOUSMAN

'Tennyson in the Moated Grange'. *Ye Rounde Table* (1878).

'Oedipus Coloneus'. *Odes from the Greek Dramatists. Translated into Lyric Metres by English Poets and Scholars*, ed. Alfred W. Pollard (1890).

'1887', 'When I watch the living meet', 'On Wenlock Edge the wood's in trouble', 'Be still, my soul, be still; the arms you bear are brittle', 'I hoed and trenched and weeded'. *A Shropshire Lad* (1896).

'Fragment of a Greek Tragedy'. *The Cornhill Magazine* (1901).*

'Oh who is that young sinner with the handcuffs on his wrists?', 'Ask me no more, for fear I should reply', 'He would not stay for me; and who can wonder?'. Laurence Housman, *A.E.H.: Some Poems, Some Letters and a Personal Memoir* (1937).

'When the eye of day is shut', 'Yonder see the morning blink'. *Last Poems* (1922).

'From far, from eve and morning'. *More Poems* (1936).

'I did not lose my heart in summer's even'. *Collected Poems* (1939).

MAURICE BARING

Collected Poems (1925).

ALEISTER CROWLEY

Songs of the Spirit (1898).

MUHAMMAD IQBAL [dates provided for first publication of respective English translation]

'The Night and the Poet'. *Tulip in the Desert: A Selection of the Poetry of Muhammad Iqbal*, ed. and trans. Mustansir Mir (2000).

All others from *Poems from Iqbal*, trans. V. G. Kiernan (1955).

A. A. MILNE

'Halfway Down', 'Disobedience'. *When We Were Very Young* (1924).

'The Old Sailor'. *Now We Are Six* (1927).

'Lines Written by a Bear of Very Little Brain'. *Winnie The Pooh* (1926).

'The more it SNOWS', 'Noise, by Pooh', 'Here lies a tree which Owl (a bird)', 'Poem'. *The House at Pooh Corner* (1928).

EDWARD SHANKS

Collected Poems (1926).

VLADIMIR NABOKOV

Lolita (1955).

Eugene Onegin: A Novel in Verse (1964).

'On Translating "Eugene Onegin"', 'A Literary Dinner', 'Ode to a Model'. *Poems and Problems* (1969).

'The University Poem', 'Spring'. *Collected Poems* (2012).

JOHN LEHMANN

'Greek Landscape with Figures'. *Collected Poems* (1963).

All other poems first published in *The Age of the Dragon: Poems, 1930–1951* (1952).

THOM GUNN

'The Secret Sharer'. *Fighting Terms* (1954).

'The Outdoor Concert'. *Jack Straw's Castle* (1976).

'The Missed Beat'. *The Missed Beat* (1976).

'The Hug', 'The Man with Night Sweats', 'Lament'. *The Man with Night Sweats* (1992).

'The Gas-Poker'. *Boss Cupid* (2000).

KIT WRIGHT

'George Herbert's Other Self in Africa'. *Short Afternoons* (1989).

All other poems first published in *Ode to Didcot Power Station* (2014).

PETER ROBINSON

'Autobiography', 'A Woman a Poem a Picture'. *Overdrawn Account* (1980).

'Cleaning'. *This Other Life* (1988).

'Convalescent Days'. *Lost and Found* (1997).

'Unheimlich Leben'. *The Look of Goodbye* (2008).

'Like a Railway Station'. *Buried Music* (2015).

ANGELA LEIGHTON

'Crack-Willow', 'Library'. *The Messages* (2012).

'Sluice', 'Crocus', 'Sicilian Road', 'Even-Song', '"Aftermath: Parasite"'. *Spills* (2016).

JAMES HARPUR

'Cranborne Woods (17 May, 1994)'. *Oracle Bones* (2001).

BEN OKRI

'An Undeserved Sweetness'. *An African Elegy* (1992).
'Migrations', 'Heraclitus' Golden River'. *Wild* (2012).

SOPHIE HANNAH

'Long For This World', 'The Cancellation'. *First of the Last Chances*
(2003).

All other poems first published in *Marrying the Ugly Millionaire* (2015).

SEAN BORODALE

'2nd May', '23rd July: Noise & Waste', '7th August: Property'. *Bee
Journal* (2012).

'Apple Jelly (On-going)', 'Washing-Up'. *Human Work: A Poet's
Cookbook* (2015).

JACOB POLLEY

'A Jar of Honey'. *The Brink* (2003).
'The Owls', 'You'. *Little Gods* (2006).
'Langley Lane'. *The Havocs* (2012).
'Peewit'. *Jackself* (2016).

EMMA JONES

'Farming', 'Conversation'. *The Striped World* (2009).

REBECCA WATTS

The Met Office Advises Caution (2016).

INDEX OF AUTHORS

INDEX OF TITLES

INDEX OF FIRST LINES